LEADERSHIP

STERLING W. SILL

LEADERSHIP

by

STERLING W. SILL

BOOKCRAFT, INC.

SALT LAKE CITY, UTAH

Copyright
Bookcraft, Inc.
1958

13th Printing, 1977

LITHOGRAPHED IN U.S.A.
BY

PUBLISHERS PRESS

SALT LAKE CITY, UTAH

PREFACE

THE WRITER was recently asked to prepare a series of articles for *The Improvement Era* under the title of "Leadership Development." This assignment proved such an interesting one that it was not very long before a fairly large number of extra articles had been prepared. It was then suggested that a useful purpose might be served by putting them together in book form.

In the main, there is only one real problem in the world, and it doesn't matter very much whether the desired accomplishment lies in doing church work or in building a business or in running an empire. The problem is always the same—leadership. But because of the tremendous consequences which are involved, the importance of leadership is greatly magnified when it applies to the work of the Lord.

Henry Ford has suggested a helpful method of attack by his statement that "There are no big problems. There are just a lot of little problems." And one of the most helpful success procedures is to divide up what seems to be the big problem into its parts and then deal with each, one at a time. It has been suggested that if you want to eat an elephant you should first cut it up into little pieces.

This is also a good leadership procedure. It is closely related to the old military stratagem of "divide and conquer." Any problem may be reduced in size by division and subdivision until each part is small enough that we may obtain mastery of it.

The following articles have been prepared as some individual leadership need has suggested itself. With two exceptions, these have been arranged in alphabetical order. The subdivisions of leadership might be thought of as a jeweler would think of the parts of a watch, where there is no specific order of importance making a rank of first, second, and third possible. Yet like the parts of a watch, each part of leadership is important and each is dependent upon the other. The hands of the watch cannot say to the mainspring, "I have no need of thee." The same applies to the "parts" of leadership.

In Benjamin Franklin's *Autobiography* he presents a very interesting plan which he used so successfully to bring about his own personal development. He took one particular personality trait which he desired to make his own and concentrated on its development for an allotted period. Then, without losing sight of the first, he went on to the second, etc. This is an excellent procedure which we might very profitably follow in the development of our leadership. It is, therefore, suggested that inasmuch as the week is the logical unit of time in church work, we give weekly consideration to each of these short chapters.

Most ideas are not only important for themselves; they are even more important for what they stimulate us to think and do. The greatest good may therefore be brought about not only by reading each chapter of this manual, but by doing some research and thinking of our own as we consider each subject. We should write down and make decisions about our own thoughts and determinations as they come to us. The next step, of course, is to put them into regular and useful practice. If this procedure is faithfully followed through fifty-two weeks, it is expected that a very pleasing and valuable growth in leadership ability will be experienced. It is only hoped that the consideration of these pages will be half as pleasant and rewarding as their preparation has been.

The ideas presented here have been taken from my own study and experience. I have frequently referred to my own written notebooks compiled over many years. Sometimes the source of a particular idea has been lost, so that it has not always been possible to give proper credit, though I very gratefully acknowledge an innumerable host of benefactors.

CONTENTS

The Laws of Leadership

THERE IS a child's book entitled *The Chance World*. It pictures a world in which everything happens by chance. The sun may come up in the morning or it may not. If you jump up into the air you may come down or you may keep on going. If water runs out to the edge of a cliff it may fall down or it may fall up. If you plant your field with wheat you will have no way to determine in advance whether or not it will grow, but if it does come up it may be wheat or it may be barley or it may be asparagus or rosebushes or apple trees, and there is no way to tell which in advance.

One of the most fortunate things about our world is that it is not *a chance world*. It is a world of law and order. The operation of its laws may be predicted in advance. There are many kinds of laws. One set of laws comes by legislative enactment. They may be and often are arbitrary rules and regulations to control the actions of people. These laws may be enforced by courts. They may be just or unjust, helpful or injurious. They may be established by whim, compromise, custom, precedent, justice or force, and they may be repealed the same way. Some of these laws are called the laws of nations, or international laws. They include any rules that may be agreed upon regulating the intercourse between nations in peace or war. They may be arbitrary and unfair. Small nations may be divided and subjugated, imposed upon or benefited without notice. These laws may be disregarded, suspended or changed by the whim of those possessing the necessary power of enforcement.

Then there is another set of laws called natural law, or the laws of nature. These laws remain constant and unalterable under all circumstances. Man did not make them; man cannot change them. From their verdict there is no appeal. If they are at times hurtful, at least they are constant. They are never influenced by whim or change of mood. They are always reasonable and always predictable. Man can learn to discover them and live in harmony with them in such a way as to insure his greatest benefit.

Successful farming, for example, is governed by these laws. They demand that crops must be planted during certain seasons, that the seed bed must not be too wet or too dry, that the proper cultivation must follow. These laws have governed since the earliest man turned the first furrow. They are an integral part of the fabric of life. If, therefore, one is to be a succesful farmer he must learn, catalog and harness the elemental certainty of the laws governing successful farming. He must first recognize their existence and their power. He must realize the utter folly of neglecting or disregarding them. He must be aware of the fact that these laws may be either a curse or a blessing to him, depending upon his attitude toward them.

Suppose that a farmer should choose to ignore these fundamental laws or remain in ignorance of them. For example, suppose that he plants his corn in the chill of the autumn rain, not in the gracious warmth of the May sunshine. In such a case there will be no crop to harvest. It is utterly useless to imagine for a moment that by some chance or mischance his labor may succeed. In his blindness, ignorance or stubbornness he may work until he falls exhausted in the furrow, but he cannot succeed, for the laws of successful farming are working against him.

The wise man learns to understand these laws. Then he may be able not only to predict events in advance, but he will know how to bring about the desired result. By means of this scientific prophecy, he may cause or prevent specific events. For example, one may learn that water will freeze at 32 degrees above zero. But if one adds 20 percent salt, the resulting solution will not freeze until 2.4 degrees above zero. Alcohol will not freeze until the temperature reaches 30 degrees below zero. It is also possible to know in advance that when the water freezes it will expand with a power so tremendous that the strongest steel may be shattered.

We don't necessarily need to know *why* this is so, but only that it is the law. We may think that water would be better off if it did not freeze until 32 degrees below zero. We may not even understand how the water tells when it is cold enough to freeze. But it never makes a mistake; it never forgets; it never alters its course because of someone's opinion, influence or need.

Isaac Newton discovered and explained the laws of gravity. Kepler discovered the laws of planetary distances, the laws of falling bodies, etc. These natural laws are never repealed; they are never suspended. The verdict is always handed down even before the act is performed. The keenest lawyer or the most sympathetic witness has no power to change the verdict in the slightest degree. The sentence is not softened because of mental or physical incompetence; there is no time off for good behavior. The effect of these laws always takes place in exactly the same way, with the result that the events can be known with certainty in advance. This ability to foretell consequences gives one a tremendous natural advantage in any work he may undertake.

Now our business is leadership. We work with human beings, under the direction of our Father in heaven. He is the God of nature and the God of our being. He also works according to law. He has said, "There is a law, irrevocably decreed in heaven before the foundations of this world, upon which all blessings are predicated, and when we obtain any blessing from God, it is by obedience to that law upon which it is predicated." (D&C 130:20-21) God is the author of human nature, and human beings also behave according to a pattern which we can learn to discover in advance.

However, because of the many influences working in the lives of human beings, the laws of human nature may in some instances be a little more complex than the laws of gravity or electricity. This, of course, makes it even more necessary that we learn to understand the laws by which we bring about our own accomplishment or our own downfall.

Almost all education is about ourselves. We study medicine to learn how to keep ourselves well physically. The studies of the mind—psychology, psychiatry, etc.— are to teach us how to keep ourselves well mentally. So-ciology is to teach us how to live together. We study agriculture to find out how to feed ourselves. Business shows us how to deal agreeably with each other. The wide field of religion teaches us how to develop our spiritual health and vitality.

Then we have the great undertaking which we call human leadership. Leadership is a science, and it is also an art. It is certainly the most important enterprise ever undertaken. It is also the one supremely difficult thing to develop. Goods can be manufactured on a formula; guided missiles can reach their own targets. We can bake our bread, make our clothes, plow our ground with machines. But it takes a human being to be a leader, and great leadership requires a human being at his best.

Each person must develop his own leadership. Lead-ership cannot be bought. It cannot be conferred. It cannot be inherited. It knows no divine right. It cannot be passed on by any process of succession. It is always stamped with the label, "Not Transferable." It is acquired only by the personal mastery of each individual aspirant. Once this ability is acquired, one may then touch the keys regulating human behavior and help to bring about the most important responses in human beings.

Jesus tried to teach us some of these laws of leadership, most of which we have not made much of an attempt to master. For example, he gave an almost all-powerful law of success by which we may bring about in others almost any response we desire. This law is made up of just fifteen words. Some have called it the Golden Rule; others have called it the Law of the Boomerang; others have called it the Law of Retaliation. This law says, "Whatsoever ye would that men should do unto you, do ye even so unto them." If we could only learn to put this one law into effect, it would transform our lives and the world in thirty days.

If you want someone to punch you on the nose, you don't need to make a formal request or argue or reason with him about it. The quickest and most certain method of getting this response is simply to punch him on the nose. If you want someone to send you a Christmas card, all you need to do is to send him a Christmas card. If you want him to invite you to his house to dinner, you invite him to your house for dinner, and very shortly you will receive an invitation to his house for a little better dinner than he received at your house. If you want someone to like you, all you have to do is to like him. If you want him to trust you, trust him. We are all human magnets. Our deeds, our attitudes and even our thoughts attract in kind. If you frown at someone he scowls back at you. If you want smiles, give smiles. You can know in advance how everybody will react to a given situation. Therefore, a great power is placed in your hands if you choose to use it. Just figure out what you want, and then give accordingly.

Everyone gets back with compound interest exactly what he sends. The chickens come home to roost and bring their offspring along. If, therefore, you would like to possess great personal power, if you would like to be trusted, respected, loved and followed, just learn to practice the Law of the Boomerang.

How simple this law makes it for us to control others. If you want to wipe out an enemy, just be friendly to him. The hottest coals of fire ever heaped upon the head of one who has wronged you are the coals of human kindness. To return good for evil is a method of attack which he does not understand. This procedure of giving good for evil leaves him baffled and powerless, so that you can easily dominate him. Jesus said, "Love your enemies." Someone has stated that one reason we should love our enemies is that we made them ourselves; another reason is that they keep us on our toes; a third reason is that we should make them our friends.

But when we learn to practice these fifteen simple words, we will know about all there is to know about religion. We will know almost all there is to know about human relations. We will know almost all there is to know about philosophy, and we will know about all there is to know about leadership. It is a leadership technique too powerful for anyone to resist; it conquers everything before it. If we can learn to handle it, this one great law alone will give us a wonderful power to lead.

There are dozens of other very helpful laws found in "the book of leadership." There is the law of motivation, the law of ego-recognition, the law of example, the law of self-discipline, the laws of learning, the laws of interest, the laws of enthusiasm.

A large part of the work of leaders is done in the personal interview. Just think of the wonders that can be accomplished by a personal, face-to-face contact. The doctor is more helpful if he meets his patient face-to-face. Why does the patient always feel better when the doctor is present? How can a psychiatrist heal a mind merely by a few face-to-face interviews? God, our Creator, has given great power to human personality. The greatest accomplishment can only be made on a face-to-face basis, where our full God-given powers can be brought into play.

But we need to understand the governing law. We need to know of the powers resting within ourselves and how to use them. If we do not understand that the radiator water freezes at 32 degrees above zero, we may ruin the most valuable engine in a single night. Very similarly we may bring serious consequences upon ourselves because we do not understand the laws of our own being. On the other hand, we may bring about the greatest possible transformations merely by learning the laws governing our own lives. The laws of leadership extend to us the greatest of all opportunities. It is our job to know them and become effective in their use.

There is a basic, fundamental law upon which all of the others rest. Called the law of the harvest, it says that "as a man soweth so shall he also reap." And just as one can learn the laws of successful farming to bring about an abundant harvest, so he can by learning the laws of leadership reap an even more wonderful harvest in the service of the Master.

What Must I Do to Succeed?

Paul and Silas had an interesting experience in the prison at Philippi. At midnight as they prayed and sang, there was a great earthquake, shaking the foundations of the prison. All of the prison doors were opened, and every prisoner's bands were loosened. The keeper of the prison, awaking out of his sleep, drew his sword and would have killed himself, supposing that his prisoners had fled. But Paul assured him that the prisoners were all safe. Then the jailor fell down before Paul and Silas and said, "Sirs, what must I do to be saved?"

Paul instructed the jailor what he ought to do, and the jailor did as he was told. He started out his new life by being baptized that very night. The jailor first felt that he had *a need*. He asked for information from someone who he felt had the answers. Then all he had to do was to follow instructions.

That is a pretty good formula to solve most problems. It fits with the counsel of Jesus, who said, "Ask and ye shall receive." The jailor wanted to know. Knowledge comes from explanation, discussion, reading, thinking. One thought expressed to our minds may start a chain of reactions. Then like an electric calculator when the machinery finally comes to a stop, our minds may have an answer all worked out for us to put into operation. We may get answers to many problems by this process. Sometimes the facts may already be in our minds, but an expression from someone else acts as a sort of catalyst to make our thoughts crystalize, and puts them in a form suitable to our mental machinery.

That question, "What must I do to be saved?" is made up of seven little one-syllable words. But the answer was probably worth salvation itself to the jailor. "What must I do to be saved?" is probably the most important question in the world.

What might be the second most important question is very similar. It is also made up of seven words. It is, "What must I do to be successful?" To those of us who assist in doing the work of the Lord, these seven words might be changed to ask, "What must I do to save others?" It is the responsibility of leadership in the Church to see to it that everyone under our direction qualifies for the celestial kingdom. That is the biggest and most important assignment in the world. We think and talk about being saviors upon Mt. Zion. That is not a simple task. Probably the only way to be a savior is to save someone. That was what Jesus said was the most worthwhile thing, even if it took a lifetime. To save someone is a pretty complicated procedure. Yet it may not be any more complicated to save others than it is to save ourselves. Many people spend a lifetime of effort and fail to save their own souls.

In answering the question for the jailor, Paul indicated, as Jesus had done before him, that there are certain very definite things that must be done to bring about eternal exaltation. But success, like exaltation, is also based on a pretty definite set of requirements. The process of saving ourselves has been called the process of salvation. But this process of saving others is called *leadership*. These two involve the most important known abilities. The priesthood gives us the *authority* to save souls, but leadership gives us the *ability* to save souls. Either one largely loses its value in the absence of the other.

We have the *authority*. Now our big problem is to get the *ability*. Successful leadership therefore becomes our most important problem. It has been demonstrated

over and over again that a soldier can fight harder, a salesman can sell more goods, a missionary can make more
converts, if he works under the direction of someone who
can *teach* and *train* and *supervise* and *organize* and
deputize and *inspire* and *motivate.* That is a short
description of leadership.

Some time ago I was in a stake where in one ward 87
per cent of the members of the Aaronic Priesthood received
an individual certificate of award. That might be taken
as the best measurement we have to identify those who
are currently on schedule to get into the celestial kingdom.
In another ward in the same stake, with the same kind of
boys, 10 per cent received an award. The difference is
entirely a difference in leadership. If you change the
leaders and put the 87 per cent leaders in the ward with
the 10 per cent accomplishment, you will undoubtedly see
the achievement of the low ward rise to approximately
87 per cent, as that is the stature of the leadership. If you
put the 10 per cent leaders in the 87 per cent ward, it will
probably not be long before that accomplishment would
settle at 10 per cent.

The jailor asked, "What must I do to be saved?" Many
volumes of scripture and thousands of other books and
sermons have been written and preached to help us with
the answer. If we ask, "What must I do to succeed?" the
answer is of about the same length, though probably not
quite as clear in our minds. Most church writings and
discussions have to do with church doctrine, philosophy
or history. We are not so well supplied in the Church with
ideas, methods, and procedures as to how we can actually
put the doctrine in force in the lives of people. Leadership
covers the whole field of administrative skills, executive
procedures, training methods, morale building, means of
bettering human relations, etc. Leadership includes the
power of example. It strives to harness every resource of

the personality, the spirit, the faculties and the senses, to bring about this one end, the eternal exaltation of the human family.

But however "effective leadership" may be defined, it is clearly the greatest power in the world. By its use, one man can, if he will, change the morale of a whole community. To be a leader is far more than just to be a good man. Leadership is the ability to make goodness operate in the lives of others. For a quorum president or a bishop or a stake president to qualify for the celestial kingdom is a great accomplishment, but not as great as their ability to get many others to qualify. To know all of the doctrines of the Church by heart and live them to the letter is not equal to the ability to put these doctrines in force in the lives of others.

Our lack of leadership is our chief limiting factor in the Church or in life. The one business of life is to succeed. We are not placed here to waste our lives in failure. Failure is a sin, not for itself alone, but for what it is a sign of. If the jailor had failed to follow instructions it would have been a sign of weakness in him. But when we fail to do those things necessary to save others, it is a sign of weakness in us. These weaknesses must be overcome; they must be changed into strengths. We sometimes sing a song which says, "If we fail we fail in glory." That is ridiculous. No failure is glorious. Every failure is a tragedy. We must not fail. We cannot afford to fail. Eternal lives depend upon our success. Exaltation through all eternity is a tremendous idea. Joseph Addison once exclaimed, "Eternity, thou pleasing dreadful thought." Therefore, one of the most important questions in the world is one that we should ask ourselves, "What can I do to succeed?" Just think how much depends upon our finding the right answers.

Leadership is both an art and a science, and probably no one ever masters either part very well. No one in a lifetime can learn nearly all there is to know about medicine. We learn even less about leadership for two reasons: first, leadership in all of its aspects is so much more expansive than any other science; and second, unfortunately, we are usually not so devoted to our work of leadership. At any rate, we come far short of reaching the limits of our possibilities.

I think it was Edison who said that no one knew more than one-half of one per cent about anything. Yet to be discouraged because of the size of our field would be one of the most disastrous things that we could do. Probably the best place to start our accomplishment is where the jailor started, and ask ourselves the question, "What must I do to succeed?" And then if, as we get the answers, we get started as soon as the jailor did and keep working at it diligently for the rest of our lives, we will undoubtedly receive the appropriate reward of success.

Suppose then that each week we take one little corner of leadership and try to find some answers that we can immediately put into practice. We will gradually develop the skills that go with leadership success. We can get help from many sources. The following discussions will help us to center our minds on a problem. Additional reading and thinking will greatly help us. One of the best sources for our learning is to study the lives of great leaders. Some of these leaders are written about in the scriptures; some work contemporaneously with us in the Church; many great leaders are in other fields. But the principles of leadership success are very similar no matter where we find them, and they may be selected and adapted and used by us in the work of the Lord.

Here is one great idea that will help us. There is a tradition that comes down to us from ancient Greece about a great painter named Apelles. Apelles lived in the 4th century B.C. He painted a portrait, *The Goddess of*

Beauty, which enchanted the world. For many years he traveled widely in many lands, observing the fairest features of the most beautiful women. He then painted the most attractive qualities that could be found in each, getting an eye here, a forehead there. Here he captured a particular grace and there he painted a rare turn of beauty, which all together gave him his great masterpiece, a portrait of a perfect woman, the beauty of which enthralled the world.

Every great leader is also a composite. Each person is "many in one." It has been said that if you subtracted from each of us that which properly belonged to someone else, there would not be much of any of us left. But only by this process of getting the best from everyone we meet can individuals be raised to their highest leadership power.

Everyone and everything has something to teach us. We can adopt and adapt all that is finest and most worthy. And as we hold these ideas up for consideration, they can be stamped into our own brain cells, and we can build our leadership as we do our knowledge of the gospel, line upon line, precept upon precept. Then we will experience this greatest of all natural phenomenon, which we call growth.

Probably the best single way to improve our leadership qualities is to be aware of our needs. That consciousness by itself will help us to pick up the good points in others. It will help us to get the greatest benefit from what we read and hear and think. As we regularly nibble at the whole problem, we will be led to the necessary abilities. The inspiration and blessing of the Lord will sanctify and enrich the whole, and we will gain new powers and ambitions for this greatest of all enterprises, *leadership* in the work of the Lord. Our abilities to lead will help us to answer both of the two greatest questions of our lives, "What must I do to be saved?" and "What must I do to save others?"

Almost

THERE IS ONE little word in our language that probably has as much tragedy packed into it as can be contained in any single word. It is a very innocent-looking little word called "almost." An illustration of its potential tragedy is indicated by an experience of the Apostle Paul. Paul had been imprisoned at Caesarea, and it was the responsibility of Festus, the procurator of Judea, to conduct Paul's trial. Festus was very interested in Paul and his message. When Agrippa paid a visit to Festus, he told Agrippa about this unusual Christian missionary who was a prisoner in his custody. Agrippa expressed a desire to hear Paul's testimony. Paul was brought before them, and he said to Paul, "Thou art permitted to speak for thyself." Then Paul told Festus and Agrippa about his extraordinary experience on the road to Damascus. He told them exactly what had happened, and bore a firm and convincing testimony of the truth. Agrippa was impressed and interested. How could he doubt Paul's sincerity or the accuracy of his statement? But he turned his back on his opportunity by a method still very common among us. He would not make a decision to conform with the evidence. He disposed of the whole question by merely saying to Paul, "Almost thou persuadest me to be a Christian."

Paul, of course, knew what this "almost" meant. It meant that even though Agrippa was within reach of his own salvation, he would do nothing about it. Paul said to the king, "I would to God that not only thou but all who hear me this day were both almost and altogether such as I am, except these bonds." If Agrippa had been

as Paul was, he would not have been "almost" persuaded
There was no "almost" so far as Paul was concerned. Paul
had always been either one thing or the other. There was
no middle ground. Either Christianity was true or it was
not true. "Partial conversion" or "fractional devotion" must
have been an unintelligible concept to Paul. Paul was
altogether. He went all of the way. What kind of logic
would suggest that one halt midway between the issues?

But there are many people like Agrippa who are
"almost" something. The king was "almost" persuaded,
but not quite. He "almost" decided to think this matter
through and make some decisions about it. But he didn't
quite get that far, and so the great blessings that he might
have had died before they were born. "Almost" sounds
very near to accomplishment, yet it is sometimes so far
away that it really doesn't count for very much. The Jews
who lived contemporaneously with Jesus were so *near* and
yet they were so *far* away. How often someone gets close
enough to say, "I *almost* quit smoking," or "I *almost* went
to church," or "I *almost* repented," or "I *almost* succeeded."

Recently a salesman said that he had "almost" made
a sale. He was asked how near he came to it and he said
that the sale was 98 per cent made. He was then asked how
much commission his company paid on sales that he had
almost made. Just think how all-important that other 2
per cent is when added to a 98 per cent accomplishment.
This same principle operates in most of our activities.
There is a very fine line which separates failure from success, and when we stop just short of the line we are often
not much better off than if the start had never been made.
It is that extra 2 per cent that gets the job done and is so
all-important.

Probably one of the most unfortunate of all of our
leadership traits is that we so often lack this small balance
of power that gets us over the top. So often we stop just

a little short of success after we have actually gone most
of the way. The world is full of half-finished work and
half-finished decisions. We are surrounded by minds that
are only partly made up. Ralph Waldo Emerson once said
that he had never seen a whole man. Mostly we are just
parts of men. There are many whole birds and many whole
flowers. That is, they fill the purpose of their creation on
a 100 per cent basis. But so far as man, the masterpiece
of creation, is concerned, we frequently fall far below our
possibilities. Often the most damaging soft spot in our success is this bad habit of being "almost." We do things by
fragments; we start a lot of things that we never finish.
We do many things poorly, but never become very effective
in any one thing.

A young man, supplied with letters of introduction
from prominent references, once presented himself before
Chief Engineer Parkinson of the Rapid Transit Commission
of New York, as a candidates for a position. "What can
you do?" asked Mr. Parkinson. "Have you any specialty?"
The young man answered, "I can do almost anything."
The chief engineer ended the interview by saying, "I have
no use for anyone who can do *almost* anything. I prefer
someone who can actually do one thing thoroughly."

What a blessing to civilization are the men and women
who can do things to a finish, who complete what they
undertake, who leave nothing just half planned or half
thought out or half decided or half done. Think of all the
people who start out to go to school and then quit before
they have finished, or think of the people who start out
for the celestial kingdom and then get sidetracked before
they have "endured to the end."

"Fragmentation" and "unfinished business" are among
the biggest problems of our world. The great rewards of
life go to those who finish what they start. It is interesting
to watch a horse race and see how everybody wants to

be at the finish line. People are interested in how the race starts, but they are a lot more interested in how it is finished.

The story is told about the first race horse ever to win a million dollars in prizes for its owner. In the particular race which made the winner a millionaire, there was another horse which came in second place. This second-place horse had consistently finished close to the leader, race after race, but his total earnings were only $75,000. The "also ran" was "almost" as good as the champion—never farther behind than a length or two—and yet the champion had won thirteen times as much money. He was not thirteen times as fast; he was not twice as fast; he was not even 2 per cent faster— just a nose or a length in a mile.

We see illustrations of this phenomenon all around us. If the job in hand is to generate steam, you must heat the water with a good fire to 212 degrees. That is where the expansion takes place. If the temperature of the water in the cylinders of a locomotive rises only to 210 degrees, you have wasted your fire. When you "almost" have steam up, you really don't have anything very worthwhile.

It is about the same with success; it is the same in the development of our leadership. It is the one who goes the extra mile—who does more than is expected—who is most likely to get the job done. He is the one who generates that extra balance of power. He is the one that changes a weak "almost" into a powerful "altogether."

Accomplishment is easiest when we work the hardest; it is the hardest when we work the easiest. One who works twice as hard will have four times as much accomplishment. If he works three times as hard he will find that he has nine times as much accomplishment, and he will surely have nine times as much fun in the process.

If we are going to be leaders in the work of the Lord, we ought to be thorough-going leaders, or not take upon

ourselves a task on which so much depends. Certainly
God will not be kindly disposed toward triflers in places
of such overwhelming responsibility. There is probably
no place where this hazard of "almost" is more evident
or more costly than in the work of the Church. Many
people are "almost" early for meetings. They are "almost"
prepared. They "almost" know their business. They
"almost" have their minds made up. They "almost" have
faith. To just "almost" succeed in the work of the Lord
is pretty serious business. What does it profit to have
"almost" succeeded in saving the souls of those for whom
we have responsibility?

Judas almost repented before it was too late. It was
after dark on Thursday night when Judas "went out" and
betrayed Jesus, and it was early Friday morning when he
came back and repented. Matthew said: "When the
morning was come all the chief priests and elders of the
people took counsel against Jesus to put him to death . . .
and . . . (they) delivered him to Pontius Pilate, the governor. Then Judas who had betrayed him when he saw
that he was condemned, repented himself and brought
again the thirty pieces of silver to the chief priests and
elders saying, I have sinned in that I have betrayed innocent blood. And they said, What is that to us? See thou
to that. And he cast down the pieces of silver in the
temple and departed and went out and hanged himself."
(Matt. 27:1-5)

The remorse and repentance of Judas were certainly
sincere, but they weren't quite soon enough. If his repentance had taken place the night before, things might
have been different for him. There are a lot of people
who commit sins at night and repent before morning.
They belong to the "almost" crowd. How much does it
help if we "almost" have enough strength to keep us from
falling into sin?

What we need above most other things is that little extra power, that little extra determination, that little extra training, that little extra devotion, and we need it a little sooner so that we can get out of the "almost" category into the "altogether" class.

Paul had an "almost" missionary companion. His name was Demas. Paul wrote his entire history in nine words. He says: "Demas has forsaken me, having loved this present world." Demas almost made the grade; he had enough power to get himself into the right orbit, but he lacked the power to maintain that position.

Just think how often this tragedy is repeated. A leader accepts a position in the Church. He lacks only 2 per cent of being able to keep himself on the job. His chain of leadership has only a *few* weak links. But when the strain is on, when things are not going quite as smoothly as expected, then like Demas, those who lack the 2 per cent are pulled out of the orbit by some counterattraction.

When a good engineer designs a bridge he makes it three times as strong as necessary to carry the usual load. The bridge is made strong enough to take the maximum strain and then some besides. What confidence it gives if in a bridge or in a leader you can feel unwavering, certain strength. You don't like the feeling that a bridge or a leader is "almost" to break down. You like to feel that if you doubled the load of either it would continue to stand as firm and strong and true as before, with no buckling or breaking even in the weakest places. What a thrill to feel that even in the greatest trials you yourself have more than adequate strength to meet the crisis.

This needed extra strength can be developed. At the trial of Jesus, Peter denied the Master three times. At that point he wasn't strong enough to take the load without buckling. Later when he was sentenced to be crucified, tradition has it that he not only met his end valiantly but he went further. He asked that he might be crucified with his head downward because he felt himself unworthy to be crucified in the same manner as the Lord. Peter now had a great reserve of power. He could take any load that they decided to give him.

The development of this extra strength has in it the spirit of the great American patriot, Nathan Hale, sentenced to be shot as a spy at age 21. He did not buckle nor even bend, but said, "I regret that I have but one life to give for my country." There was no spirit of "almost" about Nathan Hale.

We are the designers of our own leadership qualities. We ought to figure out what strength is needed and where, and then we should make provision in the specifications to build ourselves to carry 300 per cent of the expected load. This strength will be a great blessing to us, and it will help all of those with whom we have to work. Our job is to put ourselves in the "altogether" class with Peter and Paul and Nathan Hale.

THE CHAMPION

The average runner sprints
Until the breath in him is gone;
But the champion has the iron will
That makes him carry on.

For rest, the average runner begs
When limp his muscles grow;
But the champion runs on leaden legs,
His spirit makes him go.

The average man's complacent
When he does his best to score,
But the champion does his best
And then—he does a little more.

As If

MANY YEARS AGO the great psychologist William James announced his famous "as if" principle. That is, if you want a virtue act "as if" you already have it. That is a most constructive idea which we should put into practice. If you want to be brave, act brave. If you want to develop a warm, friendly, happy disposition, don't go around with a scowl on your face and hatred in your heart. Our mental and spiritual faculties are like servants. They always serve us with exactly what we request. If we act as though we expected to be "a nobody," life assumes that we are in earnest and grants our prayer.

In *As You Like It* William Shakespeare says: "All the world's a stage, and all the men and women merely players. . . And one man in his time plays many parts." Suppose you were going to take the part of Hamlet or Macbeth or King Lear in one of Shakespeare's plays. You would first fill your mind with the words and attitudes and spirit of your role. Then you would live the part. You would not only speak and think and act like Hamlet or Macbeth or Lear, but in your mind you would actually *be* Hamlet or Macbeth or Lear.

A recent news release told of the "Passion Play" given every ten years in the little Bavarian village of Oberammergau wherein a group of players re-enact the last week in the life of Christ. The play has been put on regularly since the year 1633. Each player accepts the part he is to play, and then he lives that part and nothing else, until that is what he becomes. The one who plays the part of Jesus must think like Jesus and act like Jesus and feel like Jesus. Can you imagine what the result would be in his life? Or can you imagine the possible power of this "as if" principle in our individual lives if we would just select the role in life that we wished to play and then live the part twenty-four hours per day?

This particular news report of the "Passion Play" gave an interesting item about a man who recently committed suicide. For the previous five years he had been taking the part of Judas. But that is not all. This was the third Judas in recent years who had come to his death by suicide. If he had lived like Judas and thought like Judas, what is more natural than that he should have died like Judas?

Think of the danger that would be involved if you were to pick out some degraded person and then really live his life —fill your mind with his thoughts, adopt his attitudes and habits. What would you expect the outcome to be? No one really knows how far the mind can actually go in influencing our lives. We know it can change our facial expression. It can determine our bodily appearance. It can produce great spirituality within us. It can stamp our personality qualities in any desired denomination. It can send us insane, or it can lift us up to any height of accomplishment, merely by controlling what and how we think.

The "as if" principle is one of the most potent ideas in the world. Pick out any part in life that you wish to play and then play it with all your heart, and that is what you will become. It is as simple as that. Just suppose that a play has been written for you in which your part is to represent a man in the process of making a great fortune. This part requires a man of character, vigor, integrity and enthusiasm, one in whom everyone has confidence, who

conquers by his very presence. But suppose that in playing this part you were to dress in the role of a slouchy,
shiftless, irresponsible person, and that you drag yourself
onto the stage in a lazy, irresolute manner as though you
had no ambition, no determination, no plan and no faith
that you could ever accomplish any worthwhile thing.
Suppose that you went around the stage with an apologetic
manner, completely lacking in self-confidence, and suppose
you kept saying to yourself, "I can't do it." "I am afraid."
"This is too big for me." "I wasn't cut out to be prosperous
and industrious and successful." "Good things were never
meant for me." What kind of impression would you make?
What kind of person would you become? What kind of
success would you get?

How long would it take a young man to become successful if he put himself in an atmosphere of failure and
remained there until he was thoroughly saturated? How
long would it take a man to become a success while continually depreciating himself, thinking failure, talking
failure, dressing like a failure and always complaining of
his insurmountable difficulties? How long would it take
him to arrive at a success which he himself never believed
he could reach? The greatest artist in the world could not
paint the face of a beautiful madonna while he held a
model of depravity in his mind.

And yet this is about what thousands of people are
actually trying to do every day. It is true of their daily
work; it is true of their church work; and it is true of their
lives generally. There are many people who seem almost
completely satisfied to remain in spiritual or material pov-
erty. At least they have ceased any desperate attempt to
rise out of it. Many have lost the expectation or even the
hope of being successful. You can almost gage the quality of a man's outlook on life the first time you meet him.
We can tell how big the streaks of pessimism are in his

life and to what extent he has been soured by a few unfortunate experiences. Some people are too easily disheartened. They sometimes come to look upon everybody with suspicion and believe the worst about everyone, including themselves. As long as a man carries about with him this poorhouse atmosphere, he will always make a poorhouse impression. If we are always overemphasizing the bad in ourselves, if we are always criticizing our own shortcomings and weaknesses and castigating ourselves for not doing better, we only deepen the unfortunate pictures in our consciousness and make them more influential in our lives.

We are too often crippled by the old sectarian idea of man's depravity and inferiority. There is nothing depraved or inferior about the man that God has made. The only inferiority that is in us is what we ourselves put there. God made us in his image. He endowed us with his attributes, and he gave us dominion over everything upon the earth, including ourselves. Man was made to hold up his head and be like God and not like a slave. He was intended to be a success, not a failure. Self-depreciation is a sin. You may be very sure that your success will never rise higher than your confidence in yourself. You must *see* a better world before you can ever hope to live in it. You get the role in life which you yourself select.

What else but the "as if" principle did Isaiah have in mind when he said, "As a man thinketh in his heart so is he"? Isaiah didn't say, "As a man thinketh in his *mind* so is he." The heart was thought of as the seat of consciousness. That is where we feel and live. That is also where we "become."

This "as if" philosophy reached its highest expression in the life and teachings of the Master himself. Jesus said, "All things are possible to him that believeth." It would be difficult to get a stronger expression than this. He didn't just say *a few things* are possible. He said *all* things are possible. It might have been said, "As a man expecteth in his heart so is he." Be very careful about what you expect, for you will probably get it.

Confidence and faith are the very basis of all achievement. What tremendous power there is in a genuine conviction. Jesus said, "According to your faith, be it unto you." This tremendous idea is reiterated throughout the scripture and is the original "as if" principle. This expression of central faith doubles one's power and multiplies his ability. It reached its greatest height in the great objective held up by Jesus when he said, "Be ye therefore perfect, even as your Father which is in heaven is perfect."

Theodore Roosevelt started out in life as a weak, sickly boy. But he "thought" health and courage, and he rose to the highest position his countrymen could give him. Once when he was decorating a soldier for bravery, Roosevelt is reported to have said in substance: "This is the bravest man I have ever seen. He followed right behind me all the way up San Juan Hill." President Roosevelt believed in his soldier but he also believed in himself.

If we don't get courage inside of us, how can it ever come out? It is wonderful for us to believe in God, but it might be even more wonderful to live so that God can also believe in us, and so that we can believe in ourselves. You must believe in yourself and you must like yourself. You must believe in your work and you must like your work. If you want to be great, believe in greatness and live the part. A courageous spirit and an alert, happy mind produce a body to match. There is very little physical sickness among people who are mentally and emotionally robust and in love with life and with what they are doing.

In the Church and out of the Church we see many people who are ruining their lives by negative thinking. We play and live the parts of cowards and sinners and weaklings. We assume a false modesty and say, "I am not capable. I am not worthy. I am not prepared." We become "alibiers" and procrastinators and triflers with God. We accept an assignment with reluctance and perform it with half a heart. Thereby we mold ourselves into deformity.

If we are going to call ourselves servants of the Master, we ought to act like servants of the Master. We should remember who we are, that we are the children of God. If we are ever going to be like God, why should we put off getting started to act that way? Certainly God is not weak nor poor nor sinful nor incapable. If we want to be like him, we had better get started.

Most of the sectarian world believes that God is incomprehensible, unknowable, formless, shapeless, feelingless. If we were formed in the image of nothing, there might be some justification for negative thinking, but that is not true. God is an all-knowing, all-powerful, glorified personage. He is literally the father of our spirits, and according to the laws of heredity we may become like our Father. In possibility we are already like him. We possess every potential power. Therefore we should act the part. Why should we continually think of weakness and failure? Why should we keep our minds operating in reverse by insisting on negative thinking? We can change our lives for good by doing away with the philosophy of failure. We should stop apologizing, criticizing, procrastinating and offering excuses. We should stop forcing someone to remind us of our duty as though we were incompetents or cripples or children. We should cease our falseness and sins. If we keep acting like the devil, that is what we will become.

One of our problems in the Church is our big turnover in office. We are constantly starting and stopping, quitting one job without success and starting something else. Many people betray their attitude by being too greatly pleased when they are released from office. If we think and act like quitters and deserters, we will become quitters and deserters. If we don't get a thrill out of doing God's work, if it weighs us down rather than makes us buoyant and enthusiastic, then there is something wrong with us, and we should repent. The Lord's work is important, and it should be a lot of fun, and we ought to be happy while we are doing it.

Jesus himself said, "Be of good cheer—rejoice and be exceeding glad." The prophet Lehi said, "Men are that they might have joy." (2 Nephi 2:25) The Lord wants us to get started in that direction as soon as possible. Why not just do what he says? If we expect to be great souls in heaven, we ought to start being great souls here. If we want to be happy in eternity, we ought to get in practice. And if we want to be happy we should not act as though we disliked everybody and everything. Rather, we should act "as if" we were already happy.

We ought to study and read and think and work as befits our calling. We ought to know what we are talking about. What a thrilling idea that if we try hard enough we can think Godly and successful thoughts. That is the way we become Godly and successful people. It is possible to turn every defect into a virtue. All we need to do is to understand who we are and then live the part.

Boy Wanted

A POOR BOY from the country, looking for work in the city, saw a sign hanging outside of a store saying, "Boy Wanted." He took the sign down, put it under his arm and walked into the store. The proprietor met him indignantly and asked what he meant by taking down his sign. The boy said, "You won't need the sign any more. I am going to take the job." And he took it, and he kept it.

There are a lot of other signs hanging around the world at various places that need to be taken down, providing someone has the imagination, determination and skill to do the thing that needs to be done in the way it should be done and at the time it ought to be done. Everywhere we go and everyplace we look we see a sign with an urgent meaning which says, "Boy Wanted," or "Man Wanted" or "Woman Wanted." The greatest needs of the world lie behind these signs. James Russell Lowell said that "no man is ever born into the world whose work is not born with him." Everyone has a job to be done which he is supposed to do and which he can do better than anyone else in the world.

A young man by the name of Thomas A. Edison saw a sign which said, "Wanted: A man to light the world and fill it with electrical wonders for the latter days." Young Tom took down the sign and brought about a new day in a new world.

Another young man by the name of Charles A. Lindbergh took down the sign which said, "Wanted: A man to fly the Atlantic." Lindbergh did what had never been done before, and he did it alone, and he did it on his own initiative without being told. He thereby made his own peculiar contribution to the general progress and good of man.

In 1632 the great English architect Sir Christopher Wren was born. He saw some signs hanging around London that needed to be taken down. The great St. Paul's cathedral needed to be built. Sir Christopher Wren built not only St. Paul's, but also fifty-four other churches and thirty-six prominent buildings in London. Later he was buried beneath his great masterpiece, St. Paul's. Upon the walls of the church were written these words: "Underneath is laid the builder of this church and city, Sir Christopher Wren, who lived more than 90 years, not for himself alone, but for the public good. Reader, if you seek his monument look around you." Turn where you will in London, you find monuments to the noble genius of one of the greatest architects who ever lived. Yet he never received instruction from anyone. He needed no one to lean upon, no one to point out what ought to be done. He developed the natural possibilities within himself. He filled a place in the world that no one else could fill, and he filled London with beautiful architecture and useful buildings.

But the story of Christopher Wren is also the story of every man. Every man is unique, and every man can do best that job which only God can teach him. Where is the man who could have taught Shakespeare or Edison or Franklin or Jesus? It is just as true that no one can fill the niche that God intended for you, and someday it will also be said of you, "If you seek his monument, look around you."

In 1809 in a little backwoods Kentucky cabin with a dirt floor, a boy baby named Abraham Lincoln was born. He was "born without a chance." But he studied while others wasted their time. He worked while others played. He said, "I will prepare now and take my chances when

the opportunity arrives." Almost before he was ready he
saw the world hanging out the sign which said, "Wanted:
A man to free the slaves." Lincoln took down the sign. The
time was upon him, and he was ready.

In September, 1863, Lincoln issued his preliminary
Emancipation Proclamation, which someone called the
most sublime act of the 19th century. That day Lincoln
wrote in his diary, "I promised my God that I would do
it." No one can doubt that God had much to do with
hanging out the sign of freedom and helping to inspire
the mighty resolution in the heart of Lincoln who took it
down. It always produces a great power within us when
we promise God we will be faithful to the best that he has
placed within us, to be faithful to our destiny, to be devoted
to our calling.

Martin Luther was born into a world that badly
needed a religious reformation. He took down the sign
and went to work, almost single-handed, against overpowering opposition. When his supreme test came, he
said, "Here I stand. I cannot do otherwise. God help me.
Amen." The reformation which he started prepared the
way for still greater things to come.

Then a fourteen-year old boy in Palmyra, New York,
saw the sign which said, "Wanted: Someone to restore the
gospel and open the greatest of all the dispensations."
Joseph went into the woods to pray to ask God for direction.
He came out of the woods with the sign under his arm.
The Lord had told Joseph that he had been selected for
the job. Joseph walked across the fields to his father's
house and went into the kitchen where his mother was
working. He said to her in substance: Mother, I have seen
God. It was as simple as that. A new and final dispensation was now under way. Important assignments are
sometimes made in the most unexpected places and to the
most unexpected people. But the Lord knows what he

is doing. Joseph Smith could do this particular job better than anyone else could. Opening a new dispensation meant that many more calls would be made and many more workers would be required to carry forward the greatest enterprise ever undertaken upon the earth.

The Lord has included every one of us in the program. He said to the Prophet, "Every man who has a calling to minister to the inhabitants of this earth was ordained to that very purpose in the grand council in heaven before the world was." (*DHC* VI:364) You were high in the councils of heaven in your first estate. Your responsibility was made plain to you even before the world was created. Your sign is now being put up again. It says, "Wanted: A boy to be president of the deacon's quorum, a boy who, by his dependability, initiative, industry and faith, can lead his associates to lives of manhood and godliness by teaching them the simple duties of their office."

Another sign says, "Wanted: A faithful ward teacher, one who can effectively touch the lives of people, stimulate their activity, uncover their possibilities and help them find the place where they can serve best." Most people need someone to locate that vein of gold which is buried in every life. Sometimes we don't seem to be able to fulfill our destiny by ourselves; someone else is often the discoverer of our greater possibilities. Some of us miss our way because we do not always correctly read the message of our own lives.

Then there is another sign which says, "Woman wanted, to teach the members of a Sunday School class the gospel of Jesus Christ and by her own inspiration start them toward their eternal exaltation."

There are many other important jobs to be filled. Mrs. David McKay once saw a sign which said, "Woman wanted to be the mother of the future President of the

Church." She took down the sign and today her son stands on the very pinnacle of accomplishment.

There is another sign which says, "Man wanted to be bishop of the ward, one to select personnel, train leadership, supervise workers and see to it that every member of the ward qualifies for the celestial kingdom."

None of these signs are for midgets with stunted vision to do pigmies' work. They inquire for those who have a creator's touch and a master's sense of responsibility. They ask for men and women inspired by a noble purpose, whose minds are capable of being stretched to new and greater dimensions. The importance of our times requires that present problems be solved better than they have ever been solved before. The sign cries out:

> Bring me men to match my mountains,
> Bring me men to match my plains,
> Men with empires in their bosoms,
> And new eras in their brains.

But not every sign is heeded. Not all are taken down. "Behold, there are many called, but few are chosen. And why are they not chosen? Because their hearts are set so much upon the things of this world." We sometimes get so busy with the "hewing of wood and the drawing of water" that we miss our life's work, the work to which we were set apart in "our first estate." You were one of God's noble spirits, and if you do not do the job, there will always be a deficit in the program of the Lord, "for nobody else can do the work God has marked out for you."

Many fail because they think they are not capable and become discouraged. It will help us to remember that not all great men are brilliant; not all are handsome; not all have famous ancestors or good educations. The work of the world has always been done by imperfect men in an imperfect way and will continue to be so done until time ends. It is claimed by some that Paul was a hunch-back. He was thought of as extremely homely. He him-self says he had a "thorn in the flesh." For a long time he fought the work of the Lord. Lincoln was ungainly and awkward. Sir Christopher Wren was untaught. Thomas A. Edison was kicked out of school when he was fourteen. Thomas the Apostle was a doubter. Peter denied Jesus. The Prophet Joseph Smith would not have been on the list of those voted most likely to succeed. But each did well that part of the work which he was called to do.

The work of the world has been divided up. Some people do the inventing; some fight the battles; some dis-cover new continents; some teach the lessons; some preach the sermons. The South grows the cotton; Detroit makes the automobiles; Florida, California, Arizona and Texas supply the citrus; the midwest produces the corn. And then, as Isaiah had foretold, the mountain of the Lord's house has been established in the tops of the mountains, from whence the word of the Lord shall go forth to every kindred, nation, tongue and people. This is the responsi-bility to which we are called. The thing for which we are better suited than anything else is to assist in the work of human salvation. We have taken down the sign. It is our job. It will be our blessing.

Your work was also born with you. It is important. You have your call. Undertake it with a high ambition and a sense of responsibility that will not be denied. Then dullness will lessen, inaptitude will vanish; and day by day there will develop in you a power previously unknown. You must succeed in doing your part of the Lord's work. Before your birth your work was written down in heaven. If you work at it devotedly enough, you may find the power to do it better than like work has ever been done before.

God give us faith. We know that all things are pos-sible to him that believeth. May the Lord help us to take our proper place, that we may not leave our call unanswered or our work for someone else to do. One of the greatest possible sins would be to return to God the life which he has has given us with our abilities undiscovered and our talents undeveloped and unutilized. We remember that one of the most bitter rebukes ever given by Jesus was to him who buried his talents in the ground. Fractional devotion or partial use of our God-given talents is displeasing to our Creator. Therefore look for the sign with your name written upon it. It has a very urgent meaning. It reads, "Wanted, A Man."

Caesar's Ghost

WILLIAM SHAKESPEARE wrote thirty-seven plays and staffed them with a thousand characters. His characters were sometimes real people and sometimes the personification of personality traits. Shakespeare had an understanding of human behavior and an ability to give that behavior a voice and a personality that have seldom if ever been equaled. He said his purpose was to "hold as 'twere the mirror up to nature—to show Virtue her own features, scorn her own image." He said, "I your looking glass will be and will modestly discover to you qualities which you yourself know not of." To be clearly shown the good and the bad in success is a constructive service that our leadership may take advantage of.

Shakespeare's Julius Caesar might be called a personification of courage. Inasmuch as courage is one of the chief ingredients of leadership, we might hold it up for study while we absorb its philosophy and use its power to stiffen our spine. At any rate, here is a profile of the courage of Shakespeare's Julius Caesar.

Caesar is reported to have been an epileptic, and it is probable that there are people drawing total disability benefits who are in better physical condition. And yet in spite of his handicaps, he raised himself to be the greatest man of his day. How did he do it? If we can discover the process we may be able to use it in our own interests.

While the conspirators were plotting Caesar's overthrow, Cassius was telling them of some of Caesar's weaknesses, in the light of which he could not understand how Caesar had risen to such a great height. He told of one occasion when Caesar had challenged him to swim the Tiber, but part way across Caesar tired and cried, "Help me, Cassius, or I sink." Cassius turned around in midstream, went back and rescued the drowning Emperor and swam to shore, carrying Caesar upon his back. On another occasion while the army was in Spain, a fit of epilepsy came upon Caesar before his generals and men. Cassius told how Caesar's great eyes lost their luster, his lips lost their color, and the great tongue that bade the Romans write down his speeches in their books became as that of a sick girl.

Cassius knew of these weaknesses and was greatly disturbed that Caesar had so far outdistanced him in greatness. Cassius said:

> And this man
> Is now become a god, and Cassius is
> A wretched creature and must bend his body
> If Caesar carelessly but nod on him.
>
> * * *
>
> Why, man, he doth bestride the narrow world
> Like a Colossus; and we petty men
> Walk under his huge legs, and peep about
> To find ourselves dishonourable graves.

And then he said,

> Now, in the names of all the gods at once,
> Upon what meat doth this our Caesar feed,
> That he is grown so great?

That is a good question, because greatness does feed upon certain things, and the diet of Caesar might give us some ideas. We might begin our study by examining the words of Caesar himself. Caesar had had a premonition of approaching trouble and had been cautioned to stay at home and not go to the capital that day. He was suspicious

of several people. One of them was Cassius. He expressed
this suspicion to his friend, Mark Antony, but Antony tried
to reassure him, saying, "Fear him not, Caesar . . . He is a
noble Roman." Listen to Caesar's reply. Caesar said:

> . . . I fear him not:
> Yet if my name were liable to fear,
> I do not know the man I should avoid
> So soon as that spare Cassius.

Caesar said in substance, "I don't fear Cassius; I don't
fear anyone. My name is not even liable to fear." Again
Caesar said,

> Danger knows full well
> That Caesar is more dangerous than he:
> We are two lions litter'd in one day,
> And I the elder and more terrible:
> And Caesar shall go forth.

That may not have been good judgment, but it certainly was courage. Caesar said,

> Cowards die many times before their deaths;
> The valiant never taste of death but once.
> Of all the wonders that I yet have heard,
> It seems to me most strange that men should fear;
> Seeing that death, a necessary end,
> Will come when it will come.

Caesar thought and felt and acted courage until it
had become a part of him. Anyone with that kind of
attitude and fortitude, with the industry to back it up,
could hardly prevent himself from becoming an outstanding man, epileptic or no epileptic.

After Caesar had been stabbed, the Roman Empire
was divided into two camps, one led by Caesar's friends,
Antony and Octavius, and the other by the conspirators

under Brutus. If Caesar was the personification of courage, then Brutus was probably the personification of prestige or honor. Several men were induced to join the conspiracy only if Brutus would lead them. Casca said of Brutus,

> . . . he sits high in all the people's hearts:
> And that which would appear offence in us,
> His countenance, like richest alchemy,
> Will change to virtue and to worthiness.

Even after the death of Caesar, his courage continued to be a factor to be reckoned with. The conspirators were afraid, and fear breeds weakness in overly-fearful men. Brutus and his associates began to talk about their fear among themselves. They not only infected themselves with discouragement by their negative thoughts, but in recounting their fears, they magnified their discouragement. George Bernard Shaw says that "when we are discouraged we use our reason to support our fears and our prejudices. We have some unwholesome doubts, and doubt is the first step on the road to betrayal and surrender." These first steps the conspirators were now taking.

Just as Caesar had thought about and talked about and magnified courage, the conspirators magnified their weakness and discouragement. It was not long before in the imagination of Brutus the ghost of Caesar began paying visits to him. It is easy to build things up in our own minds until they destroy us. As Job once said, "That which I feared is come upon me." A great American president once said that the only thing we have to fear is fear itself. Fear makes us resemble one with the delirium tremens who thinks he has snakes in his bed. Real snakes may be bad, but imaginary snakes can do terrible things to people, even to sending them out of their minds. Fear can easily get out of hand and paralyze its possessor.

The conspirator leaders were following the pattern of
going from doubts to fears, to discouragement, and then to
surrender. Soon one by one, the conspirator generals began
to commit suicide. Human nature hasn't changed very
much. Last year in the United States 18,000 people committed suicide also because they were afraid. In one way
or another most failure is suicide because we ourselves
bring it about.

Cato expressed the situation thus:

> O Julius Caesar! thou art mighty yet:
> Thy spirit walks abroad, and turns our swords
> In our own . . . entrails.

Then Brutus himself, the greatest of them all, decided
to give up the fight. He did not surrender to the enemy
army nor to Antony or Octavius, but to the ghost of a
helpless but courageous Caesar. Brutus said,

> The ghost of Caesar hath appear'd to me
> Two several times by night; at Sardis once,
> And, this last night, here in Philippi fields.
> I know my hour is come.

That is the way all men feel when they get severely
discouraged and can't stop thinking and talking of failure.
All failures in the advanced stages say to themselves, "I
know my hour is come." Every leader has much in common
with a general. Both must believe in themselves to be successful. Both must have courage. A leader or a general
who is always shaking in his boots and always seeing ghosts
had better find some scheme to bolster up his courage. No
spirit from the other world has ever been known to do
anyone bodily harm. But some of the most serious obstacles
to success are the imaginary hazards which never exist,
except in our own minds. We fight the ghosts of doubt,

the ghosts of unbelief, the ghosts of failure and fear. We are afraid of what someone will think, or afraid that someone doesn't like us. We are afraid that we will not be able to put our objective over, and in one way or another we create a thousand hazards that exist only in our imagination.

Brutus indicated that the ghost came by night. That was when Brutus was not fighting and had time to be negative and scared. No one ever sees a ghost when he is on the job courageously doing his best. The ghosts that bother us are those that we see when we are not doing our duty. Brutus had let his courage get away from him, and it is a natural law that "that which we fear we bring to pass."

Finally Brutus could stand the strain no longer. Like a lot of people in other life situations, Brutus allowed doubt, fear and discouragement to give him a case of "battle fatigue." Brutus was a young man, but youth does not make one immune to either discouragement or weariness. He had lost his grip on himself. All of the fight had been taken out of him, and he wanted to "throw in the towel." He wanted to quit. He said,

> Night hangs upon mine eyes; my bones
> would rest.

When one loses his courage he always tires easily. People who live on courage and enthusiasm usually don't get tired. But how can a fearful man get rested, or where can he go to get away from his imagination and his negative mind?

Brutus decided that the only solution would be to take his own life. Some of his associates tried to dissuade him. Their arguments have been put into verse:

> O Brutus, stain not a life of glory in its end,
> Leave not thine honor and our hopes
> With thy body in the fields of Philippi.
> Wherefore dost thou say that virtue is but a shadow

When thou shalt soon enjoy its reward.
Imagine not that thou art going to die;
No, thou art going to live
To fulfill every promise that has been made to thee.

But Brutus would not be dissuaded. He had come to the end of his rope. His courage had collapsed and he could go no further. It is pretty difficult to bolster up one's mind when he feels that dead weight of discouragement and fear around his heart.

Finally Brutus said to his servant Strato,

Hold then my sword, and turn away thy face
While I do run upon it.

Then Strato held the sword while his master committed suicide. Then lying on the ground with his sword in his own heart, Brutus spoke his last words:

Ceasar, now be still:
I kill'd not thee with half so good a will.

That is, he was so pleased "to call it quits," so pleased to get out of the fight, that it was a greater satisfaction to run the sword into his own heart than overthrow Caesar for the good of Rome. Even the greatest men can fail if they allow themselves a short supply of certain character qualities.

Antony himself paid Brutus this tribute:

This was the noblest Roman of them all:
All the conspirators save only he
Did that they did in envy of great Caesar;
He only, in a general honest thought
And common good to all, made one of them.
His life was gentle, and the elements
So mix'd in him that Nature might stand up
And say to all the world, "This was a man!"

The failure of Brutus teaches what can happen when one becomes discouraged. Many of us fail in that same manner. Cato, one of the famous contemporaries of Brutus, committed suicide on the very eve of his triumph. If he had hung on until morning he would have been acclaimed a victor. That is the case with us more often than we realize. Courage, like the other great personality qualities, has a very high value, particularly in leadership. It can be developed, but we must think courage and practice courage.

Caesar lived with hardship and danger. He made his personality robust by doing the things that other men were afraid to do. His experience and his attitude of mind had given him a strong, sound, useful courage. Strength is born of the mind. Shakespeare said, "All things are ready if our minds be so." John Milton said, "The mind in its own place and of itself can make a heaven of hell or a hell of heaven." It can also help us develop courage and every other desired leadership quality.

One of the greatest messages of the Master—the most courageous leader who ever lived—says to us, "Fear not." "Be not afraid."

What a thrilling challenge to build up our strength for use in his work and never allow our leadership to be wiped out by the ghosts of doubt, fear, discouragement, or disbelief.

Can Do

WHEN YOU were a child you were probably entertained by the old stories from the *Arabian Nights* which told of flying carpets, seven-league boots and magic lanterns. The other night as I flew nonstop through the darkness high above the earth to Chicago, I marveled at how far we have surpassed the ancient wonder of flying carpets. In their wildest imagination the writers of Arabian Nights tales never dreamed of putting a windshield or a radio or food service or rubber seats or even a safety belt on a flying carpet.

There was one story out of *Arabian Nights* to which I was particularly attracted. It told about a young man by the name of Aladdin who had an unusual lamp. Every time he rubbed this lamp it summoned a giant genie to do his bidding. This very helpful servant built a beautiful palace for Aladdin; it gave him wealth, power and luxury, and made it possible for him to marry the princess.

As the years have come and gone there have been many people who have wished for some way to summon extra power to get and be what they wanted. This desire for power is still one of the strongest influences in people and has been partly responsible for the creation of the giant mechanical engines that now serve us on every hand. But we still do some daydreaming about how convenient it would be to have some dependable, willing, personal servant always at our elbow to help solve our problems, to get what we want, and promote our influence and leadership.

What we do not often realize is that we actually have available an almost unbelievable power which we allow to go largely unutilized. The greatest source of power, now as anciently, is in people. But many of our greatest human resources have never been very well understood or developed. For centuries our material lives existed by very primitive means, even though unknown wonders surrounded us on every hand. Invention and discovery have now revealed these wonders to us and transformed our world. Our biggest question now has to do with the progress of man himself. Edwin Markham might have been speaking for us all when he said—

> Why build these cities glorious
> If man unbuilded goes?
> In vain we build the world
> Unless the builder also grows.

That is our present most serious and most urgent problem. It has been variously estimated that the average man still uses only a very small percentage of his potentialities. Our powers are not only unused, but undiscovered. The thing that we probably know the least about is our own individual selves. We know how to fly through the stratosphere faster than sound; we have solved our problems of food supply, housing, transportation and communication. We have even reached into the world of the atom and released a power so fantastic as to be unbelievable. But we have not discovered enough power to stop our negative thinking or overcome our lethargy or conquer our sins. We don't know how to get 100 per cent ward teaching or make our leadership operate with an efficiency comparable to that of our most simple machines. We can't control our moods, our enthusiasms, our passions, our tempers or our thoughts.

Hundreds of people who down inside themselves want to do right are doing things to shock and embarrass their families, their friends and themselves. People are going to psychiatrists by the thousands to ask why they themselves do as they do. Dmitri Karamazov might have been voicing our feelings when he said, "I have been wretched all of my life because I have yearned to be honorable while I have continued to do unworthy things." Paul said, "When I would do good, evil is present with me." This underlines our need for more power.

Aladdin would have rubbed his lamp and given his genie orders. We also have a genie who will carry out orders. Living somewhere in the unexplored regions of the subconscious mind or the spirit, there is a wonderfully efficient helper who can transform our lives. When fully commissioned he is a marvel of accomplishment. Someone has appropriately named our genie CAN DO. It took Aladdin quite a while to find out how to handle his genie. He finally stumbled onto the secret more or less by accident. It may also take us a little while to learn how to handle CAN DO. Mostly this great power within us is bound down and helpless. If we will only set him free he will serve us gratefully all the rest of our days with a greater devotion than that with which the genie served Aladdin.

This situation comes about because for all practical purposes each of us is at least two people, not just one person. H. G. Wells said, "I am not a man but a mob." This heterogeneous population of our souls gets going in a dozen different directions at the same time and we become stalemated and confused. At best man is a very contradictory being. He has a positive and a negative pole, so to speak. Goethe says, "Two souls are lodged within my breast that struggle there for undivided reign." The psychologist says that man has a split personality. Certainly virtue and vice are strangely intermingled in human nature. Dr. Robert J. McCracken says, "We can sometimes be fully conscious of the folly of a decision and yet at the very moment be knowingly proceeding to carry it out. . . . Human nature is not fundamentally and essentially rational. It is often appallingly irrational. Nothing is more irrational than sin." We do things that just don't make sense, and then we keep exclaiming to ourselves, "Why did we do it?"

In Robert Sherwood's play, Abraham Lincoln says of himself, "You talk about a civil war. There seems to be one going on inside of me all of the time. One of these days I may just split asunder and part company with myself." That is a pretty good idea. We can probably solve our problems best by thinking of ourselves as two people. One is our better self; the other is our poorer self. Mark Twain said that everyone is like a moon which always has a dark side and a light side.

Suppose we hold up the mirror and study ourselves. The first look shows us what we are—weak, divided, undetermined, unsuccessful. But if we look again—and if we look carefully—we might see the person that God intended us to be—strong, consolidated, resolute and filled with power. Our better self is always anxious to do right, to be successful, but the darker side of our nature is always pulling in the other direction. Paul said, "That which I would I do not, and that which I would not that I do." This is a very vexing situation and continually confronts most of us.

To better understand ourselves we might remember the difficulties involved in Robert Louis Stevenson's story of Dr. Jekyll and Mr. Hyde. A kindly, generous, capable physician by day became an uncontrolled, unprincipled degenerate by night. Many people in a lesser degree re-enact this duality in their daily life and work. We say of someone, "He is not himself today," or "He was not at his best today." Our better self is always trying to build us while our "Mr. Hyde" is actually tearing us down. We express this paradox by saying, "We are our own worst enemy."

We make our mistake in allowing our better and our

poorer selves more or less equal authority. This almost always results in a stalemate. Let's imagine therefore that these two personalities "part company," as President Lincoln suggested, and then put our better self in charge and give him unlimited jurisdiction. A group of workers will always get more work done if you make the best one the boss and give him plenty of authority with which to direct the others. The mind can also be given extra authority and charged with additional power so that instead of being pushed around by the appetites, the passions, the fears and the doubts that support our less desirable selves, the mind may reign supreme. A person usually has great authority over his arms and legs. If he tells them to move they will obey. He may get that same kind of authority over the mind, the tongue, the heart and the ambition.

Now here is where CAN DO comes into the picture. The primary weakness in human personality is lack of properly directed works. We have a natural tendency to talk and think and plan, but then we let it go at that. We don't always follow through very well. We have a lot of faith that never matures into action. Many wonderful objectives are never born; ambitions die in infancy. To reduce the death rate of our accomplishment, we will charge CAN DO, our strong better self, to take the initiative, to start the ball rolling. We will make him responsible for accomplishment. He must see to it that every order is carried out.

Emerson once said, "What I need is someone to get me to do the things that I ought to do." That is what we all need. There is only one who can do that. Our own success must be an "inside job." That is, CAN DO, our better self, when properly charged, is all-powerful. He can enforce every order and make it effective among the other elements of our personality. But there must be no question about who is the boss. Our influence must always be on the right side. If we support the enemy a part of the time all morale will be destroyed. We also need to pass some firm decrees that every order must be carried out without exception, without delay and without alteration. The ward teaching must be done the first week of the month; the planning meetings must be properly held; the self-improvement program must go forward on schedule. Exceptions, if allowed, will tear us down faster than our better selves can build us up. Once we have a solid authority established, then we need to develop an effective, regular system of execution and establish some sound habits of success. Once we get reason and righteousness in force as the determining cause of action, supported by system and good habits, we will be surprised what undreamed-of powers will immediately rush to our aid. Any weakness can be overcome by appropriate action. Soon we will be on our way to becoming the man God intended us to be. This is also the man James had in mind when he said, "Be ye doers of the word and not hearers only." When we are only hearers we merely widen the split in our personality and put our weaker self back as co-captain of our soul.

We must not allow exceptions to activity and success. We must keep the emphasis exactly where James put it, on action. We must carry to the finish everything that we start. Every undone or unfinished task becomes an obstacle to our own progress. Every time we violate our conscience or stumble over an assignment we tear down our central control and weaken our CAN DO. It is a serious thing to undermine the goodness of our Dr. Jekyll and strengthen the deformity of our Mr. Hyde.

Jesus said, "If ye know these things, happy are ye if ye do them." Suppose we know a thing and don't do it. We become sinners, for "to him that knoweth to do good and doeth it not to him it is sin." Proper action generates the power to destroy sin and failure. Our own CAN DO is the most wonderful force in the world when properly established and supported. CAN DO will never fall down. He will always get the job done. He will always bring home the bacon. He will always keep us identified as our better self. Carl Erskine, the famous Brooklyn baseball pitcher, said, "I never pray to win; I just pray to be in my best form." There are no better prayers than this. Our best form is the form God intended for us.

Just think what would happen if we were *always* in our best form, if we always did just as well as we could, if we always followed every worthy program through to maturity. Then nothing would be impossible to us. To do this would mean that we would always have this powerful servant CAN DO waiting at our elbow. CAN DO knows his business; he keeps us at our peak of performance; he never has to be reminded or coaxed.

The Prophet Nephi had CAN DO. His brothers were afraid and ran away; they always sided with their poorer selves; they were always weak. But Nephi was at his best. He said, "I will go and do the things which the Lord hath commanded, for I know that the Lord giveth no commandments unto the children of men save he shall prepare a way for them that they may accomplish the things which he commanded them." (I Ne. 3:7) What great power is thus produced within us. The elder brothers of Nephi carried with them the seeds of death. They had Can't Do and Won't Do, and they infected and destroyed a whole civilization. In the conflict that went on inside of Laman and Lemuel they gave their "won't power" greater encouragement than their "will power." They thought of all of the reasons why good things should not be done. They were full of procrastination and alibis. In some of the most important things they weren't interested one way or the other. This is the process that puts CAN DO back in chains where he can accomplish nothing.

Think of all the things that we can't do without CAN DO. For example, just try to get a group of people to be on time for their meetings. They may be completely convinced that they should be punctual; they may even want to be punctual; and yet they will habitually come in late. They have locked their CAN DO down in the dungeon. People can be 100 per cent punctual with a margin to spare when catching an airplane. Then they have CAN DO, for they know there will be no exception or excuses. Then they are not divided. But in going to Sunday School 50 per cent of the same people will come in late. They have given their authority and support back to their poorer selves. We follow the same pattern in the more difficult subdivisions of our work.

Aladdin summoned his genie by rubbing a lamp. There is a more up-to-date and scientific method. The following will always work:

1. We must get a strong partiality on the side of success.

2. We must know our business.

Everything is easy when you know how. An interesting story is told of Ralph Waldo Emerson trying to get the calf into the barn. This particular calf had not been fully persuaded that he should do what Mr. Emerson wanted him to do. Mr. Emerson lacked something in know-how so far as calves were concerned. The great scholar from Concord took his logical position at the calf's rear and forcibly tried to propel the calf into the barn. The harder Mr. Emerson pushed the more firmly the calf braced himself to resist. Mr. Emerson pushed and puffed and said some uncomplimentary things about calves, but the calf held the line. The struggle left Mr. Emerson with exactly no ground gained. Then an Irish servant girl came by and seeing the predicament offered a helping hand. She put one finger of that hand into the calf's mouth and started for the barn. The calf, enticed by this maternal imitation, went along enthusiastically. As Mr. Emerson wiped the perspiration from his steaming, scholarly brow and proceeded to cleanse his hands of their bovine smell, he was heard to mutter to himself, "I like people who can do things." A good question for us to ask ourselves about our leadership is, Can we get the calf into the barn?

3. CAN DO can accomplish almost every miracle by the simple use of "the follow-through." Every job should be done to a finish. Nothing is so fatal to character or accomplishment as unfinished jobs. We believe in too many things that we do little or nothing about. We can strengthen our CAN DO by strengthening our follow-through.

4. CAN DO rule number four is TO BE, not merely to seem. Mr. Emerson says that the greatest sin is pretense. CAN DO is the son of I AM and there must be no pretense. The purpose of life is not what we can get out of it but what we can become by it. Jesus was great because of what he was. There was no place for failure to attack Jesus. He had no vulnerable spots, no insincerity, no vacillation, no indecision, no procrastination, no indifference, no lack of effort. One of the highest titles of the God of Creation is I AM.

Leadership must be genuine if it is to be worthy of its name. Jesus had the power *to be* because he developed the power *to do*. He had the power to do because he earned the power *to know* and he gave us the key when he said, "If ye know these things, happy are ye if ye do them."

Leadership must be energetic. It must be active. Aladdin summoned a powerful genie by rubbing a magic lamp. The rules have now been brought up-to-date. They are all available to us. If we follow them faithfully they will bring to our elbow a giant helper who will transform our lives and our leadership. Remember his name. It is CAN DO.

Can You Hear the Whistle?

MUCH HAS been said and written about leadership and the means by which it may be brought about. For convenient study, leadership is divided up into subheadings; first, that we might be able to better understand what it is, and second, that we might reduce it to its most simple denomination, thus making it easier to master and reproduce in our own lives.

Some of the important subheadings of leadership have to do with "selection," "training" and "discipline." The great businesses of the world are annually spending millions of dollars in aptitude testing, personal interviewing and other means of selecting the right person for the right job. Square pegs in round holes have always proven very costly. After "selection" comes "training." A trained man is always more effective than an untrained man. When we default in our leadership training, we waste our greatest resource. But in the presence of both careful selection and effective training, great accomplishment is more easily brought about. We need the best ideas and the most stimulating motivation to help us in these important processes of leadership development.

A very interesting and helpful story has been told many times about some of the procedures used in the selection and training of the finest Arabian horses. These are the horses that are to be used in important service. The horse, of course, must have intelligence and stamina. But he must also have the ability to accept rigid discipline. There must be unquestioned obedience to the command of the master. Early in the horse's training he is taught the importance of instantly responding to the master's whistle. To test the horse's discipline and to prove his power of control, each horse is given very severe selection tests, one being to see how he behaves under pressure. He is deprived of water for a long period. Then when the corral gate is finally opened, the horse makes a break for the clear, cold water near-by to quench his long thirst. But just as the horse is about to reach the water, the master's whistle is blown. It is said that when the horses are very thirsty some of them pay no attention to the whistle; others hurriedly slake their thirst and *then* obey the whistle. But there are some that, no matter what the circumstances when they hear the whistle, will immediately turn and go to the master. These horses are the honor graduates and are accepted for the most important service. The others are eliminated as culls to be used in less vital work.

Life has some leadership examinations that are very similar. These are continually being given to us who are candidates for the service of the Master. How well we pass the tests determines our assignment. Every day we are given choices to make, and by our choices we set an evaluation upon ourselves and determine our own future.

We remember one of these tests which was given to Jesus. He began his ministry by being baptized of John. Immediately thereafter he was led by the spirit into the wilderness where he fasted for forty days and forty nights in preparation for his encounter with Satan and his great test of temptation. (Matt. 4:1) When he was at the point of his greatest physical weakness and hunger, Satan offered him food, glory and power. Jesus passed all of these tests without wavering, just as he passed every other test without wavering. This was one of the marks of his greatness and certified his right to be called the Master. He was master of temptation. He was master of circumstances and, what was greater, he was master of himself.

Now, by contrast, think of some others who under far less strain do not pass the test and consequently are discarded as culls. For example, I know a returned missionary who had become very successful as a salesman and finally was placed as a junior executive with a great corporation. He had passed many tests successfully, but one very important test he did not pass. As his success seemed to him to be increasing, he began to forget the ideals of his training. He began to smoke; he drank a little and did some other things incompatible with his standards of right and wrong. He disregarded the whistle of his conscience and the still small voice of the spirit. When this came to the attention of the officers having to do with his advancement, he was dropped as a candidate for major executive responsibility and transferred to a less responsible assignment. One of these top officers was later questioned about the matter. He said that his company would never promote a member of the LDS Church to a responsible position who was not true to his ideals and training. This officer was not LDS, and he himself smoked, and drank a little. This was not a matter of religion with him; it was a matter of character and good business sense.

Men who must carry great responsibility must not have too many weak places in their character. Our actions are not only important for themselves alone; they are also important for what they are a sign of. That this young man would forsake his standards for trivial things was a sign that there was a serious weakness in his make-up. Too great a weakness classifies an Arabian horse, or a member of a business organization, or a church worker as a cull, fit only for inferior responsibility.

If the horse is not dependable under all circumstances, that fact had better be found out before he fails in some important responsibility. The same is true with any man. How important it is that we give full attention to building our strengths and eliminating weaknesses from ourselves before *they* eliminate us from the race!

It seems fairly natural that an Arabian horse might feel that slaking his own burning thirst before doing his duty was justifiable. It is also easy to imagine that we might become so absorbed in our own interests or pleasures that we fail to hear the call of duty or the voice of right. But if the still small voice of the spirit doesn't get through to us, obviously we are defective so far as the most important service is concerned. For when the corral gate is opened, so to speak, no one will be able to tell for sure what we will do, except that we will probably seek our own satisfactions in our own way as our first consideration.

The weakness in this young returned missionary disqualified him for important service and the honor and opportunity that went with it. It is pretty hard to be a cull in character and not be a cull everywhere else. This young man had fine capabilities, but he could not be trusted when the pressure of his own interests manifested themselves. He could then not be counted upon to be loyal and dependable so far as the firm was concerned. This was the considered opinion of a staff of top business men. But what do you think the Lord's opinion would have been? What do you think he would have thought of his own Son if he had not been dependable and true to the teaching of his Father under all circumstances?

We remember what Judas did when he had a chance to make thirty pieces of silver. He beat down the shouting of his conscience while he attempted to slake his greedy thirst in gold.

The Arabian horses have only the whistle of their master to guide them. They must trust that which they may not fully understand. But we have the gospel. We have our understanding and our reason. We have this wonderful little personal policeman called our conscience.

We have this still small voice of the spirit which gives us continual direction. One who gives a faithful ear to his conscience will never make very many mistakes, at least without knowing what he is doing. It is only when we won't listen or when we refuse to obey that we get into serious trouble. Our problem is to prepare our hearts and our attitudes and our ears that we will always be able to hear, and then to obey the whistle.

Jesus said, "My sheep, hear my voice." Righteousness has a familiar spirit to those who follow the Master. However, if one continually violates his conscience it will not be long before his conscience will fail to guide him. Only in continual obedience is there safety.

A shepherd's daughter as a child went with her father out onto the moors to help him tend the sheep. It was one of her greatest delights to hear her father give the shepherd's call when the sheep were scattered. It sounded loud and clear across the moors, and the sheep seemed to understand that the call was in their interests and that they must always obey it. It is certain that at times some of the sheep had not finished their grazing or for some other reason were "not quite ready" when the call came. But they responded just the same. Just suppose that one of the sheep decided not to answer the call but to spend the night on the moor away from the sheepfold. It would not be long before wolves or thieves would make short work of such an unwise sheep.

The shepherd's daughter herself when she grew older left the shelter and security of her own home and went alone to the big city. Like all such young women, she felt perfectly capable of taking care of herself, but she became involved in the big city ways and entangled in its sins. Unpleasant rumors began to circulate and soon reached back to her home. The father, true to his shepherd instincts, went to the city in search of his daughter. He walked through the city and gave the shepherd's call, which finally came to her ears. She heard the call; she understood its meaning and realized her own danger. She found her father and she found herself.

One of the greatest concerns of Jesus was for those who had ears but who could not or would not hear. It is so easy to turn a deaf ear on those things we don't want to hear. As long as we are faithful, the still small voice continually prompts us. But if we continue to disregard its voice and turn our back on its counsel, it grows more inaudible and indistinct, until we are left alone.

To excel in our work we don't need to be blessed with great mental powers. It is not necessary to win beauty prizes or popularity contests. But we must be able to hear the whistle. We must be true to the instincts that God, our Father, has provided for our benefit and guidance. Then, the possibility of success is multiplied many times. For then if we start towards some wrong deed, conscience blows its whistle. If we are slack in our duty, the whistle is our constant reminder.

Job heard the whistle and went to the Master. He said, "Though he slay me, yet will I trust in him."

Lincoln heard the whistle as the trumpet call of his life. His spirit expanded with the determination to be true to the best that he knew.

There are some men and women whose mental and moral reception is so delicately tuned that they hear the slightest whisper of their conscience. Obedience is still better than sacrifice. We very largely select ourselves for important service with the Master by the process of our own discipline. Only when we have inner spiritual perception are we really ready to make progress. It is not enough that we just hear the whistle when it suits us, but we must also hear and obey it even when we are on the edge of some great personal satisfaction which we must abandon. Then if we are champions, without hesitation we will turn from our intended pleasure and go to the master.

What a marvelous satisfaction it must be to the great Shepherd of us all to know that we are obedient, that we can be trusted, that we will do right regardless of the consequences or the enticements on the other side. Occasionally when we need some inspiration to stir up our determination, let us just remember Jesus in the hour of his greatest hunger and thirst standing before Satan himself, refusing food after his long desert fast of forty days and forty nights. He also turned down the very things for which most men strive throughout their lives. In his greatest need he was still stronger than the strongest of the adversary. After he had successfully resisted Satan, angels came and ministered unto him. That is the pattern. It will also be so with us. Therefore, we should occasionally give ourselves a listening test to find out how clearly we can hear the whistle.

Crossing the Rubicon

POMPEY THE GREAT was ruler of the vast Roman Empire half a century B.C. His most important field general was Julius Caesar. Caesar had had some differences with Pompey, and was considering marching on the capital to take matters into his own hands. In 49 B.C. Caesar came to the Rubicon, a small river in Northern Italy that served as his territorial boundary line. The Rubicon was called "the sacred and inviolable." It was the line across which no general was ever allowed to pass without special permission from the Senate. If Caesar crossed the Rubicon it would be with the idea of making the entire Roman Empire subject to his will.

That was a momentous decision. It would immediately precipitate a civil war and divide the world between Pompey and Caesar. Caesar knew what the consequences would be if he tried and failed. He knew that many lives would be lost, in any event. Surely he must have hesitated before arriving at so great a decision, for he knew there could be no hesitation after the decision was made. Caesar carefully considered every angle. He explored every possible alternative. Then he made up his mind. He would march on Rome.

One part of Caesar's power came because of his ability to analyze a situation; another part came because of his habit of always finishing what he started. He was now starting the biggest undertaking of his life, to strike down the very heart of the world. Caesar said, "The die is cast." That expression marked the point where deliberation ended and action began. There would now be no turning back.

Then Caesar threw himself into the waters of the Rubicon at the head of his legions and the whole history of the world was changed.

Since this important event 2,000 years ago, the phrase, "crossing the Rubicon," has been used to indicate some decisive action of great importance. In one way the action of Caesar might become a sort of pattern for us. Our first step is to know what we are doing; then we should carefully weigh the arguments. Then we should make a decision and be willing to stake everything upon our judgment. Once the decision has been made, every contrary thought should be banished. No energy should then be wasted in doubts, fears or reconsiderations, and nothing should be left undone which would help to bring about the projected accomplishment.

Whether Caesar was right or wrong is not the point of this discussion. The point is that every one of us also has a Rubicon to cross, and we should learn what we can about making decisions both on a personal and a group basis, and then learn how to carry them through to accomplishment.

The greatest sermon ever spoken consisted of just three words. Jesus said, "Come follow me." And one of the most important decisions we ever have to make is, What are we going to do about it? Will we follow him? Can we develop the leadership to make an adequate accomplishment possible, and if so, how?

When a Roman soldier joined the legions of Caesar, he took a pledge to hold the life of Caesar dearer than all else. That was his Rubicon. What should be our attitude who enlist in the service of the Lord? Why should our responsibility be of a lesser order? Or why should our minds be less firmly made up? Or why should our service be less devoted than those who paid their allegiance to Caesar?

A certain man once said to Jesus, "Lord, I will follow thee whithersoever thou goest." Jesus warned him to think about what was involved. That is an important part of making up our minds. What would this man do when the winds of opposition began to blow? Jesus cautioned him about the dangers of vacillation. "He who hesitates is lost." Jesus said it this way: "No man having put his hand to the plow and looking back, is fit for the kingdom of God." (Luke 9:62) That is a pretty strong statement, and it concerns every member of the Church.

It has always been one of our most difficult problems to make accurate decisions which are solid enough to stand firm under the pressures of life. So frequently we find reasons for wavering or side-stepping or turning back. Lot's wife crossed her Rubicon, but she was not quite as well prepared as Caesar was. Lot's wife hadn't quite made up her mind. Therefore she looked back and was turned into a pillar of salt. (Gen. 19:26)

There are far too many of us who are afflicted with the trait of making partial decisions. Then we are continually looking back over our shoulders. For example, ask ten people to tell you what their goal in life is and exactly what their plan is for accomplishment. Most people have no very definite answers to these important questions. We never quite get around to settling once and for all even the most important questions. How many of us actually make firm decisions about our objectives for eternity supported by concrete methods for their attainment? If some of us get to the celestial kingdom, it will be by a kind of "accident" brought on by circumstances or the continual urging of friends to do our duty. Some have not permanently resolved the question of tithing, liquor, honesty, tobacco, church attendance, or other personal church performance. Their activity depends too much upon the circumstance of the moment. How many of us have really decided about our own church leadership—its quality, quantity, continuity and method? Think about the high turnover in office, the ineffective work being done, the large number of resignations each year, the many startings and stoppings. Think how much time we spend in indecision, reconsideration, vacillation and retreat.

We often decide something one way when we are at the top of our condition and then abandon our plans when the tide begins to ebb. It is so easy to get cold feet or weak knees when a challenging set of circumstances confronts us. We become "accidental men" by putting our success even in the most important things under the control of circumstances. We get safely across the Rubicon only to begin suffering from a "faint heart," and then a retreat to the rear is the next logical step.

Real leadership cannot always be stopping to change its plans and directions. If we would succeed, we must make up our minds, not only on principles but also on methods. Even the smallest details must be perfectly clear to us. Then we can advance with the firm step of a Caesar determined to conquer our circumstances.

James Russell Lowell says:

> Once to every man and nation
> Comes a moment to decide
> In the strife of truth and falsehood
> For the good or evil side.
>
> Some great cause, God's new Messiah
> Offering each the bloom or blight
> Parts the goats upon the left hand
> And the sheep upon the right.
>
> And the choice goes on forever
> 'Twixt the darkness and the light.

There are very few things that so quickly separate the sheep from the goats or that divide failure from success as this quality of a firm determination in the right direction.

To improve the quality of our leadership, we should see to it that no day is allowed to come to its close while any personal conflicts or problems are still undecided. Again, we might get a pretty good idea from Caesar. When Caesar went to capture Britain, he first landed his men and then unloaded his supplies. Then in the night he sent out men and burned the ships in which they had come. Then death was the only Roman alternative to victory. Under such circumstances most men fight with a vigor that never knows defeat. Then men learn to depend upon their own strength. When we know that we are cut off from outside resources we fight with a vigor equal to the force of desperation. There are many advantages in "burning our ships." When we cut off our chances to retreat, we increase our chances to succeed. Then, like Caesar, once over the Rubicon, there is only one direction to go and that is forward.

Some men often make the mistake when they start on an important undertaking of purposely leaving open a way for retreat. Then if things get a little difficult, they can always change their minds and their program without embarrassment. It is not an aid to success to be able to turn back from any point along the way. No one can really accomplish his maximum until he is definitely committed to his task and his mind has closed all lines of retreat. Retreat or surrender should not be made so easy as to actually invite us.

A determined person allows no exceptions to success. Exceptions tear down a success habit faster than victories can build it up. Too often we say, as did the drunken Rip Van Winkle in Jefferson's play, "I won't count this one."

"Rip" got into his difficulty because he never really made up his mind.

Most of us, including Rip Van Winkle, know what ought to be done. It is comparatively very simple to write out the formula for almost any accomplishment. But we fail either because we haven't really made up our minds or because we allow too many exceptions. We should make a definite landing and then burn our ships.

Do we really believe the gospel? Have we whole-heartedly accepted our responsibility? Do we know in detail what is required for our particular success? Have we worked out a definite system, including all of the details of accomplishment?

When any question comes before you for decision, throw all possible light upon it; weigh it in the balances. Then make a decision and go forward. Beware of inde-cision. Look out for postponements. The temptation toward continual reconsideration is fatal to any forceful action. One of the greatest thieves this world has ever produced is procrastination, and he is still at large. The indecisive man, the vacillating man, or the procrastinator belongs to whoever can capture him. He is the tool of the last influence that had a chance at him, and just as the driftwood on the river is whirled around by every little eddy and blocked by every obstruction, so the undecided man is spun about by circumstances and other men's opin-ions. He only marches toward his objective until he gets to the first intersection. If the positive man makes a mis-take he will not be long in rectifying it, but the man who never really makes up his mind or is always hesitating, consulting and reconsidering, hasn't much chance to accom-plish. This loose-jointedness of will makes continuous effort impossible and distractions deadly. The real leader is the one who stands firm in the face of the strongest opposition.

A friend once told me of visiting a certain town the day after a cyclone had swept through it. Only the solid substantial structures were left standing. The weak rotten trees and the light flimsy buildings had collapsed and gone down before the wind. It is about that way in all departments of life. And the weakest are always the first to go. A business crisis weeds out the inefficient businessman. Sickness strikes hardest at those with the least resistance to disease. The cyclone of sin and failure first removes from the ranks of leadership the undecided, the unsure and the undetermined. Only the stalwart and vigorous withstand the storm.

The Lord said, "Once more I shake . . . the earth" and only "those things which cannot be shaken may remain." (Heb. 12:26-27) Testing is a part of our education and training. We must develop our strength on a crisis basis. Everyday faculties and abilities are sometimes not strong enough to carry us over the emergencies. Emergency strength is of a different denomination. We must have it in readiness. We can't postpone a crisis while we prepare for it.

God gave man dominion over all things, including himself. Then how pathetic to see him crumble like a rotten building before the storm of some problem or inconvenience. There are no other qualities that stand so near to genius as a resolute mind and a persistent purpose. These two have won many battles after all other qualities have surrendered. Great generals say that there is usually an indecisive period in every battle, an awful moment when the soldiers are about ready to give up. This is the supreme "psychological moment" on which everything depends. Then the courage and faith of the rank and file are ebbing, and the soldiers feel like running away. These moments sometimes come in every department of life. Then is the real test of leadership. Then is the time when the leader must make the supreme effort to turn the tide. Workers must be inspired if they are to be kept from breaking.

Such an event is told of in connection with the Civil War battle of the Shenandoah Valley in 1864. The Union troops were demoralized and scattered. A New York reporter, standing at that hour upon an eminence overlooking the valley watching the disorderly retreat, wrote: "I am watching the awful destruction of the Union." Then a man on a big white horse came racing down the valley at top speed. He was carrying a pennant with two stars; it was the pennant of the Union general, Phil Sheridan. As he came, he cried, "I am here! Turn about. We will win. We will save the Union."

It is reported that the men threw their hats into the air and cried like babies. They embraced each other shouting, "Sheridan is here." The effect was magic. The troops re-formed. By nightfall they had recaptured the Shenandoah Valley. The courage and decisiveness of one man had turned the tide for thousands. Such is the power of great leadership. Such is your power.

The most hopeful moment in any life is when there comes into it the dawning of a fixed purpose, with definite plans for accomplishment. Then we are able to say, "The die is cast," and we dive into our own Rubicon and with firm strokes head for our destination.

The Druthers

JANE ADDAMS once told an interesting story of a working girl in Chicago who for the sake of her health was put on a very strict diet. She utterly refused the rigid dietary requirements of her physician. When she was taken to task for her failure to follow the physician's prescription, she dismissed the whole matter by remarking that she'd druther eat what she'd druther.

In the natural expression of this girl's motivation we might recognize one of our own most important problems. Most of us are bothered with a fairly serious case of the "druthers." We sometimes base our actions on something no more substantial than a whim or an impulse or a feeling which does not have a very solid foundation. There are a great many people who have a basic philosophy of life consisting merely of their determination to do as they please. There is a natural temptation in human nature to follow our "druthers," against all other considerations. There is a doctrine which has some standing among us that gives almost limitless expression to our own attitudes and inclinations—this, in spite of the fact that it has been proven millions of times that our personal inclinations may not necessarily point out the course that is right or desirous even in our own interests. In fact in the past people doing as they pleased have been found to be on the wrong track many, many times.

Oscar Wilde once said that if the gods wished to punish us, they would only need to answer our prayers. Just think what would happen if all of our prayers were answered! Then no one would ever die; no one would ever be sick; we would have no opposition; there would be for us no hardship or struggle. We would in many cases even like to disconnect the unpleasant consequences from our unrighteous deeds. If all of our prayers were answered, we would soon find out what trouble really is.

Goethe once questioned the reasoning involved in the case of a man who spends his days complaining of his headaches but spends his nights drinking the wine that gave them to him. In a little larger sense that is about what we are doing with our guilt complexes, our stomach ulcers and our nervous breakdowns. "We see the devil's hook but we keep right on nibbling at his bait." If we too freely indulge these natural inclinations, it often destroys not only our pleasures, but the effectiveness of our work and our leadership.

The attitude that has probably been more destructive of leadership than any other is represented by the statement, "I don't know." The one second on the list is probably, "I don't want to." These are statements representing the "druthers" in the negative. "I don't want to" is one phrase in which we carry over into maturity the responses of childhood. The early druthers are represented by the child who doesn't want to go to bed at night, and he doesn't want to get up in the morning. He doesn't want to go to school, and then he doesn't want to come home. He needs a stimulant in the morning to get him started and a sedative at night to get him stopped. He doesn't want to study; he doesn't want to practice his lessons; and he doesn't want to eat his spinach. When we don't get rid of this handicap during childhood, we suffer during maturity. We say that we don't want to do ward teaching; we don't want to undertake any program of self-improvement; we don't want to make our lesson preparation.

Jonah furnishes a good sample of a negative statement of the "druthers." The most prominent recorded thing he said to the Lord was, "I don't want to." The Lord said to Jonah, "Arise, go to Ninevah, that great city, and cry against it; for their wickedness is come up before me." But Jonah didn't want to go to Nineveh. He hiked out for Tarshish instead. However, Jonah didn't get away from his assignment quite as easily as he had planned. He had just boarded the boat for Tarshish when a tempest arose. Those in charge of the ship soon decided that Jonah was the cause of their trouble, and Jonah was thrown overboard at his own request. He decided that he would rather be drowned than do what the Lord had asked him to do. Even his drowning didn't go off quite as expected, for a fish swallowed Jonah and gave him a free ride to shore and then obligingly deposited him back on dry land. This put Jonah right back where he had started from.

Then the word of the Lord came to Jonah a second time saying, "Arise, go unto Nineveh, that great city, and preach unto it the preaching that I bid thee." There seemed to be nothing else for him to do, and so Jonah went to Nineveh and told the people that they were going to be destroyed unless they repented. To Jonah's great surprise and dismay, the people believed the message and turned away from their sins, and the Lord spared their city. This greatly upset Jonah. The record says, "And he was very angry." And God said to Jonah, "Doest thou well to be angry?" Jonah said, "I do well to be angry even unto death." Then Jonah said, "O Lord, take, I beseech thee, my life from me; for it is better for me to die than to live."

Jonah had some pretty definite ideas of what *he* wanted to do and they seemed to have all been wrong. When Jonah didn't get his "druthers" he was in a very negative state of mind. Some of our characteristics have a close relationship to those that got Jonah into so many difficulties. Frequently we just insist on doing what we please, and the things that please us are so often the wrong things.

It might be a pretty good idea to sit down occasionally and write out a list of our "druthers" and inspect each one for its reasonableness, its saneness, and its righteousness.

Recently as I was talking with a young man about some church responsibility, he said, "I have a mind of my own." I knew the young man, and it seemed to me that he had used his mind largely to make mistakes. He had caused trouble for himself, his parents, the Lord, and almost everyone else, but he would continue to hang on to his "druthers" for dear life. Jonah also had a mind of his own, but apparently it would not work except in the wrong direction. He would rather follow his own mind and be dead than to take a suggestion from the Lord and save both himself and Nineveh. For one to have a mind of his own is wonderful—if he uses it to help himself and others in the right direction. But to use one's mind merely to get himself thrown into the ocean may have some disadvantages. Certainly such a mind is not an unmixed blessing.

Another young man, when asked to fill a church teaching assignment, declined on the grounds that he "did not think he would enjoy it." Merely not to enjoy something does not seem adequate grounds for declination. It is entirely natural that he should not enjoy it. In the first place, he had had no experience in teaching; he didn't know how to do it. As the price of enjoyment in any job, we must learn to do it well, as "we are always down on what we ain't up on." But if we turn everything down merely because we don't enjoy it, we soon get into serious trouble. We may not enjoy getting up in the morning or brushing our teeth or going to work, but we do these things just the same. In these things we are influenced by our necessities, to look beyond our "druthers" at least until next pay day.

There was another reason this young man would not enjoy teaching, and that was that he himself was not converted. Again, that may be exactly the reason why he should have accepted it.

When we get a little training and the wisdom that should go with it, many experiences that we think we wouldn't like give us great pleasure. There are some people whose natural inclinations prompt them to go fishing on Sunday, to stay away from stake conference, to refrain from fasting and prayer. But this action may not bring them lasting happiness. In fact, they may lose for eternity the companionship of the members of their families whom by their bad example they have led away from the Church. As a consequence of the "druthers" many people continue to live loose, uncontrolled, unsuccessful and unhappy lives. Liberty without direction or restraint can be very harmful. Liberty is not the ability to do as we please under all circumstances.

This philosophy of liberty without proper direction was pretty well expressed by Satan himself, who said in effect, "Lie a little, steal a little, lay a snare for thy neighbor. There is no harm in this. God will punish thee with a few stripes but in the end all will be well." Satan says to us: "Live your own life. Do as you please. Never limit your natural inclinations. If they were not supposed to be indulged you wouldn't have them. Why should you worry about a sense of responsibility? It is nobody's business but your own."

Sometimes under careful parental guidance with the necessary restraints, a young person gets the "druthers" and says, "Just wait till I grow up, when I can do as I please!" But usually the most unfortunate moment in anyone's life, young or old, is that moment when he decides that he can and should do as he pleases. Often that means that in some of the important duties of life he intends to coast, and the only way that anyone ever coasted was downhill. Once on the roller coaster of "Do as you please" you may find it pretty hard to stop, and before you know it, Satan takes over. No one has ever been *sent* to hell; he goes there in the chute-the-chute of his own "druthers." Sometimes all we need to do is to turn off the power and follow the line of least resistance. "It is the line of least resistance that makes both rivers and men crooked."

Our "druthers" can make us dislike work. They tell us not to think of our unrighteous acts as sins. They will not allow us to admit or think about our mistakes. They prevent us from growing up or assuming our proper responsibility. We sometimes tend to be like James M. Barrie's little character, Peter Pan, who wanted to remain a perpetual child, forever carefree and unencumbered. The thought of going to work and assuming responsibility, of practicing obedience, justice, honor, sobriety and purity, is not very appealing if the "druthers" get too much of a head start. When we do only the things that we want to do, disaster is inescapable, for what we ardently wish we soon actually believe. When the urge within us is great enough, it usually seems to us to be right. Then our conscience gives no guidance; advice can't help us much, and even our own experience is of little value when we look at it through the distorted perspective of the "druthers."

We had better see that our "druthers" are carefully checked and regulated by duty and good sense. For we are only truly happy when our reasoning rises to the high level of right rather than rests on the low bottom of desire. Jesus expressed a great success attitude when he said, "My meat is to do the will of him that sent me." That was the secret of his greatness. He *wanted* to do right, even though not everything was pleasant, even to Jesus. In his supreme trial, he said to his Father, "If it be possible let this cup pass from me; Nevertheless, not my will, but thine, be done." The "druthers" didn't bother Jesus. If he had conducted his life on a basis of the expediency of the moment, he would probably have called his twelve legions of angels and while they fought for him, he could have turned back from the cross and failed in his greatest opportunity. Jesus made his own wishes secondary to the will of his Father. They were also secondary to his own wisdom and sense of right. That is an important formula for us to keep in mind. What a wonderful thing, if we could always follow it!

It is certain there will be times when we would rather go fishing than attend to our duties. There will be occasions when it would best suit our convenience to pass the preparation of the Sunday School lesson, or fail to hold the council meeting, or skip the payment of our tithing. We can argue with our conscience by saying, "If we fall down a little, there is no harm in this. We will not be beaten with many stripes." Or we might bolster our conscience up and excuse our lethargy by saying, "All is well in Zion. Yea, Zion prospereth, all is well." It is usually thus through our own "druthers" that "the devil cheateth our souls and leadeth us away carefully down into hell."

When we believe in our "druthers" too devoutly, we strengthen them against our own interests. With our "druthers" in power it becomes very difficult for us to do right, for then we will not allow any conflict with our own inclinations. To try to act contrary to what we believe in is like seeing ourselves through the deception of a side show mirror. Because of this distortion, it is difficult to believe that a sin is as black in us as it is in our neighbor, and it is almost impossible for us even to imagine that eventually *we* may be lost eternally. We usually have an irrational optimism that no matter what we do, there will be a happy ending.

Ignorance is bad; sin is harmful; sloth is destructive. But just don't forget to watch your "druthers." They add self-deception to the other problems. This self-deception prompts us to think of ourselves only in the highest terms, regardless of what we may actually do.

Satan himself has no power to force us to do wrong without our consent. He has no power to destroy our leadership. He has no ability to limit the amount of good that we may do, except by his fifth column procedure of infiltration. But if Satan can fill our minds with the "druthers" he can pretty well guarantee our failure. Then we say to ourselves, "I'd druther do what I'd druther."

The Executive

CERTAINLY the most important part of any successful organization is the leader. He is the one who works at the head and carries the responsibility. He is the executive, the one who puts the program in force. He is the one who guarantees accomplishment for the organization as well as the individual success of the other members of organization. If the leader really leads, accomplishment is assured, for "as with the priest, so with the people." Marshal Foch once said that it was not an army that crossed the Alps, but Hannibal.

The dictionary says that the executive is the one who executes. He is the "guarantee" that the work will be done, not only effectively, but on time. The word "execute" literally means to follow out or to pursue—and effectively describes what a good executive must do.

The executive is the one who determines goals, devises strategy and decides on methods. He is the one who blueprints accomplishment and provides a suitable and effective motivation. The executive is responsible for the climate in which success may grow. In business or in the army or in the Church, the *esprit de corps* doesn't usually bubble up from the bottom; it filters down from the top. An organization tends to be what its commanding officer is, and the best executive is the one who can most nearly release the full potential of the entire management team. Maximum success requires that every member of the team must be kept at his best, for when one falls down, he tends to pull the team down. One basketball player can lose for the entire team. That is also true in church work, where there are no one-man teams.

It is the responsibility of the real executive to prevent failure before it occurs; therefore, he must study the causes of failure. For we never really know a thing until we know it by its causes. And the function of the effective executive is to destroy the causes of failure. He constantly guides and motivates his organization toward the predetermined goal.

Recently a man related a boyhood experience on the farm. His father hauled sugar beets to the factory in a wagon drawn by four horses. The boy held the reins while the wagon was being loaded, until the load began to get heavy. Then the father took over the driving, because the horses could pull more with the father holding the reins.

With horses or with men, the ease with which the load is moved is determined in large part by who holds the reins, and how they are held. A skillful driver knows how to communicate to the team by means of the reins, his voice, manner, etc. He makes accomplishment easy, because the members of the team are then able to coordinate their effort and to work in unison. Even horses soon learn to have confidence in a capable master. They know that he will not ask anything impossible or unreasonable. But they also know that he knows what the maximum effort is of which each is capable, and that he will not tolerate a balky or a lazy horse who would destroy team efficiency.

When the father held the reins, the horses were at their best. Then they were organized and united. Their spirit was at its peak. They knew that the one holding the reins acted in their best interests. It is the same with a good executive. The members of the team are inspired by his ability, fairness and purpose. The team is stronger then than the total strength of the individual members. For each has his own strength, but he also draws from the strength of the others including the leader.

The team spirit usually breaks down when the leader lacks competence. This competence is more than ordinarily important, for it is a very common thing to see otherwise good men fail in their executive function.

"Are you able," said Jesus to his followers, "to drink the cup that I drink of?" In addition he might also ask of us: Are *you able* to get the enlistment work done? Are you *able* to get spirituality to grow in the hearts of people? Are you *able* to get accurate reports in, and on time? Are you *able* to carry your share of the responsibility without always being reminded? Are you *able* (so to speak) to get the ship into port? God is best served only as we develop our talents to their utmost.

After the French had been conquered by the Nazis in June, 1940, Marshal Petain, referring to the years before the war, announced this requiem over a lost France: "Our spirit of enjoyment was stronger than our spirit of sacrifice. We wanted to have more than we wanted to give. We tried to spare effort and we met disaster."

Sometimes our purpose is conquered by evil, for the same reasons given by Marshal Petain, and we may eventually find ourselves face to face with a far greater tragedy than overtook the French, if we fail in our stewardship because we were not able. In the work of salvation, mere goodness is not enough; we also need ability and know-how, and the determination to follow through.

In our day the Lord pointed out one of the greatest sins of the sectarians when he said, "They draw near to me with their lips but their hearts are far from me." This great evil still walks up and down among us, seeking to destroy.

Mostly we are only partially faithful. So often we choose to walk the easy pathway of minimum performance, whereas the work of God demands our best effort. It was not a "fractional devotion" intended by the line of scripture saying, "See that ye serve him with all your heart, might, mind and strength." God re-emphasized the importance of our spiritual success when he said, "It would be better to be drowned in the depths of the sea, than to offend one of these little ones."

A good leader must be expert in *human engineering*, inasmuch as the most important problems in the world are human problems. A recent survey indicated that of all the automobile wrecks where lives were lost, 4 per cent of the wrecks were caused by mechanical failure, and 96 per cent by human failure, indicating a far greater need for human mechanics than for auto mechanics. The Air Force maintains "flight surgeons" to keep men at their best and to "ground" them when inefficiency warns of failure.

The leader in church work is supposed to bring men to their best and then keep them there. His job is to draw ideas from others, and help to perfect their knowledge and purpose. He must be able to induce their greatest effort. He is responsible for team integration and balance, to get average men to achieve above the average. Every member of the group suffers a character loss if the leader lets down so that the program does not go over.

Executive ability is the most valuable known ability. Workers always do better with a good leader. It has been proven many times that a sales force under an ordinary leader will sell only a fraction of the goods that can be sold by the same sales force under a leader who can maintain high morale, promote a sense of responsibility, give effective training, and provide stimulating supervision and motivation.

With good leadership, the Aaronic Priesthood boys of one stake get five times as many awards as the same kind of boys do under poor leaders. Missionaries make more converts when they are better trained and more effectively led. And in a ward where a bishopric is effective in its executive and administrative functions, many more people may qualify for the celestial kingdom. What ability is greater than this?

It is comparatively easy to secure technicians or skilled workmen, but real executive leadership is a quality of a higher denomination. The executive must know many things. He must know how to work on his own power. He must be able to develop the ideas and harness the imagination of others. It is the job of the executive to think, plan, invent, direct, check and inspire. He watches the sky for enemy aircraft, so to speak. He knocks down the problem before it drops its bombs. He pours oil on the troubled waters. He has a sense of honesty and fair dealing. He must be a self-starter, a good manager of himself, and set a good example. He must be "loaded" with industry, and be an expert in human relations.

Walter Gifford once said that "The successful general is one under whose leadership the staff, as well as the rank and file, will work and die with enthusiasm." History tells us that the very presence of Napoleon meant a victory for his soldiers. In his presence his troops could not be defeated. The Duke of Wellington estimated that the presence of Napoleon on the field was the equivalent of a reinforcement of forty thousand additional men.

Because this ability is all-important, we ought to do more about developing it on every level of church responsibility. This can be done through thorough training, constant study, thoughtful effort and experience. Leadership cannot be placed upon one's shoulders like a mantle. It cannot be bestowed. It can only be acquired. One cannot become an effective executive simply by being so designated. Executive ability is something that each must bestow upon himself. And even then, it is available only on a temporary basis. You cannot own it; it is only yours for as long as it is continuously earned. When the leader begins to slip, morale and accomplishment begin to slip also. When the leader improves, the work of the Lord over which he has charge will prosper accordingly.

What a thrilling thought, that we may qualify as executive officers of the Lord, assigned to put his program in force in the lives of people!

Following are some suggestions for those who have, or will have, executive and administrative responsibility in the Church:

1. The church executive must see to it that his organization is properly and continually staffed. An army or a business organization can be annihilated or bankrupt in just a few hours if left without proper officers.

2. It is the executive's responsibility to see that the organization functions effectively. Proper functioning covers the whole field of management. Planning meetings must be continuously held and duties must be accepted and carried out. The captain of a ship cannot tie his steering gear fast and hope to reach the desired port. It takes constant steering to go in a straight line.

3. The executive must not be so tied down with details that he is unable to do his own work. If the mind of the executive is littered with a hundred petty distractions, success is impossible. He must give the necessary hours of thought and work to his executive function. No one would trust a banker who spent his time doing everyone else's work except his own, or a general who abandoned his command to run errands.

4. The executive must be a good judge of men, and must make certain that each understands his duty, accepts it wholeheartedly and follows through to satisfactory accomplishment.

5. Everyone must be made to see his place in the enterprise and know that he is a part of the management. Even the skillful man will do a poor job unless he knows *why* he is doing it. The executive is the one who divides up the work and follows through to see that the job is done. He should never give an assignment and then fail to check up. This follow-through is one of the most important parts of training. It is one of the most important parts of supervision.

6. The executive must be able to initiate, guide, measure and control work. The executive must guarantee success, though he must not try to do all of the work himself. The driver of a four-horse team makes his greatest contribution by skillfully holding the reins, not by abandoning the reins to try to push the wagon personally.

7. He must always have an objective. Thomas Watson, the late president of IBM, said that every executive should start with a goal and work backward to accomplishment.

8. The executive must know the program and the problems and the solutions involved in the work of those immediately answerable to him, so that he can give them technical help. He should know the top contribution of which each worker is capable.

9. A good executive must be a good student. The field of his activity is so important and so vast that he must be constantly getting new ideas, better methods and more productive skills. Good tools are of little value in the hands of a bad carpenter. To grow as an executive, one must also grow as an individual.

10. Alfred Sloan said, "The most important thing I have learned about management is that an executive must arouse the individual initiative of the men working under him." This requires a good example, great understanding, and a lot of personal, individual help. The highest form

of leadership is the leadership of persuasion, not the leadership of command.

The greatest ability known in the world is executive ability, and our greatest contribution to the work of the Lord can only be made as we develop our abilities to their highest possible denomination.

My Father's Business

WE HAVE MARVELED many times at the wonder of the world which we call American business. It has raised our standard of living; it has lifted the burden of toil from the backs of many people; it has helped to win the wars and has provided men and women with conveniences and luxuries never before known in the world. We now have a higher standard of living than any king had just a hundred years ago.

But if you would like to think of "big business" in its most stupendous terms, think of that great enterprise which Jesus called "My Father's business." The largest corporation in the world has assets of some 18 billion dollars. Compare this in importance with even the most humble church worker who helps to mold the soft clay in the lives of immortal souls. It is the responsibility of an effective church worker to raise the standard of thinking and the standard of activity and the standard of living the gospel, in such a way as to bring about the highest possible standard of living, which is eternal life in the celestial kingdom.

Much of the teaching of Jesus was by parable. He took an idea that everyone understood, and by comparison, helped them to understand some similar idea which might not have been clear otherwise. Many of the parables of Jesus had to do with money or property. Some examples are the ten pieces of silver, the tribute money, the lost coin, the talents, the pearl of great price, etc. Jesus probably used money as the basis for his comparisons because people, then as now, understood money better than almost any other thing. Even a six-year-old child thoroughly understands a $10 bill. He knows what its uses and limitations are. We are not always equally familiar with the value of spiritual things. But if the proper comparison is clear to our understanding, material values may help us to understand spiritual values. This is what Jesus had in mind when he talked about "treasures in heaven." To teach spiritual truth is also the aim of the parable of the sower, the good Samaritan, the prodigal son, etc. Certainly the Master would have had difficulty to find a more expressive term for our day than "My Father's business."

Most people quickly understand the need for effectiveness in business relationships. A responsible person would not think of being "unbusinesslike" in his business. We can readily understand the cost of business failure when placed in contrast with the advantages of business success. We spend years in education and training to learn how business progress may be brought about. We recognize the importance of individual industry, capable leadership and professional competence in those doing the work. We therefore make constant effort to upgrade efficiency in the many specialized fields of the 2,100,000 individual business organizations in the United States.

However, in spite of all of the care and study that we put into our business effort, there are still approximately 378,000 of these companies, or one-sixth of the total, that fail every year. The loss of capital is tremendous; the frustration of the human spirit is pathetic. But interestingly enough the cause of failure is not primarily in the products, or the markets, or the financing, or even in business conditions; the cause of failure is in the men who run the businesses. The main cause of business failure is man failure. This fact emphasizes the necessity for care in the selection of personnel, thorough on-the-job training, continual supervision, and effective control. For where people learn to work effectively and harmoniously together, much of this pathetic waste can be eliminated.

But how much more important it is to eliminate the waste in the work of the Lord where the eternal salvation of his children is at stake. Failure in *our* business may lower our standard of living here, but failure in our "Father's business" will lower our "standard of living" throughout all eternity. What a tremendous return it would be on any investment we might make in our leadership effectiveness if we could bring about the exaltation of even one additional soul. But such an accomplishment can actually be multiplied many times by properly utilizing those proven management techniques and administrative skills that have brought about such wonders in the world of business.

The principles of success are much the same in all accomplishment. We borrow the knowledge and skills developed by great educators to help us with our religious education. We use the knowledge developed by agricultural colleges and experiment stations to make our welfare farms more productive. Why not also take advantage of effective business procedures and administrative skills to save souls?

A great literature has been built up and made available to us under such interesting titles as: *How to Increase Your Executive Ability, Effective Methods of Organization and Administration, Increasing Personal Efficiency, Proper Selection of Personnel, The Art of Motivation, How to Create High Morale*, etc. These and many other great books that are available offer many valuable suggestions which may be used by us to increase our effectiveness in the work of the Lord.

The most important business in the world is "My Father's business," and we who are engaged therein should be the most "businesslike." The great truth that no one can be saved in ignorance has a significant application and additional meaning to church leaders. For as it is true that no one can be saved in ignorance, it is also true that no one can save others in ignorance.

The Fire in Leadership

A PART OF THE literature of our age includes what has been called "useful fiction." We have fables, myths, stories, etc., to help illustrate ideas, teach principles and induce action. For example, we learn from the famous fable of the tortoise and the hare. The story of the blind men and the elephant also has much to teach us. The purely fictional characters of Shakespeare and Dickens can be very helpful in developing our principles and attitudes. The learning process is made more simple when we have language with unusual meaning, interesting pictures and impressive emphasis to make thoughts clear. During the Civil War, one general was nicknamed "Stonewall Jackson." This title helps us to visualize the man. Shakespeare gets his ideas over largely because of his picturesque phrases and striking figures of speech. We see ourselves on the program when he says, "All the world's a stage." This use of words in a non-literal sense sometimes helps to give beauty, meaning and vividness to ideas.

The ancient Greeks built a significant culture and wrote a colorful literature, as an important part of which they assigned personalities to the forces of nature, personifying great ideas in some human or superhuman form. This helped to dispel vagueness of thought and made ideas more vivid to their minds. These stories usually centered around the exploits of the Titans and heroes who peopled the top of ancient Mt. Olympus.

One of these legends concerns Prometheus, who distinguished himself as one of the best friends mortals ever had. He was a fighter against injustice and unrighteous power. "Prometheus" means "forethought," and he was given credit for being very wise. But he is best known in the myths of the Greeks because he brought fire from the sun and gave it to men. Our own scripture tells us that God "is the sun and the light of the sun and the power thereof by which it was made." (D&C 88:7) And it is through that power that our eyes are enlightened and our understandings quickened.

But from time immemorial "fire" has been used as an expressive and helpful figure of speech. "Fire" or "heat" has served us as the symbol of ardor, fervor, enthusiasm. We say of one, "He is on fire"; of another, "He has a burning desire." We say, "Strike while the iron is hot." We talk about a "heated emotion" or a "warm friendship." We call an energetic person a "ball of fire." If he is very successful we say he is "setting the world on fire."

This particular use of these phrases gives a helpful vividness and feeling to our thinking. We all understand that a little fire in the personality is often its most valuable characteristic. To be able to develop this fire in ourselves is one of the best ways to promote our leadership and accomplishment.

A leader is very much like an automobile: he never gets very far or has very much power until he gets "warmed up." By way of contrast, we often think of the traits that bring failure as having a lower temperature. We say that the members of a losing basketball team were "cold." They just couldn't "get up steam." The term "frigid" is descriptive of certain unfavorable, unfriendly attitudes. We understand what is meant when we talk about one whose enthusiasm is "zero."

Probably the most undesirable place on the thermometer, from some points of view, is that area midway between hot and cold. Then one is neither one thing nor the other. It is recorded in the "Book of Revelation" that the Lord said to the members of the Church at Laodicea, "Thou art neither cold nor hot; I would that thou wert cold or hot. Because thou art lukewarm, I will spew thee out of my mouth." This quality of being on the fence, of being neither one thing nor the other, aroused even in God a feeling of disgust.

If we want to be successful in the work of the Lord, we must "get up steam." Our enthusiasm must develop a "fever" if it is to have power. We use the figure of "heat" or "fire" to indicate a wholehearted and wholesouled devotion. In fact, fire is used many times in the scriptures as an indication of the presence of God himself. When the Lord descended onto the top of Mt. Sinai to give the Law of Israel, the historian said, "And Mt. Sinai was altogether on a smoke because the Lord descended upon it in fire, and the smoke thereof ascended as the smoke of a furnace and the whole mountain did quake greatly. And it came to pass on the third day in the morning that there were thunders and lightnings." The Bible uses this interesting metaphor in referring to God himself by saying, "God is a consuming fire." The figure is a good one and helps us to get the spirit of accomplishment. Certainly we get a clear contrast between the "fire" of God and the lukewarm indifference of the Laodiceans.

The Bible uses this figure of fire to represent God's glory, his holiness, his presence, his holy spirit, his judgment and his punishment. "And who shall abide the day of his coming and who shall stand when he appeareth? For he is like a refiner's fire and like fuller's soap." If one wanted to try a pun he might say those who are not on fire will be burned.

Prometheus brought fire from the sun to the ancients. The reason the Laodiceans got into trouble was that they lacked fire. Apparently they needed some Prometheus to perform this fire-carrying service for them. Good fire carriers are also *our* greatest need. We need someone to make the sparks fly and get the flame going. Jesus baptized with "the Holy Ghost and with fire." (Matt. 3:11) We need to make that fire burn effectively. Every great leader needs to cultivate fire-producing and fire-carrying abilities. To help bring the spark of divine fire to men is an office of the greatest importance. Not only should this spark be kindled in the hearts of people, but it should be continuously cared for until it becomes a brightly burning flame. Good leaders are not only "fire possessors" and "fire carriers" but they also should have a substantial "fire power."

A scientific explanation of an actual rise in temperature indicates that there has been an increase in molecular activity. An increased activity within ourselves will also raise our temperature. Increased spiritual activity brings greater devotion to our minds, an increased fervor in our hearts, and an increased accomplishment to our efforts.

The nearest word to "fire" in meaning and function is probably "enthusiasm," which is a kind of fire in the soul, producing soul power. The word "enthusiasm" came from the Greek words "en" and "theos" which mean "God in us" or "divine inspiration."

We talk a great deal about our right to receive inspiration from God. What we don't understand so well is our right and ability to give inspiration to others. We are the children of God, created in his image and endowed with his attributes. We are recipients of his authority and a measure of his power. Our need is to give out more. We are not merely receiving stations; we are also centers of distribution. When once we get possession of this enthusiasm of fire, then, Prometheus-like, we may give it to others. This is one of those things that we can not only give without losing, but the more we give away, the more we actually have left. Here is a place where we can re-enact the miracle of feeding the multitude. We may start out with five loaves and two fishes and after we have fed the five thousand, we find we have twelve basketfuls left. (Matt. 14:17-20)

This ability to fill ourselves and others with enthusiasm carries with it a great power of accomplishment. It is one of the most valuable abilities with which God has endowed us. But its value is still further increased because it is so rare. It is one of the potentialities which is often left undeveloped in men. There are many *good* men; there are many *wise* men; there are many *industrious* men. There are not many fire kindlers, not many fire carriers, not many who bring us sparks from the divine, even in a symbolic sense.

A genuine enthusiasm is one of the best of all guarantees that any assignment will be accomplished. Intelligent enthusiasm probably makes a greater contribution to success than any other single trait. Sir Edward Appleton, Nobel prize winner, said, "I regard enthusiasm as more valuable even than professional skill." Professional skill in spiritual leadership is tremendously important, but its effectiveness is multiplied when powered by intelligent enthusiasm.

Cold water in the cylinders of a leader brings no more accomplishment than it does in the cylinders of a steam locomotive. Even when the water in the boiler has been heated to 200 degrees it is still merely hot water. But when the temperature rises to 212 degrees, then the water expands and becomes live steam. The same water, which at a lower temperature had no power, can now drag a half mile of loaded freight cars back and forth across the Rocky Mountains. A comparable increase in the temperature of the human spirit brings about a corresponding increase in the leadership result.

Not only does well-directed, intelligent enthusiasm guarantee almost any accomplishment, but like the fire from which it gets its strength, it can be passed around from one to another. There is no label saying, "Not Transferable," stamped on enthusiasm. Enthusiasm is completely negotiable. "A heart can inspire other hearts with its fire." John Wesley said, "I set myself on fire and people come to see me burn." Many people had their own lives set ablaze by listening to John Wesley. John Wesley extensively carried out this process of lighting fires in the lives of people and finally started one of the greatest conflagrations in history, which still goes on spreading throughout the world. John Wesley was "a carrier of fire."

Fire has been used as the sign of God, but enthusiasm, or "God in us" is also a sign. Enthusiasm in our church work is a sign of our devotion. It is a sign that we are living the principles of the gospel, that we are in tune with the source of spiritual fire. It is a sign that we believe in what we are doing and have the necessary fervor and eagerness required for accomplishment. This enthusiasm wakes us up and makes us vital and untiring. The red men told Columbus that they had an herb that would take away fatigue. Enthusiasm will do the same thing. It also produces in people that quality of being "valiant," which is the primary requirement for the celestial kingdom.

It has been said that men, like automobiles, go forward by a series of explosions. Enthusiasm might be said to be the explosive power of the personality. It is the fuse that connects with the train of powder. Every leader needs enthusiasm to explode his industry. Enthusiasm acts as an emotional generator to set industry in motion. It supplies the initiative, determination and persistence for the proposed accomplishment.

When the spirit leaves the body, the body gets cold. That is also what happens when enthusiasm leaves the leadership. To retain enthusiasm we must feed it on accomplishment. If accomplishment is allowed to dwindle, then our initiative gets weak and our industry runs low. When we fail to care for this valuable possession of "God in us," even for a short time, our spiritual thermometer begins to drop and our progress tends to come to a standstill.

A captain of industry once said that he wanted every member of his organization to be fired with enthusiasm. He said that if he had an employee who was not fired with enthusiasm he would try to fire him with enthusiasm. But if he could not fire him with enthusiasm, then he would fire him, with enthusiasm. The Lord probably feels that same way.

The chief ingredients in the spirit of the two greatest commandments are the qualities of friendliness, fervor, ardor, devotion, love and enthusiasm. These are the qualities with a temperature. They are the fire qualities that we should get into our leadership. Someone has said that whenever the pulse goes over eighty the industry goes like sixty.

Too many leaders, even in the work of the Lord, do grudgingly and with reluctance what should be done under substantial voltage and at high temperatures. More than almost anything else the fires in our souls need rekindling. We need to ignite the sparks of our God-given faith; we need to put fuel on the flames of our interest in the work of the Lord. Our spirits need to be aroused and then set ablaze. Our ambitions need to be inflamed in such a way that we will have more fire power in our leadership.

"Get Thee Up—Be Illuminated"

SOCRATES SAID, "Let him who would move the world, first move himself."

One of the most profound secrets of success in church work, or in any other work, begins with a vigorous, continuous, physical activity. The great British Prime Minister, Disraeli, once defined genius as "the power to make continuous effort." This is also one of the most important parts of church leadership. It is one of the most important teachings of the gospel. Our eternal exaltation in large measure depends upon it.

The Lord has said, "He that is slothful shall not be counted worthy to stand." (D&C 107:100) "Thou shalt not be idle." (D&C 42:42) "The idler shall not have place in the church except he repent and mend his ways." (D&C 75:29) "Now I, the Lord, am not well pleased with the inhabitants of Zion, for there are idlers among them." (D&C 68:31) "Idleness is wickedness." We must "work" out our salvation. Only the "valiant" shall inherit the celestial kingdom. (D&C 76:79) "Let every man be diligent in all things." (D&C 75:29)

One of our most vital problems is how best to promote this all-important diligence in our own lives. Some try to achieve it by driving themselves from the outside; that is very difficult to do. There are others who propel themselves by an enthusiasm generated within themselves; that is much easier. The most effective leader is usually the one who can generate to its maximum this great internal driving power. These are the leaders who "do many things of their own free will, and bring to pass much righteousness" of their own accord. But be that as it may, we need to remember that one of the most important elements in our lives and in our leadership is just plain, simple, honest industry.

There is a great verse in the sixtieth chapter of Isaiah in which the prophet says, "Arise and shine, for thy light is come." This verse was translated by Cloverdale to say, "Get thee up—Be illuminated."

Sometimes our own experience gives additional emphasis to some particular idea. I recently visited a stake which had some of the problems of the Laodiceans, to whom the Lord referred as being neither hot nor cold. As I observed the lack of fire in this particular stake I was impressed that this line from Isaiah was probably the most thrilling line in all of the scriptures. The members of this particular stake seemed to be "dead on their feet." They had many of the earmarks of a first-class cemetery, where the living sleep above the ground almost as soundly as the dead do beneath.

The greatest opportunity of our lives is to shake off our lethargy, to wake ourselves up and get going. There is so much to be done and so little time in which to do it. We should impress ourselves with the seriousness of slothfulness and be aware of the fact that our "greatest sin is to be conscious of none."

The army has taught us something about the seriousness of sleeping at the post. Sleep is the original state of man. The human embryo sleeps continuously. The infant sleeps most of the time. Life is a constant struggle against sleep, which has been described as "a morsel of death." If this spiritual drowsiness is too much indulged in in our religious lives, it brings about spiritual death. "Idleness is wickedness" because it brings failure to every accomplishment, and in the work of the Lord we must not fail.

Recently a man was priding himself on how successfully he had resisted appointment to church responsibility.

He acted as though this were his greatest virtue. He did not seem even to be aware of his own spiritual insensibilities. Most of our problems come from a partial awareness of things. Even when we are supposed to be awake, sleep partially possesses most of us. The chosen disciples could not stay awake to sustain the Son of God in the very hour when, under the burden of their sins, he sweat great drops of blood at every pore. We have not improved very much. We not only sleep in church where we have gone to worship God and do his will, but we often make common jokes about it. How appropriate, therefore, are the timely words of Isaiah, coming down across the centuries to inspire us to throw off this spiritual lethargy and produce within ourselves that kind of ambition which foretells a happy immortality and a glorious exaltation.

When Alice was exploring the mysteries of Wonderland, she met a strange-looking lock in the garden, with feet and hands that made it resemble a human being. It was running around frantically looking behind trees, bushes and under stones, as though it were searching for something. At length, overcome by curiosity, Alice asked, "What are you searching for?" The lock said, "I am searching for the key with which to unlock myself. If I do not find that key I am doomed to remain shut up within myself all of my life. I shall never get out. Therefore, I must find the key to unlock myself."

Almost more than anything else, we need to get ourselves unlocked, to break the cords of inertia which hold us bound, and release that God-given potential with which each of us has been endowed. Effective activity is the roadway to every accomplishment. Probably the bitterest denunciation that Jesus ever heaped upon the head of anyone was upon him who hid his talents in the ground. He said, "Thou wicked and slothful servant." What a great sin is sloth, and how effortlessly we can bring its penalties upon ourselves.

To become what we sometimes call "lost" one need not necessarily be a wicked or notorious sinner. He needs only to be overcome by the fumes of sleep. Sometimes we get what has been called "grey sickness." That is described as a state of being half asleep and half awake, half dead and half alive. In this condition a child of God, intended to be the masterpiece of creation, sinks into this "partial death" and is overcome by lack of interest, inertia, boredom, ignorance, indecision and indifference. Death is inactivity. Life is intelligent enthusiasm and vigorous, continuous effort.

Just think how many good members of the Church depend for their exaltation upon the prodding, encouragement, and continual reminding of someone else. The Bible says that a deep sleep fell upon Adam. Unfortunately Adam is not the only one who has had that experience— except some of us have never learned to arouse ourselves. But "If we really believe as we believe, then why do we do as we do?"

It was reported that one bishop formed the habit of going down to the railroad station every morning to see the train pull out. Someone asked him why, and he said that it just made him feel so good to see something move on its own power, without his having to push it.

We ought to make up our minds about our faith, and then back up our convictions with our whole hearts. The difference between half a heart and a whole heart makes the difference between signal defeat and splendid victory. Someone said that a tired businessman is one whose business is not successful; and a tired church worker is one whose heart is not in what he is doing.

One is not always lost because he does wrong; one

may be lost only because he does nothing. Neglect itself is often fatal, just as a man who has been poisoned needs only to neglect to take the antidote, and he will die.

Faith without works is dead; when we try to isolate faith from its appropriate task, it always dies. Faith cannot survive without activity. When the proper activity is absent, death comes to our leadership, our convictions, our faith, our knowledge, our skills, our good habits, and our testimonies. And every man who refuses the activity loses the benefit that goes therewith.

We generate doubts, negative attitudes and bad habits in periods of inactivity. An inactive man cannot realize his potentialities only because he will not. Degeneration of the spirit is the failure to use properly the faculties that God has implanted within us. Man has been compared to the old Model T Ford; when you turn off the engine the lights go out.

The gospel of Jesus Christ is far more than a set of great ideas; it is also a set of activities. The letters "LDS" stand for Latter-day Saints. They could also stand for "Let's do something."

If we fail in our activity, we automatically bring ourselves under the sentence of "death by disuse." The spirituality withers when, like an unused arm, it is carried constantly in a sling. In all of nature, disuse is as mortal a sin as abuse. The mole refuses to use his eyes, and he thereby loses his sight, just as surely as if his eyes were shot out by a bullet. Everyone is under bond for the effective use of his talents. The law says, "Use them or lose them." The penalty says, "From him that hath not, shall be taken away even that which he hath." To everyone who buries his talents life says, "Take therefore the talent from him, and give it to him who has ten talents." It is a great sin to hide one's light under a bushel, and it is one of the greatest Christian virtues to "arise and shine," for your light will come only as your need and activity shall call it forth.

An explorer was once traveling through a cold Arctic winter night. He was not particularly uncomfortable, but as he proceeded he felt a sluggish, drowsy feeling coming over him. He decided to lie down and rest. Then all of a sudden he realized that he was freezing to death. The thought so startled him that he got up and began to run with all his might. The excitement and vigorous exertion quickened the heart action and soon had a good supply of warm blood circulating through his body. Then the danger was past. His life had been saved because he "got up" and increased his activity.

This experience has its counterpart in our spiritual affairs. It is not uncommon to see spiritual lethargy resembling the numbness that precedes the death of a freezing man. From this dread malady there is one certain prevention, and one sure cure. It is the inspired formula of Isaiah, "Get thee up—Be illuminated." Run for your life. Get your blood circulating. Step on the gas. Be active. Get on the ball. Use your talents to their utmost. Talk about a spiritual "wonder drug"! Isaiah has given us a formula that will solve almost all of our leadership problems and almost every other problem in and out of the Church.

Goethe said, "An idle life is death anticipated." It is an easy thing for God to raise the dead; it is not quite so simple to put new life in a lazy, disinterested, slothful servant. How tragic is the oppression of the spiritual drowsiness preceding decay. Then we get the feeling of one of old who said, "Lo, I am weary in mind and weak in spirit and little strength is there in me." Then always comes the natural judgment saying, "Woe to him of fearful heart and faint hands, for he believeth not; therefore he bringeth damnation to his own soul." Such a one also tends to bring damnation to the souls of all of those for whom he has leadership responsibilities, for "as with the priest, so with the people." It is far more difficult to lead than to mislead. When we go in the wrong direction, then Lucifer-like we draw others away after us.

There are a great many stowaways in the Church who hide out in spiritual idleness, hoping to make the journey without either working or paying their way.

Woe to him who has lost his initiative. Woe to him who develops battle fatigue. Woe to him who does nothing. The law says, "Get thee up and be illuminated." The alternative is to stay down and be eliminated, for spiritual death is banishment from the presence of God.

Someone prayed, "O mighty God, hear the voice of one forlorn, and deliver me from my sloth." But God has done more than that. He has put in our own hands the power to deliver ourselves. The secret is just to get started. Solomon said, "With all thy getting get wisdom." Then someone who must have been a little wiser than Solomon, said, "With all thy getting get going." Industry is the "mustard seed" that moves mountains. Leonardo da Vinci said, "Thou Oh God doth sell us all good things at the price of labor." Goethe said that "genius is nine-tenths industry."

It is probable that these five words from Isaiah may be to us the most important words in scripture. It is seldom that we cannot find the way, but only that we will not walk therein. J. Allergy wrote an epitaph for himself saying: "He lived in the world of going-to-do but died with nothing done."

"The fellow who watches the clock doesn't need to worry about his future. He hasn't any."

Matthew Arnold said that "Religion is mortality touched by emotion." We need a powerized testimony of the gospel. Activity is the key to leadership. It is the foundation of spiritual accomplishment.

Because of their importance, we ought to write these thrilling words of Isaiah across our minds, engrave them in our hearts, and then get them into our muscles, our nervous system and our blood stream. Not only should we set our light upon the hill, but we should see to it that it burns brightly enough to do some good. Isaiah said, "Arise and shine, for thy light is come."

> Don't grumble, don't bluster,
> Don't sleep and don't shirk;
> Don't think of your worries—
> Just think of your work.
>
> Then your worries will vanish,
> The work will be done;
> For no man sees his shadow
> Who faces the sun.

And if you need a morning prayer to harmonize with the spirit and power of Isaiah, here it is:

> Now I get me up to work;
> I pray the Lord I may not shirk.
> If I should die before the night
> I pray the Lord my work's all right.

The Gift of Translation

A SCHOLAR was once asked which of all the translations of the Bible he liked the best. His reply was that he liked his mother's translation best. His mother had translated the Bible into her own life. That is the translation that really counts. The Bible seemed far more important to the scholar as it manifested itself in the personality, faith and actual daily performance of his mother. She lived the Bible precepts. Its spirit was her spirit. She was the visual representative of the message and attitude of Holy Writ.

A successful follower of the Master must be able not only to translate the words of the scriptures into deeds, but he must also translate the spirit of the gospel into his heart and then acquire the leadership techniques to make it effective in his work. One of our greatest responsibilities is to develop the skill to get Christianity out of the scriptures and into the lives of people, particularly our own. We must be able to translate the spirit of the life of Christ into actual accomplishment.

"The only Bible that some folks ever read is the Bible of our lives." What more fruitful meaning could attach to the term "translation" than to think of it as transferring the greatest ideas from the printed page into our actual daily conduct? Or what greater failure could attend us than to lack the ability so to translate? It has been claimed to our discredit that many Christians are only "Bible Christians," which means that the Christianity remains mostly in the Bible and only a small amount gets into us. The Christianity that is confined to the printed page or to a mere verbal expression does not have great practical value. In fact, it is often actually sinful, as "the greatest blasphemy is not profanity but lip service." Of the vine-dresser's son who said, "I go," but went not, Jesus said, "Verily I say unto you that the publicans and harlots go into the kingdom of God before you."

One of our greatest deficiencies is our inability to make an appropriate translation. There are some people who can hear a great gospel message and not be deeply stirred. There are some who can stand on holy ground and have no desire to take off their shoes. There may even be some who could read the Bible from cover to cover and then go on about their usual affairs much as they did before, without appreciable change either in attitude, conduct or devotion. There are some who can be outstandingly efficient in their own daily work but who are unable to use those same abilities to do the work of the Lord effectively.

But then there are some people who, like the scholar's mother, have developed the ability to take ideas and translate them into attitudes, activities and godliness. They can take the abilities that make them effective in the work of the world and use them with even greater effectiveness in the work of the Lord.

The dictionary says that "to translate is to change the form." "It is to give meaning to thoughts" and "make feelings profitable in the lives of others." We speak of a "translated being" as one who is taken into heaven without tasting death. The definition of a "translated idea" might be very closely related, except that many ideas die en route. They never live through the process or ordeal of being translated into action. Yet it is this ability to get ideas successfully through the early stages of their metamorphosis to where they become faith and action that has real value. To get ideas and feelings across the border of usefulness

and make them negotiable is real religion. That skill is also
one of the all-important characteristics of constructive
leadership. It is our main job to see to it that this ability
to translate is fully developed and effectively used.

In several places in the scripture the phrase, "the gift
of translation," is used. The Lord said that Joseph Smith
was to be called a translator. He said to Oliver Cowdery,
"Behold I grant unto you a gift if you desire of me, to
translate even as my servant, Joseph." The gift referred
to, of course, is the gift of translating from one language
to another. But there is another gift of translation, that
of translating from language into feelings and from feelings
into action and from action into accomplishment. Determination in leaders can be translated into eternal glory
for those led. The word of the Lord serves its highest
purpose only when it is translated into faith and godliness.

But most of the greatest men of the world in every
field might in one way be called translators. James Watt
translated an idea from a boiling teakettle into a powerful
steam engine. A spider spinning his web gave a construction engineer the inspiration for one of the first great
suspension bridges. Brigham Young, while cracking the
shell of the boiled egg he was about to eat for his breakfast,
got an idea which he translated into the oval roof for the
Salt Lake Tabernacle, which did not require inside supports.
Knute Rockne translated the rhythm and harmony of movement of a line of chorus girls into the symmetry and power
of his famous backfield called "The Four Horsemen." The
same ideas that brought people to the theatre every night
were used by Mr. Rockne to bring them to the football
stadium every Saturday afternoon. The greatest inventors,
writers, thinkers and leaders are those who can adapt the
best ideas from the greatest number of sources and make
them productive in their own work. John Stuart Mill
thought that the chief function of the mind was making

inferences. One is up against an insurmountable obstacle who tries to build his success only upon his own original ideas.

This also applies to those of us who work in the Church. A teacher would not be rated very high who was not familiar with the methods and ideas of the most up-to-date educators. We also want teachers to be familiar with the researches of the leading teachers' colleges. But probably beyond this, a good teacher needs to be able to take the everyday experiences and translate them into character, ambition and righteousness, as did "the great Teacher."

Jesus himself was the master translator. He had the greatest skill in using to the best purpose everything that he saw around him. The parable was one of the most prominent teaching methods of Jesus. The whole list of his parables might very properly come under the heading of "translation." He used the ideas that people understood to make clear the truths which he wanted them to understand better.

For example, the parable of the sower was given to a group of people familiar with the operations of the farmer. Jesus pointed out that they should not plant their seeds on the hard ground or allow the thorns to choke out the tender plants once they started to grow. This idea with which they were already familiar was then easily translated for their use in promoting their own spiritual interests. With great effect he taught from the experiences of the prodigal son and the good Samaritan and the foolish virgins. Jesus transformed even the most ordinary experiences and ideas into something uplifting and beautiful.

He is the best example of great leadership, and we should follow his example in learning from those things nearest to us. The more capable the man, the more he learns from everything around him. But learning is of little value unless some practical application can be made of it. For those who can see beyond the event itself, there are "tongues in trees, books in running brooks, sermons in stones, and good in everything." If we lacked the mind and heart of the translator we might see only the stones and miss the sermons. With the mind of a translator the benefit of even ordinary experiences is multiplied in us. It connects us up with other important links in the chain of constructive thought.

Every wind helps the boat go toward its objectives, if its sails are properly set. Paul said, "All things work together for the good of them that love God." Everything has something to teach us, if we have our eyes open and set our sails to take advantage of it. Every experience can be our benefactor. Sickness is as important as health; death is as much a part of the plan as birth; night is as necessary as day; struggle is as much in our interest as ease. One set of facts teaches us what to avoid; another set of facts teaches us what to do. An effective, well-adjusted, stable personality takes all of the incidents in its experience and translates them into the attitudes, skills, habits, devotion and other qualities of leadership and success.

It is possible for us to do in the field of leadership what the ancient alchemists failed to do in the field of metallurgy. For many years alchemists tried to transmute the baser metals of iron and lead into the more valuable metals of silver and gold. In this they were doomed to failure. But there is a kind of spiritual alchemy where we may be guaranteed an outstanding success. For if we desire it sincerely enough, and work vigorously with the right attitude, we can gain the ability to translate our every experience into some good. "Success is merely a matter of buying experience and selling it at a profit."

In his story of "The Great Stone Face," Nathaniel Hawthorne tells of a young boy who daily looked up to and admired the noble features and kindly characteristics of a natural stone image on the mountainside, and every day he became more and more like the image which he admired, not only in personality traits but in actual physical characteristics. This young man had the power to translate for his own good the worthwhile personality factors and character qualities which he identified and admired in the image on the mountainside. These he made negotiable for others through his own life.

Lincoln did the same thing. His earliest years were spent reading good books. The most important of these was the Bible, which could always thereafter be identified as a part of the character of Lincoln. One of the other sources of his strength came from a book written about the life of George Washington. Lincoln adapted attributes from Washington, as Hawthorne's Ernest did from the Great Stone Face, and as we can do from everything around us.

The Bible records that the mantle of Elijah fell upon Elisha. The mantle of Joseph Smith fell upon Brigham Young. It is our responsibility to see to it that the mantle of leadership falls upon us. The Lord will give us the power of great leadership if we will only make ourselves worthy.

An important part of our qualification is to develop and use this gift and power of translation. With every experience and every idea we ought to say: How will this help me in the work of the Lord? How can I use this to build up my faith and my attitude? How can I use the principles of successful teaching and good public relations and business success to save souls? A worth-while church leader is responsible to see that every member under his charge qualifies for the celestial kingdom. That will challenge our gift of translation to its greatest productivity.

"Have To"

IN A RURAL section of Southern California a Mexican mother died, leaving a family of eight children. The oldest girl, not yet seventeen, was a small child upon whose frail shoulders fell the burden of caring for the family. The neighbors watched her as she took up the task with courage and ability. She kept all of the other children clean, well fed and in school. She did her task with unusual competence. One day a neighbor woman complimented her on her substantial achievement. The girl replied, "I can take no credit for something that I have to do." "But, my dear," said the friend, "you don't have to. No one can require this of you." The girl thought for a moment and then said, "That may be true, but what about the 'have to' inside of me?"

In the utterance of this unschooled Mexican girl is found one of the most important phases of leadership success. It consists of an "internal pressure of responsibility." It is a sense of urgency to do right. It is what made Socrates say, "Whatever duty thou assignest me, sooner will I die a thousand times than to forsake it."

There are people who develop to a high degree this powerful sense of voluntary determination to do their duty. This quality is far more than just initiative. It is a combination of enterprise and conscience at its best. These two great traits join hands to form a wonderful internal spiritual power.

During the first world war, the captain of a gunboat gave the order for his ship to go to the rescue of a stricken comrade. The mate pointed out the hazards to the captain.

Their return would surely be cut off, leaving little chance for them to get back to port. The captain replied, "We have to go out; we don't have to come back." This captain had the same spirit and sense of responsibility possessed by his little Mexican sister.

This quality attains its highest rank among the traits of leadership. It was one of the important characteristics that distinguished the life of Abraham Lincoln. Lincoln had lots of "have to." He said, "I am not bound to win, but I am bound to be true. I am not bound to succeed, but I am bound to live by the best light that I have. I will stand with anybody that stands right, and I will part from anybody when he goes wrong." It was the "have to" in Lincoln that kept him going against great odds until the cause was finally won.

This quality reached its highest denomination in the Master himself, who took it with him to the cross. He didn't have to, but he did. He did what he did voluntarily and of his own will. He said, "I lay down my life of myself. . . . No man taketh it from me." We can hardly imagine anyone reminding Jesus to do his duty.

Recently a member of the Church said to me that he was going to quit smoking. I asked him why, and he showed me an article that he had just clipped out of the paper about the tremendous increase in lung cancer, and the fact that scientists are now agreed that smoking causes many horrible cancerous deaths. That is, the possibility of suffering and death had scared him into doing right. He was not going to quit smoking because it was wrong; nor was he going to quit because it would please God. He was not quitting because of a righteous "have to" in his heart. He was quitting merely because he feared the pain and death that he was bringing upon himself. And while it was a good idea for him to quit, regardless of the reason, I thought how much more thrilling it would have been if he had quit smoking because of the word of the Lord. Certainly his motive ranks far below that which actuated the Mexican girl and the gunboat captain.

In our own day, Jesus has reimpressed upon us this principle of voluntary action. We ought to give it careful consideration. From the following how do you think Jesus feels about our developing some "have to"? On August 1, 1831, he said to Joseph Smith:

26. For behold it is not meet that I should command in all things, for he that is compelled in all things, the same is a slothful and not a wise servant, wherefore he receiveth no reward.

27. Verily, I say, men should be anxiously engaged in a good cause and do many things of their own free will and bring to pass much righteousness.

28. For the power is in them wherein they are agents unto themselves and inasmuch as men do good, they shall in no wise lose their reward.

29. And he that doeth not anything until he is commanded and receiveth the commandment with doubtful heart and keepeth it with slothfulness, the same is damned. (D&C 58:26-29)

That is pretty strong language. Certainly it is clear. We should keep in mind that we can damn ourselves by doing nothing. There is a law to the effect that if a person is drowning and if we are able to go to his assistance but do not do so, we are legally responsible. Our citizenship would be questioned if someone always had to give us a pep talk or in other ways wind us up to get us to go to the aid of a drowning man. We should also be fully aware of the place that initiative and aggressive self-action have in the leadership activities of the Church. The above four verses are a very important part of our responsibility. If we listen closely, our conscience will tell us what ought to be done. Our initiative can carry any accomplishment, if we will only use it. Anyway, the responsibility is up to us.

Our minds and our ambitions can be stretched to new dimensions when the right ideas are put into them. Leadership reaches its highest level only when we develop the ability to do important things under our own power.

There was a farmer in South Carolina trying to hire a satisfactory farm hand. His only qualifying question was, "How many tellings do you take?" That is one of the important traits the Lord needs to know about us. Someone said a little caustically that a genius was one who could do a thing with only three tellings.

But I know of a ward teacher who has to be told that many times every month. Someone must call him and remind him and stir up his enthusiasm to get one month's teaching done. But it is extremely difficult to keep him active for long at a time. He is like a tire with half a dozen slow leaks. Everytime any service is required, he must be pumped up again. But he loses his pressure about as fast as he gets it. He is greatly handicapped because he must depend upon power from outside himself. Can you see in your imagination the kind of man that the Lord had in mind when he said, "He that doeth not anything until he is commanded and receiveth the commandment with a doubtful heart and keepeth it with slothfulness, the same is damned"?

There are some people who can't hold their welfare meetings until pressure is brought to bear from the outside. An emergency comparable to the fear of lung cancer is often necessary to force a reluctant mind to get going. There are some who cannot even get to church without assistance or some kind of artificial respiration of the spirit. Even when they get there they are often late and unprepared to make or receive a worth-while contribution.

Elbert Hubbard once wrote a famous story entitled, "A Message to Garcia," wherein Rowan was given a very important assignment. He accepted the assignment, made his preparations and carried them to a successful completion without all of the inquiry and assistance so often required in even the most simple tasks. Mr. Hubbard's message caught on in people's minds like wildfire. Employers bought copies for their employees. It was immediately translated into dozens of foreign languages. People gave it for graduation presents, wedding gifts, birthdays, etc. The popularity of this message was so great because of the general awareness of the importance of this rare quality.

Few things so excite our admiration as someone who can do things on his own power without being coaxed or begged or reminded or helped. Think how the little Mexican girl inspires our pride and friendship, as she takes over in her youth the heavy responsibilities of maturity. It would have been easy for her to have found many reasons why she should look out only for herself. But her "have to" took over, and the family was kept united and in good condition and the girl herself was blessed above them all.

Now think of our situation. Our Father in Heaven also has children. Many of them are in even greater need than these little Mexican children. Many of our Father's children are in danger of losing their blessings. All of the principles of the gospel have to do with the celestial kingdom. The purpose of the Church is to help everyone to qualify. Yet we are told that only a few will reach that high objective. The reason is often an inadequate leadership. With one kind of leadership, accomplishment may rise to a very high level; with another kind of leadership accomplishment almost sinks out of sight. Still another kind of leadership *misleads*. Jesus said, "But woe unto you, scribes and Pharisees, hypocrites! for you shut up the kingdom of heaven against men: for ye neither go in yourselves, neither suffer ye them that are entering to go in." (Matt. 23:13)

The artist Rembrandt once painted a picture of the crucifixion. As you look at the painting your eyes first rest naturally upon the central figure in the scene. But as you look into the shadows you see another figure. Those who know the story of the picture and the artist say that Rembrandt painted a picture of himself in the background. There is no question about his intention. Rembrandt was showing himself as helping to crucify Christ by his thoughtlessness, his unintended sins, his misdirected effort and bad example.

Most people do not actually mean to do harm. The ward teacher who slights his duty or the leader who fails to hold his planning meetings or the teacher who passes up the preparation of his lesson has no intention to harm anyone. But the lives of people are adversely affected just the same. It is an inspiring idea that Rembrandt was able to think of himself in the role that many of us unintentionally assume at times. At least Rembrandt was not fooling himself. Somewhere there in the shadowy background we also may be assisting the forces of evil. It is a possibility that we should be aware of.

We speak of ourselves as saviors on Mt. Zion. We cannot be saviors unless we save someone, and the first soul that anyone should bring to God is his own soul. We will not be saviors to very many people if someone always has to push us from behind.

I know of two boys of the same age in the same ward. One gets to his priesthood and other meetings fifteen minutes ahead of time, on his own power. The other boy's parents can't get him up in the morning. The one boy was asked to teach a Sunday School class at a very early age. Someday someone will be asking him to be a bishop or stake president. It never occurs to anyone to ask the other boy to do these important jobs. The difference between them is a personal, private sense of urgency or "have to."

Every time I see this first boy I feel like saluting. This quality in him is a prediction of great accomplishment to come.

Peter and John were once accused and brought before the leaders of the Jews. They said to their captors, "Whether it be right in the sight of God to harken unto you more than unto God, judge ye. For we cannot but speak the things which we have seen and heard." (Acts 4:19-20) They felt impelled to go forward. This quality gave them power, and it will do the same for us.

We can also develop this sense of urgency, this helpful inner pressure in our lives by living it. Then like the little Mexican girl we will develop a "have to" sufficient to guarantee our every success and happiness.

Here Am I. Send Me.

THE PROPHET ISAIAH gives a partial account of a vision which he had of the grand council in heaven. It was of the time when the savior was being chosen for what was as yet an unborn race of mortals. He was to redeem a world yet in its formative stages of development. Isaiah said, "And I heard the voice of the Lord saying, Whom shall I send and who shall go for us?" (Isaiah 6:8)

Modern revelation tells us that there were two who responded. One was the first-begotten Son of God who was particularly qualified for this special mission. He answered and said, "Here am I. Send me. Father, thy will be done and the glory be thine forever." (Moses 4:2) But another also spoke. It was Lucifer, the brilliant Son of the Morning, and he said, "Behold here am I. Send me. I will be thy son and I will redeem all mankind and not one soul shall be lost. And surely I will do it; therefore, give me thine honor." (Moses 4:1; D&C 76:26; Isaiah 14:12-14)

Here we see initiated two opposing philosophies which have continued with us ever since. The first-begotten Son of God offered to come to the earth in the interests of others. Lucifer offered to come in the interests of his own glory.

And God said, "I will send the first." And the record says that "the second was angry and kept not his first estate." (Abr. 3:27-28) Because Lucifer did not get his own way to serve his own interests, he became rebellious, and ever since he has fought against the work of God. Lucifer was cast out of heaven, and one-third of the hosts of heaven were cast out with him. By their disobedience

125

and rebellion, they disqualified themselves for advancement to what would have been their second estate. (D&C 29:36)

This disqualification by disobedience is still going on —and for about the same reasons. Our hearts sometimes get pretty solidly set on our own short-termed personal gain. This was not only the biggest problem that God had with his children in the pre-existence, but it is also the biggest problem he has with us here. "Many are called but few are chosen." Few are chosen simply because we disqualify ourselves. The Lord's present work is still the work of human redemption for which he was set apart in heaven, and his biggest problem is still getting people to qualify for their high calling in becoming the right kind of leaders. Because his work must always be based on the law of free agency, God is as of old still confronting us with that same great question: "Whom shall I send? And who shall go for us?" And as in the grand council, our reply will largely determine our own future and the futures of those who follow our lead.

What can we do about it? Perhaps more than anything else, we need to develop within ourselves an aggressive enthusiasm, patterned after the volunteer spirit of the premortal Christ who said, "Father, here am I. Send me. Thy will be done and the glory be thine forever." This and the extent to which we can develop this spirit in ourselves will determine our blessings and our usefulness.

The Lord gave us the key when he said, "If ye have desires to serve God, ye are called to the work." (D&C 4:3) "Desire is the pilot of the soul." If our desires to serve God are not strong enough, then we may let personal interests crowd out eternal considerations. We need to develop more aggressiveness of spirit. We need to increase our own individual initiative and resourcefulness. The Lord doesn't like us to wait until we are "commanded in all things." The work of salvation is not only his cause; it is our cause also.

There may be some people who think it smart to be "hard to get" in doing church work. There are some who resist church appointment or accept it with reluctance and lack of interest. I once heard a man say in stake conference that he had been considered for a certain position on two occasions and each time he had found out about it in advance and had sold his home and moved out of the stake. But this last time he hadn't found out about it in time and was "stuck with the job." His words and attitude were that he did not desire to serve God. How do you think the Lord would feel about such an attitude?

If this is the work of the Lord, why shouldn't we get excited about it and want above everything else to have a part in it? That spirit was recently indicated by an elderly brother who was an Aaronic Priesthood adviser. He said, "I hope the bishop won't think I am too old for this assignment. I love this work and I don't know what I would do if I could not be a part of it."

Brigham Young once said, "Every man and woman is expected to aid the work of the Lord with all the ability that God has given them." This is the philosophy that President Young himself practiced vigorously all of his life. We voluntarily took upon ourselves a covenant of service when we were in the grand council in heaven. But each of us must renew his covenant here.

The work of the Lord has not yet been finished. Many of the most important assignments are yet to be filled, and as of old, one of the most important questions is, "Whom shall I send and who shall go for us?" Our reply should reflect our desire to serve. Our *desire* is still one of our most important qualifications. There are some in our day who are responding with eagerness and saying, "Here am I. Send me." Some, Lucifer-like, desert the work of the

Lord and draw others away after them. But there are some who do not respond at all. It is not that they disbelieve the word of the Lord; their problem is more serious—they just don't think about it one way or the other. They are too involved in their own interests or have sunk too deep in their own lethargy. But whatever the reason, the consequence is that some of the most important opportunities ever offered to men are being pushed aside and left without takers.

How many positions in the Church are presently unfilled? How many auxiliaries are not fully organized? How many workers are not excited about their work? How many will resign this year? We need more stick-to-it-iveness. We need to stir ourselves up. We need a lot more practice in being "anxiously engaged in a good cause." We need to be more aggressive and run to meet our opportunities.

The Savior was chosen and ordained in the first estate to be our Redeemer in the second estate. But in the grand council in heaven, many others were also selected and ordained for mortal leadership responsibilities. God referred to a group where there were *many* noble and great and he said, "These I will make my rulers." The Lord told Abraham that he was one of these. The Lord also ordained Jeremiah to be a prophet unto the nations before he was born. (Jeremiah 1:5) But Joseph Smith added some very significant additional information when he told us that "every man who has a calling to administer to the inhabitants of the earth was ordained to that very purpose in the grand council in heaven before the world was." (*DHC* VI:364)

That includes us. In all probability we were also among the noble and great. We were probably high in the council of heaven and carried great responsibility. Undoubtedly we then enjoyed the full confidence of God. There was probably a very good reason why we were reserved to perform our mission in this age of wonders and enlightenment known to us as the Dispensation of the Fullness of Times. What a great challenge it is to know that we were sent here by the direct action of God and that grand council over which he presided!

Now just suppose that after all of this advantage, we miss our calling. We have been called, but suppose we fail to be *chosen* because we ourselves do not respond. John A. Widtsoe wrote: "Those who receive the message of the gospel are obligated not only by divine command to warn every man his neighbor, but also by that ageless agreement made before this world was organized, that those who were privileged to seek and find the gospel during their earthly career would do all in their power to bring it to the attention of others." That certainly means that we must magnify the position of leadership to which we were ordained in heaven.

But sometimes it takes the greatest effort for us to rise to our most simple responsibilities. Sometimes we resemble a flying fish that can soar for only a little way above the surface before it drops back into the water again. Sometimes we make a brief effort to rise to meet our calling and then drop back into our mediocrity.

What a thrilling thing it is to see an aggressive, resourceful, willing, untiring, well-directed spiritual leader who can do the right things on his own initiative and keep on doing them to the end!

Very frequently we speak of the fact that God has given us the authority to officiate in his work. But we ourselves must develop the desire and the stick-to-it-iveness, the sense of responsibility and the industry to make that authority effective. What does it profit us if we have the authority but lack the resourcefulness and ability to make it operative? What an inspiration to see one with enough self-confidence to know in advance that he will succeed, that he is prepared and ready to do whatever is necessary to bring accomplishment about. Then he knows that he will not fail, because he will not permit himself to fail. "I Will" is a more important quality than "IQ."

Occasionally the Lord has referred to some particular person or group as his "friends." (D&C 84:63; 84:77; 94:1) To be the friend of the Savior of the world would seem to imply a similarity of interests—a similarity of responsibility and enough strength to stand firmly and untiringly in our calling. It has been said that in addition to merely obeying God we ought to "agree with God," to see things from the correct point of view, and then do the things to qualify us for the rank of "friends."

When Jesus said, "Father, here am I. Send me," he knew it meant suffering and opposition and even death. But he was prepared. That has been true of other great leaders. When someone was needed to carry on after the crucifixion, Simon Peter said in substance: "Here am I. Send me." When someone was needed to carry the gospel to the gentiles, Saul of Tarsus said, "Lord, what wouldst thou have me do?" Or in other words, "Here am I. Send me." He didn't say, "I will try it out for a little while and see how I like it."

Joseph Smith was only fourteen and a half years old when he said in spirit, "Here am I. Send me." And thereafter he never wavered until his blood had been spilled by assassins. The persistence to stay with the call is just as important as the initiative that gets it started. We see this great quality of perseverance and determination manifest itself in great leaders in every field. Madame Curie spent her life in a successful effort to discover radium. After the 487th experiment had failed wherein she and her husband Pierre had tried to isolate radium from pitchblende, Pierre threw up his hands in despair and said, "It will never be done. Maybe in a hundred years but never in our day."

Madame Curie confronted him with a resolute face and said, "If it takes a hundred years it will be a pity, but I will not cease to work for it as long as I live." What a thrilling attitude!

Should our devotion be any less? It is up to us. We are the architects of our own fate. We may have any blessing we are willing to live. God's great question is still before us. It is his greatest question and his most important challenge. "Whom shall I send? And who shall go for us?" Let us run to meet the call with the greatest of all answers, the one given by the Redeemer himself, "Father, here am I. Send me. Thy will be done and the glory be thine forever."

Hold Up Your Hands

THERE WAS ONCE a blind man who had an operation performed on his eyes. The first thing that his new vision rested upon was his own hand. He said he thought no sight could be more wonderful than his hand, with its veins, its muscles, its wonderfully efficient bony structure, its marvelous covering of skin, etc.

The hands are soft and pliable, and yet in them and by them are forged the great instruments and machinery by which we carry on the work of the world. With the hands we build tanks, battleships, and skyscrapers. We also perform the most delicate surgical operations. These soft white hands are capable of literally moving mountains, and yet they can do the most intricate and refined tasks. The sensitive nervous system in the hands picks up the slightest impulse and transmits it to the brain. Helen Keller even used her hands for eyes. She said, "I thrust my hands into my great Braille volumes and draw them out filled with the secrets of the spiritual world."

The hand may be invested with additional significance through its symbolism. A ring on the finger may stand for the most important things in life. Outstretched to a brother, the hand speaks welcome and greeting. Laid upon the shoulder of a friend, it gives encouragement and hope. Upon the head of the sick, it is a manifestation of faith and confers the blessings of health. Struck in salute, it signifies loyalty and obedience. With the right hand raised to the square and the left hand anchored upon the Bible, we take the oath of office, and thereby give our most convincing outward expression of our integrity and devotion.

132

By shaking hands we bind ourselves and give our words greater meaning. The hand, like the heart, renders some of its greatest services through its symbolic offices.

In the Church we are asked at specified times to hold up our hands to support and sustain those who hold official position in the Church. This ceremony at its best is endowed with particular significance. It is an expression of unity and faith. But we really sustain others best only when we do our own assignment well. When we hold up our hand as a token that we will support others, we also take our own oath of office and promise that we will be faithful to God to whom we have already sworn allegiance. There are many who would rather lose their lives than fail their responsibility even in their ordinary affairs. Socrates said, "Whatsoever place thou assignest me, sooner will I die a thousand deaths than to forsake it."

Major Martin Treptow was killed in the battle of Chateau-Thierry in 1918. In the diary that was found on his body were written these words: "I will work; I will save; I will sacrifice; I will endure. I will fight cheerfully and do my utmost as though the entire conflict depended upon me alone." His pledge of allegiance lived in his life and in his death. He held his own hands up high and thereby he held up the honor and ability of his country and his countrymen. Such a pledge promises an industry and loyalty that will not fail.

Edith Cavell was a British nurse serving in a Belgian hospital in the first world war. She met her death before a German firing squad in 1915 for assisting some 200 Allied prisoners to escape. Just before the German bullets tore through her quivering flesh, Edith Cavell said, "Patriotism is not enough." Can any service be enough which has as its purpose to serve God, our country and our fellow men?

Edith Cavell, like Nathan Hale and Martin Treptow, gave her life for what she believed. Should we do less?

When we accept any responsibility in the Church, the Lord and everyone else, including ourselves, have a right to know in advance exactly where we stand and what we mean to do about it. Therefore, at regular intervals, we hold up our hands to indicate that we will uphold those in office with every ability that we possess. Then that is exactly what we ought to do.

Much of the benefit of the promise reverts to those who make it. We increase our loyalties when we declare them. We add to our determination by expressing it. And our own effectiveness will grow if we earnestly make a heartfelt promise to be faithful. It is then easier to put the full force of our vigor behind the sign that we have made.

I am reminded of the motorman who used to run the old trolley car. He got the power for his motor by putting his trolley pole up against the electric wire. Then he drew down for utilization the mysterious electric current which flowed from the powerhouse many miles away. If he dropped his trolley pole, or if he allowed it to lose contact with the wire, the power stopped. The significance of the uplifted hand serves us as a kind of spiritual trolley pole or antenna to bring down the power of God to help us do his work.

We remember the interesting account in the Book of Kings of the battle between the Amalekites and the hosts of ancient Israel. Joshua led the Israelites and was supported by the uplifted hands of Moses. The record says: "And it came to pass that when Moses held up his hands Israel prevailed; when he let down his hands Amalek prevailed. But Moses' hands were heavy." So Aaron got on one side of Moses and Hur on the other side, and they held his hands "steady until the going down of the sun." Then victory was placed in their hands.

How like our own situation! When we hold up our hands with all that that means the Church moves forward. The uplifted hand is not only a requirement of the Lord, but it makes stronger the very hands that are upheld. Like Moses', sometimes our own hands get heavy, but when we let them down progress stops. Loyalty not only increases our own strength, but it also increases the strength of those who work with us, as they know that they are supported on their flanks and in their rear by capable, loyal co-workers whose faith and devotion are solidly united with their own. "In unity there is strength." There is also satisfaction and progress. The Lord himself has said, "If ye are not one, ye are not mine."

Great strength and power can come from symbols. It may be a light in the window, or it may be a star in the flag, or it may be Old Glory itself symbolizing a nation of free men and women. It may be the insignia of the uniform or our own oath of office. Man himself draws his greatest importance largely from what he stands for. Abraham Lincoln was important because of what he stood for. Joseph Smith made his great contribution to the world by what he stood for. The Savior drew down from God the blessings of salvation for all of mankind because of what he lived and died for.

It has always been an exciting experience to me to see someone take the oath of office. On January 21, 1957, Dwight D. Eisenhower raised his right hand to God while his left hand rested upon the Bible opened to the 12th verse of the 33rd Psalm which says, "Blessed is the nation whose God is the Lord." When Theodore Roosevelt took the oath of office, his left hand rested on the Bible opened to James 1:22, which says, "Be ye doers of the word and not hearers only." As each president raises his right hand to God and promises to protect the constitution of this land which God has established, he seems to me like a national trolley pole, bringing down upon us our national blessings, as from his heart come those significant words: "I do solemnly swear that I will faithfully execute the office of the President of the United States. . . ."

In our work of salvation, why shouldn't we also have the stimulating strength that comes from a fervent oath of office? When one makes such a promise with every faculty of mind participating in the covenant, he is putting up his spiritual antenna to the source of all power.

The Lord has always placed great importance in covenants. We made a covenant at the time of baptism; we made a covenant when we received the priesthood; we made a covenant when we were married. We make a covenant when we partake of the sacrament, and we make a covenant when we hold up our hands. The ancient Israelites, in accepting God's covenant in their day, declared in unison, "All that the Lord hath said, we will do." In our own day the Lord has said, "Therefore, oh ye that embark in the service of God, see that ye serve him with all your heart, might, mind and strength, that ye may stand blameless before God at the last day." All of us who desire to do so may hold up our hands to God.

Certainly we should never accept a position in the Church with only a vague idea of what our duty is and how we are going to do it. Just suppose that whenever we accept a position in the Church we go before the bishop, or before God, and on our own responsibility, raise our right hand and covenant that we will faithfully execute the duties of the office to which we have been called; that we will allow no exceptions to our devotion; that we will accept no bribes from sloth, and that we will do only that which is right. We promise to love the work of the Lord and accept full responsibility therefore.

When we are sustained in office, probably the most important vote that is cast is our own. Certainly when voting to sustain ourselves, we ought to put our hands all the way up and maybe stand on our tiptoes while we do it.

One of our biggest problems in developing effectiveness in leadership comes because we haven't thought hard enough and seriously enough about our work. We spend too much of our lives in vagueness. We sometimes live and die, vague about objectives and procedures for our own personal program of work in the Church. To illustrate, a recent survey by a great national magazine indicated that in America 95 percent of the people believe in God, but only a few have more than a very vague conception of the kind of a God they believe in. Even about our most simple duties and the procedures for carrying them out, we are often far from clear even in our own minds.

Success comes when we replace vagueness with definiteness. We are the children of God, created by God, responsible to God. The effects of our work will last throughout eternity. We are preparing the kingdom for presentation to the King, and we must make some firm commitments about what part we wish to play. When this has been decided, we ought to put up our hands, and put them up good and high.

There are few things that are more disconcerting to us, (and they must also be disconcerting to God,) than not to know where a person stands. There are some who, if they are going to hold up their hands at all, would not put them up so high that they couldn't get them down in a hurry if the wind should start to blow from some other direction. Their loyalties are not strong enough that they are willing to put themselves on record. Too many say, "I will try it out for a little while," or "I will see how I like it,"—rather than, "I will accept the full responsibility and then carry it through in spite of obstacles."

The law of cause and effect is still in operation. All we need to do is to find out what is required for success and then spend whatever effort is necessary to bring it about.

There is an interesting scripture which says, "The Lord thy God will lead thee by the hand." If we keep our hands in our pockets, the Lord may not be able to get hold of them. Or if our expression is timid, halfhearted, undecided and barely audible, the Lord may not be able to tell exactly where we stand, or which way we are going. Let's let the Lord and everyone else know our position. The man who does not openly declare himself does the cause as well as himself an injustice and becomes little more than an onlooker.

There is some danger of getting ourselves inoculated with such a mild form of religion that we will make ourselves immune to the genuine article. The best way to avoid that calamity is to put up our trolley poles high enough that we get the full charge of power.

What a thrilling idea that we can stand for the most important principles and activities in the world, those having to do with the immortality and eternal life of man. And so, at regular intervals, it is our privilege to hold up clean, capable, powerful hands, to express our own determination and promise God to do our best in our own assignment and to support every other person so engaged in carrying on the Lord's work.

The Hour of Decision

PROBABLY the most important thing that we ever have to do in our lives is to make decisions. We have the great responsibility of being agents unto ourselves. We must decide between good and evil, success and failure, industry and sloth, happiness and misery. We must make our own determinations as to our direction, our speed, and our destination. This is the greatest blessing that we have in the world, as well as the greatest responsibility.

The part of creation which lives under the control and direction of natural instincts does not have any such responsibility. A cow behaves as cows have always behaved. The hexagon cell built by the honeybee today is of exactly the same design and the same measurements as were those cells built by honeybees a thousand years ago. Roosters crow in the same language and in the same manner and for the same reasons, all over the world. Many of the various forms of nature conform to a definite pattern as they are born, feed, breed and die.

But each individual person is different. In fact, it has been said that there is only one point at which all men are exactly alike and that is that they are all different. The reason for the difference is that man must act for himself; and the biggest business of any life is the business of deciding issues. That is also our hardest job and the place where we make or break our success.

The dictionary says that we make a decision by giving one side the victory over the other. To decide is to "bring an end to vacillation." It is the "termination of doubt or controversy." To decide means to "conclude" after careful investigation or reasoning. And a real decision implies a degree of firmness which enables us to carry it through to its conclusion.

Sometimes we confuse an intention with a decision. An intention, no matter how good it is, is a poor substitute for its more solid, determined brother. Almost everyone *intends* to do right. It is said that hell is paved with good intentions. Isn't it interesting to know that down the long way to hell most people carry with them a heart filled with the very best of good intentions? If these had been matured a little more they could have become decisions, with enough influence to have carried their possessor to the celestial kingdom. But a decision is a mental condition that is far more advanced and has greater power than a mere intention. But the right kind of decisions are sometimes very difficult to make. Even the Apostle Paul seemed to have some trouble. He said, "When I would do good, evil is present with me." Again he said, "That which I would not, that I do."

I once heard a lawyer indicate another problem in making decisions. He said that he had a "judicial mind." For many years he had trained himself to look with equal favor on both sides of the proposition. If someone robbed the bank or beat his wife, he tried to understand and appreciate that peculiar point of view. Eventually he got to the point where he had great difficulty getting his mind to take sides at all. It seemed to be permanently neutralized.

Neutrality or impartiality is not always a virtue. Winston Churchill was once accused of being partial on a certain matter. After admitting the charge, he expressed his wholehearted favor for partiality. He said he thought impartiality the cause of many of our problems. For example, he thought it a little ridiculous to be impartial as between the fire brigade and the fire. Probably hell also gets most of its devotees from the ranks of those having a strong impartiality. We are sometimes impartial between right and wrong, between industry and sloth, between God and Satan. Impartiality leaves many of our good intentions in a state of arrested development, whereas a little more partiality would mature them into decisions.

Another neutral term is "indecision," which means that a good intention is just left dangling. Sometimes one receives some help by having his decision forced by circumstances. If the train leaves at three minutes after four, that fact exerts pressure to get him to make up his mind. The fact that Sunday School starts at 10:30 gives a reluctant mind a push in the direction of a decision.

Many of our decisions are lost by postponement. If we were forced to decide an issue, the decision would undoubtedly be a good one. But we don't decide because it is so easy to put off making up our minds. That is sometimes so, even in regard to such things as honesty, temperance, industry, etc. It is also true in simple matters of procedure and administration. If the pressure of circumstances is not sufficient, then the decisions are usually not made at all or they are made for us by default. That is, if the train leaves at three minutes after four and if we don't decide to get on the train before it leaves, then we find that we have automatically decided to stay off the train. We decide some of the most important questions in our lives by this process. For example, if we fail to decide on a program of self-improvement, we automatically decide *against* a program of self-improvement. If we fail to decide to get married in the temple, we automatically decide to get married out of the temple. If we fail to decide to be a good leader, we automatically decide to be a poor leader.

One of the biggest influences in our lives is the power that habit gets over us. Habit is stronger than determination or will power, and one of the most harmful of all of our habits is the habit of indecision. With some people, indecision is their leading characteristic. It is also their greatest source of weakness and trouble. For example, no one ever deliberately starts out to become a poor leader any more than one deliberately starts out to be a drunkard. A drunkard just takes a little social drink at first. He wants to be friendly. His intentions are of the very best. He just hasn't decided *against* intemperance, so he takes a few more drinks. None of them, in his opinion, are very serious. He feels that he can stop at any time. But before he knows it, "the habit that was once too light to be felt is now too strong to be broken." He has become a drunkard without meaning to. He has become a drunkard by default. He has become a drunkard because he didn't make up his mind not to become a drunkard. He threw his life away only because he didn't make up his mind what else to do with it. He lost his temperance without even knowing it.

In the same way it is possible for one to lose his integrity and his spirituality and his leadership. He can lose them without knowing thy are gone. It is possible for one to lose eternal life by that same process. It has been pointed out that there is little possibility of losing eternal life by a blowout. It is always just a series of slow leaks—a little sin, a little procrastination, a little indecision, a little indifference, a little lethargy, and before we know it, we have lost eternal life by default—all because we didn't make a few firm decisions not to lose eternal life.

Emerson says that "the world belongs to the energetic." That truth has a significant religious application that we ought always to keep in mind. Very few things are as invigorating as work; very few things are as healthful as work; very few things so quickly destroy the germs of failure as work. Therefore, says Emerson, "Work every hour, paid or unpaid. See only that you work, and you cannot escape your reward. Whether your work be fine or coarse, planting corn or writing epics, honest work, done to your own approbation, shall earn for you the greatest rewards known to the senses." Honest work also earns the greatest rewards known to leadership and the greatest rewards known to spirituality.

But even industry must always be preceded by decision. Therefore, Emerson might have said that "the world belongs to the one who can make up his mind." But what a wonderful team decision and industry make when working together.

We need to know *what* to decide and *how* to decide. But we also need to know *when* to decide. For example, the time to decide not to become a drunkard is before the insidious habit has fastened itself upon you. "There are only two stages in the life of a drinker: when he could stop if he would and when he would stop if he could." It is the same with accomplishment; it is the same with leadership. One should make his decisions about leadership as early in life as possible.

Every prospective leader should carefully avoid indulging the practice of indecision. There is no other habit that so grows on the soul. It is one of the most difficult things for the undecided man to bring his mind to a focus. In developing our ability to make decisions, we should remember that "as the twig is bent, so the tree is inclined," also applies to habits and personality traits. If we wait until the twig is a giant redwood the problem becomes more difficult. Therefore, "the hour of decision" is now. It is the earliest hour. Sometime the hour of decision will pass. Sometime the power to choose will be taken away from us. While this ability to decide is one of our most valuable blessings, it is highly subject to lapse.

In certain sections of India each year a very large number of natives are killed by pythons. Pythons lay their eggs in the spring of the year in the sand and grass, and each year the natives conduct an intensive search to destroy the python eggs while they are eggs, for they know that if they do not destroy the eggs, they will run the risk of being destroyed by the pythons.

The same principle applies to those influences that work against our leadership. Whether consciously or unconsciously, we ourselves often warm into life the very germs of sin and failure that eventually destroy us. Once they begin to grow we have only to wait. Soon the deadly pythons have their coils about us. Who would ever suspect the potency concealed within a harmless-looking python egg? We may not be greatly frightened even to see a few helpless pythons hatched out. Only when we are being crushed by the deadly embrace of the pythons' maturity do we fully realize that the best time to destroy pythons is while they are in the egg stage. The destructive power of pythons is a convincing argument against the folly of default. It might also illustrate what it might be like to lose our power of choice.

The time to start teaching a child to be honest is as soon as he is born. If he is molded in dishonesty and sin for fifty years, then any very extensive remodeling job becomes most difficult. In building our leadership, we should also be aware that *this* is the hour of decision. We bring upon ourselves our greatest problems by merely failing to make up our minds. For as problems of thrift must be decided before we arrive at the poor farm, and as we need to decide about temperance before our names appear on the list of alcoholics, and as we need to decide about virtue before our lives have been pitted and pocked with immorality, so we need to decide about developing our leadership before the opportunity arrives or the test comes. Neither the opportunity nor the test will wait very long for us to get ready for them.

We need to develop a strong, vigorous partiality for the right things. We need to make all of the issues in our lives clear-cut and then make firm decisions about each one of them. The smallest issues are far too important to be left undecided. We need to decide now. Our greatest hour is this hour. It is the hour of decision.

The Three I's

ONE OF THE FIRST steps toward any accomplishment is to find out what the problem involved in that accomplishment is. Effective leadership, in or out of the Church, must know the goal to be reached and the difficulties that must be overcome. In church work we need to know why some people are not "on schedule" for the celestial kingdom and what to do about it. Effective treatment must always be preceded by an accurate diagnosis. We should therefore ask ourselves, what are the sins that make people lose their blessings?

The Lord has made it clear that the two most grievous sins are: first, the sin against the Holy Ghost, and second, the shedding of innocent blood. Now suppose that we figure out about what percentage of the people in our particular ward or stake will be kept out of the celestial kingdom because of these two most serious sins. Fortunately we would find the percentage to be very small. Yet we know that "broad is the gate and wide the way that leadeth unto destruction, and many there be that go in thereat." That is, a very large percentage of people will disqualify themselves for the celestial kingdom for other reasons. We must know what those reasons are, if we plan to give effective help.

We all know about the subheadings of learning called "The Three R's." But how much do we know about the subheadings of sin called "The Three I's"? The Three I's are particularly dangerous because they are usually regarded as "the little sins." Yet they undoubtedly cause more people to lose their exaltation than all of the other sins combined. That is, "it is not the giant redwoods that trip us up as we walk through the forest; it is the vines and the underbrush." In fact, the Three I's might appropriately qualify among the sins as "The Big Three." They are—

IGNORANCE   INDECISION   INDIFFERENCE

Ignorance

To become a son of perdition, one must sin against great knowledge. That is the sin of the greatest *enormity*. But the sin of the greatest *frequency* is ignorance—that is not to know in the first place. The religion of Jesus has always suffered more from those who did not understand than from those who opposed. It is largely our ignorance that stands between us and our blessings.

Upon the cross Jesus said, "Father, forgive them; for they know not what they do." The sin of the Jews was the sin of ignorance. They didn't understand. Pilate didn't know the real identity or importance of this young peasant carpenter who was standing before him. But why didn't he know? There is only one logical answer, and that is that he had not invested the time nor the honest effort necessary to find the truth. Pilate could have found out who Jesus was if he had made an earnest and adequate investigation. For "they never sought in vain who sought the Lord aright." They only fail to find who fail to seek.

Almost all of the sins in the world are in one way or another the sins of ignorance. This was true in the days of Noah; it was true in the days of Jesus; it is true in our own day. The young man who disobeys the ten commandments doesn't really understand what he is doing. The young woman who fails to develop her spirituality by not obeying the word of the Lord doesn't know what she is doing, nor does she realize what the consequences are going to be.

Some sins may be forgiven, but who can forgive us of our ignorance?

There is an old fable that tells of a horse that once ran away from its master. Then the horse repented and returned and said to its master, "I have come back." The master said, "Yes, you have come back, but the field is unplowed." It is very difficult to repent of unplowed ground, and it is very difficult to repent of lessons not learned and self-improvement not made. To dispel ignorance is one of the great challenges to those who have church leadership responsibilities.

Indecision

The second "I" is indecision. Some sins are committed because we do wrong; other sins are committed because we do nothing. Some people just don't make up their minds one way or the other. In consequence, they develop a kind of permanently "suspended judgment." Ancient Israel had this problem. Elijah said to them, "How long halt ye between two opinions? If the Lord be God follow him; but if Baal, then follow him." (I Kings 18:21) In other words, Elijah said, "Make up your minds." But the record says, "And the people answered him not a word." That is the pattern of most indecision. We just don't move, one way or the other. Our minds are left dangling between choices.

Procrastination is a part of indecision. When we can't or won't make up our minds we just postpone action, sometimes permanently. Just think how many people lose their blessings because of procrastination. So far as frequency is concerned, procrastination is a far greater sin than murder. No one would deliberately choose to miss the celestial kingdom, but exactly the same result can be achieved by just a series of postponements, until our will gets weak and our interest dies. Everyone wants to go to the celestial kingdom sometime; they just don't want to go right now.

Recently a mission president talked with an 89-year-old investigator who kept putting off joining the Church. The mission president said, "Do you believe the gospel is true?" The investigator said, "I know it is true as well as you do." The president said, "Do you believe that Joseph Smith was a prophet?" The investigator said, "I know that as well as you do." The mission president said, "Then why aren't you baptized?" The investigator said, "Don't rush me. I'll let you know when I am ready." He is already 89. Think of the blessings he has already lost by procrastination.

After too much procrastination and vacillation, some actually lose the power to make a decision. I know of one man whose mind is so perfectly balanced between the positive and the negative that he has great difficulty getting an opinion either one way or the other. His mind resembles a teeter-totter in perfect balance. There is as much weight pressing down on one side as on the other. He has difficulty getting enough of a majority on either side to get a conviction. Another man just about wears himself out every morning trying to make up his mind whether or not he is going to shave. He rubs his chin and makes up such a perfect mental balance sheet of pros and cons that his mind locks in neutral.

This same infirmity holds some of us back in our church work. We have difficulties making firm decisions about things. There are some people who haven't made up their minds as to whether or not they are going to church next Sunday. In fact, that question is not usually decided in their minds at all. They wait to see how much weight will be put on the teeter-totter on Sunday morning by the weather, how they feel, and what the other external conditions will be. There are some people who have not decided whether or not they are going to be honest, or whether or not they are going to be tithe-payers, or do their ward teaching. They wait to see what pressures will be applied by circumstances.

One of the functions of leadership is to help people make firm decisions about things, draw answers out of their minds so that important questions may be settled once and for all. For as no one can be saved in ignorance, just so, no one can be saved in indecision.

Indifference

The worst sin of many people is not that they disbelieve in God; their skepticism is more serious—they just haven't thought about him one way or the other. It isn't that they disbelieve the doctrines of the Church; what is far worse, they just don't care. It is one thing to lack faith, but it is still worse to lack interest.

There are some people who call themselves by the rather fancy name of agnostic. They seem to take pride in saying, "I don't believe, but I don't disbelieve." That is, they are neither one thing nor the other. Someone said there is one folly greater than that of the fool who says in his heart there is no God, and that is the folly of him who says that he doesn't know whether there is a God or not. In some measure, agnosticism is a mere confession of indifference, indicating a lack of ambition or a lack of enough interest to try to find the truth.

When one is indifferent, the spirit remains apathetic and detached. There is then a natural lack of any involvement that would lead to faith. No one deliberately decides to be ignorant. Ignorance is indifference to learning. Sloth is indifference to industry. Weakness is indifference to strength. One man had an "indifferent" automobile horn. He said it just didn't give a hoot.

Certainly no man can be saved in indifference.

These three sins probably rob more people of their blessings than do all of the other sins combined.

Recently I talked with a man who told me that he had never read one single book in the last five years. Woodrow Wilson indicated this natural weakness when he said, "The greatest ability of the American people is their ability to resist instruction." Unfortunately most of us have our share of this unprofitable talent.

Thomas A. Edison makes our problem seem more difficult when he said, "There is no limit to which a man will not go to avoid thinking." And yet the scripture reminds us that "as a man thinketh in his heart so is he." Now if we are what we think, and then if we don't think, the seriousness of our situation is evident.

Emerson was also conscious of the problem when he said, "On the brink of the ocean of life and truth we are miserably dying. . . . Sometimes we are furtherest away when we are closest by. . . . We stand on the brink of an ocean of power, but each must take the steps that would bring him there." . . . "Sometimes we are furtherest away when we are closest by." Those who lived contemporaneously with Jesus were so near and yet they were so far away. We must not repeat their mistake. We live in this great age of wonders and enlightenment. We have three great volumes of new scripture. But what good does it do us if we are not familiar with it so that we can make it a part of our lives? We are so near and yet we may be so far away.

The Athenians put Socrates to death principally for his attempts to deliver them from the oppression of the three I's. Jesus was crucified for the same reason. We seem to hang on to our ignorance, indecision and indifference for dear life. One cried out, "O God, why dost thou take so much interest in our welfare when we take so little in our own?"

The three I's have always been our biggest problem. We remain stricken with ignorance and poisoned by a continuous succession of small thoughts We become centers of indifference. This prevents our progress. The three I's develop a sort of "inactivity in perpetuity."

Now what are we going to do about it? The logical solution is to learn how to develop antidotes for the three I's. We need to learn how to get people to study and think and ponder and pray and make decisions about important things and then carry the decisions through to their proper conclusion. When we break the oppression of the three I's our lives will take on new meaning.

Branch Rickey was once asked what was the greatest thrill he had ever had in baseball. His reply was, "I haven't had it yet." Our greatest thrill has also been reserved for the future. It will come when we have learned to free ourselves and others from the degradation of The Big Three, "The Three I's."

The Idea Bank

Probably one of the most important businesses in the world is the banking business. A bank is a place in which we keep things safe for future use. We have money banks; we have blood banks; we have soil banks. And on many occasions in many ways it has been suggested that everyone ought to have an idea bank.

One of the reasons that we have banks to put our money in is to keep it from slipping through our fingers and getting lost. That is exactly the reason for an idea bank. One's pocket is not a very suitable place to keep valuable possessions, nor is one's head a very good place to keep ideas. In the first place, the brain was never intended as a warehouse; it is a workroom. The brain does not serve very well as an idea bank because it is so full of leaks. Ideas in the brain are like water in a leaky cask. Just try holding a lot of ideas in your mind over a long period and see what happens.

One of our difficulties is that the forgetting process is an unconscious process. The moment of learning is a conscious moment, but that of forgetting is unconscious. It is like the moment of birth. We never know that we are being born until some time after it has happened. It is the same with forgetting. We are not conscious of the thoughts that are slipping away from us, and therefore, fail to take adequate precautions against their loss. For a great many people old ideas are being lost far more rapidly than new ones are being acquired. We can easily figure out where this will lead us.

The scriptures suggest that we should have a "book of remembrance" to help us keep track of important things.

When the Lord visited John the Revelator on the Isle of Patmos he indicated the importance of preserving ideas. He said, "Write the things which thou hast seen and the things which are and the things which shall be hereafter." By writing an idea down, we can keep it forever in all of its youthful bloom and impressiveness of meaning. Just think what a tragedy it would have been if John had tried to keep the Book of Revelation in his head instead of putting it down on paper!

When the Lord was giving the great revelation to Joseph Smith and Sidney Rigdon recorded in the 76th section of the *Doctrine and Covenants,* he told them four times to write down the things that they had seen and heard. In the 28th verse is recorded the following: "And while we were yet in the spirit, the Lord commanded us that we should write the vision which we beheld." Substantially the same admonition was given again in the 49th verse, the 80th verse and the 113th verse. And each time the Lord said it should be written down "while they were still in the spirit."

The Lord had a good reason for this. Words quickly slip through the memory; impressions fade; ideas lose their meaning and impressiveness with the passage of time. One way to avoid losing our money is to hurry and put it in the bank while we still have it. A good way to avoid losing ideas is to write them down while they are fresh and "we are still in the spirit." Great men have always been bankers of ideas. Hawthorne's notebooks show that he never let a thought or circumstance escape his pen. Robert Louis Stevenson always carried with him two books: one to read from and one to write in. It is told that during an important interview, Goethe suddenly excused himself and went into an adjoining room where he wrote down a thought for his *Faust,* lest it should be forgotten before the interview was over.

Soon after Alma was made the chief judge of his people he inquired of the Lord what he should do concerning certain matters. After the instructions had been given, the following was recorded: "And it came to pass when Alma heard these words, he wrote them down so that he might have them." (Mosiah 27:33) Alma knew that his memory was not to be trusted even with the words of the Lord, so he simply wrote them down to preserve them not only for himself but for us also.

The Lord commanded the brother of Jared to write the things which he had seen. (Ether 4:1) At the time of the Lord's visit to this continent after his resurrection he said, "I command you that ye shall write these sayings." (3 Nephi 16:4) This repetition emphasizes the fact that ideas are very perishable and extremely valuable. In fact, one of the most important differences in people is found in the number and quality of their ideas. The difference between Saul of Tarsus before and after his conversion was in the way his ideas had changed. Thomas A. Edison was different from some other people because of the nature and quality of his ideas.

There are certain ideas that can be of particular value to us. They may be in prose or verse or song, but if we get the right ones and then really get them into our system, they will inspire, instruct, and charm us. Just as there are certain kinds of food that vitalize and build us up, so everyone has natural sympathies to and susceptibilities for ideas. There are certain pieces of music that have great power to arouse the enthusiasm of certain people and set their accomplishment in motion. There are ideas like that. They may be our own ideas, or they may belong to someone else. Our own ideas sometimes fit into our own mental and emotional machinery a little better than do the ideas of others, yet even our own ideas are subject to a terrible shrinkage if we don't bank them in a safe place.

Idea stimulants in the form of poems, bits of philosophy or quotations have the ability to stir us up and develop our enthusiasm and our faith. We ought to memorize not only the words of the ideas but the spirit as well. This will help us bring our accomplishment to its highest point. But in addition, we ought to make sure that we also have these precious gems of thought in the bank for permanent safe-keeping. There are particular quotations from other people that serve a special need in us. We should get possession of these ideas that have a peculiar affinity for our minds and put them in the bank where they can be adapted and harnessed to do our work.

The fact that an idea may have belonged to someone else originally does not lessen its value to us. We do not write our own music or paint our own pictures, yet they play a constructive role in our lives. The scriptures have been put into words by other people, yet we use them for our own uplift. Emerson says that next to him who first expresses a great truth is he who quotes it. He might have said that he who *lives* a great truth is even ahead of him who first expresses it.

Suppose, therefore, that we get some kind of idea file and earnestly go into the business of banking ideas. The repository itself may be a set of folders or it may be an 8½" x 11" loose-leaf binder with a good quality of paper, where we can write and paste or otherwise deposit our ideas in a permanent collection, for otherwise the vividness and power of a mental impression fades with time. The rate of fading is not uniform. One section of a thought may completely drop from view in an instant; with another the rate of loss is more gradual. But in any event, our lives are poorer as a consequence of every loss. "A good file and a poor memory are a far better leadership combination than a good memory and a poor file." Therefore, one of the first investments that every aspiring leader should make is in a pair of scissors and a pot of glue.

A person may have great learning but "miss the boat" because he has "little remembering." Ordinarily people may acquire the equivalent of several college educations during a lifetime, but never have on hand more than a smattering of education at any one time. We often reach a plateau early in life from which we never rise substantially, because our forgetting processes become more active than our learning processes.

Words and thoughts are not to be used just once, but many times. You would not listen to a stirring piece of music just once and then throw it away, nor would you just take one look at a beautiful painting and discard it. Rather, you would try to get possession of it where it could uplift you many times. Great ideas can serve us again and again to instruct and inspire our minds.

One great man says that when he wants to give himself a lift, he always turns to these selected ideas, some of which he has written himself. They are like his own children or his trusted friends. The people that we call friends have more power to lift us up and give us pleasure. But there are also ideas that are particularly friendly to us personally. It is a great tragedy to lose a friend, and yet a fortune is lost every day in friendly, helpful ideas, simply because we have no banking system and have not formed the right banking habits.

Ideas often earn a far greater rate of interest than money in the bank. But we must first capture and learn to control them. This requires skill. Sometimes ideas come in flashes of inspiration; they sometimes hesitate in our minds for only an instant and then like a bird that lights for a moment in your tree, they are gone. Ideas sometimes come in chains of thought. Sometimes they come in clusters or family groups. They sometimes form a phalanx that pounds and forces its way, pushing everything else out of our minds. Sometimes we have thoughts of optimism, courage and devotion, capable of changing our lives. A certain kind of idea in the mind sends a tingle through the emotions and quickens the whole personality. Thoughts are carriers of ambition and ability. They can rejuvenate us and put us on our feet with a new lease on life.

These thoughts should be written down "while we are still in the spirit." For ideas furnish the substance out of which life and successful leadership are made. When we lose a good idea we have lost a part of ourselves. When we add the right kind of thoughts we have increased our life's volume. We should make them our permanent property so that we can control them. We can acquire them originally under a sort of homestead act by putting a fence around them and settling on them long enough to get a permanent title.

Suppose that you went to a great conference, a banquet of ideas, that lasted for a week. It was a thrilling experience for you. Suppose that during this five-day period you received fifty really worth-while ideas. But the only receptacle you had in which to store these ideas was your head. Even before the conference was over 50 percent of these valuable possessions would already have passed beyond recall. In six months 80 percent would have slipped through the fingers of your mind. Two years later 99 percent have been lost.

If they were not valuable, why spend valuable time acquiring them? If they are valuable why not take steps to retain them? Sir Henry Sidney said: "If you hear a wise sentence or an apt phrase, write it down." It will then form associations with other ideas in your mind to build the unity that gives strength. It has been said that one reason ideas die so quickly in some heads is because they can't stand solitary confinement. "Quotable quotes" are not more valuable than your own "notable notes." Montaigne said, "I quote others the better to express myself."

But when ideas are first received in the mind they are likely to feel insecure. They have not yet established a well-developed root system. If they are reviewed and thought about frequently they will in time securely establish themselves.

It is a great sight to see a bank with the shelves loaded with money. It is a greater sight to see an idea bank with the shelves loaded with inspiration, power and know-how. Making money loses much of its significance if we don't save some of it. And money that is put in the bank earns more interest than does that which is kept in the pocket. Don't worry if you haven't much to save at first. Once you get the habit, the amounts will increase rapidly. It is also true that ideas, like money in the bank, can soon grow into a surprising estate.

Sometimes we use the word "impression" in speaking of a thought which we have just received. The word is an apt one. Receiving a thought is like making a scratch on the surface of the mind. The deeper it is cut the longer it will last.

Ideas and ideals, like everything else, are born small. Little babies cannot work as hard as grown-ups. So a baby thought, newly arrived in your mind, needs to be cared for and carefully brought to maturity.

Early-day civilization was plagued with a very high rate of infant mortality. We should see to it that our leadership is not plagued by an excessive rate of infant mortality among our ideas, ideals and leadership traits. The one procedure that will reduce this waste is to have the mind get hold of as many good ideas as it can and then "write them down while we are still in the spirit." Then we are in the banking business in the most profitable meaning of the phrase.

I Got a Glory

ARCHIBALD RUTLEDGE once wrote a delightful little book entitled *My Colonel and His Lady*. In his book he tells of an interesting experience which he had as a lad on the Santee River in Central South Carolina. This particular occasion has to do with an old Negro river boat captain who piloted the ferry boat *Foam*. The boat was dirty, odorous and badly kept. But one day when Dr. Rutledge went down to the river, he found the *Foam* completely transformed. It was clean from stem to stern. It fairly gleamed and glistened in the sunlight. The boat's brass had been polished until it shone like so many mirrors. The bilge water had gone from behind the seats, and the deck had been scoured to the raw wood. No less miraculous was the transformation in the Negro captain himself. He was shining and immaculate. His face beamed; his eyes sparkled; he sat behind the *Foam's* wheel with an open Bible on his lap.

When Dr. Rutledge asked him the reason for this wonderful transformation, he said, "I got a glory." Some great ideas had gotten into the captain's thinking, and some great aspirations had gotten into his blood stream. These had made him a different man. He now had the glory of a lighted mind, the glory of a quickened personality. He had the glory of a great ambition. Religion had touched him in exactly the right places. The transformation so apparent in the river boat was only a manifestation of a more important transformation in the captain. His work itself had not changed; he was still a river boat captain. But he was now the best river boat captain on the

Santee. Henceforth, whatever he did would indicate his own change of life, and his life's work would indicate his life's glory.

But the story of the Negro river boat captain is in one way the story of every man, for every man manifests his greatness in his work. If he isn't great in what he does, he isn't great. "No man can have a high and noble character while engaged in petty or mean employment, for whatever the pursuits of men are, their characters will be similar." You can't have a glory while you have bilge water under your seats or a sour attitude about life, or a chronic case of battle fatigue.

The term "glory" may mean different things to different people under different circumstances. The dictionary defines "glory" as "the condition of highest achievement, the highest degree of pleasure, satisfaction, splendor, magnificence, radiance." A glory is represented in art by a halo of light over one's head. But in our church work and in life, it isn't just *over* one's head—it is *in* his head and in his heart and in his habits and in his nervous system.

We should not wait until the next world to think about getting a glory. If we want to be great in heaven, we had better be great here. If we are going to be better later, we had better start being better now. We may not know all about the glory of eternity, but we can understand the kind of glory the old captain had. It is the kind of glory that gets things done. It shines out through your eyes and gets into your handshake. It becomes a part of your lesson presentation and your planning and your industry. We need to learn how to live with a glory. It will help us to make our lives different. It will help us to be "born again." Then the usual confusions, indecisions, and frustrations don't bother us so much. Weariness is banished. We then live above the distractions and problems of ordinary things.

As the condition of the *Foam* was merely a visible

expression of the condition of the captain, just so, how we do our ward teaching or present our Sunday School lesson, or manage the administrative functions of our office in the Church will be a visible expression of what we are.

We cannot improve our circumstances unless we first improve ourselves. Success cannot be found in San Francisco or New York or Cincinnati until it is first found inside of us. That is where most important things are found. It doesn't matter very much what is behind you or what is before you. The thing that is important is what is inside of you. It is very important that the Church gets into people.

Jesus said, "The kingdom of God is within you." There is a note in the King James version that says he meant "among you." And that may be what he meant if he was referring to a "place." But if he was referring to a "condition" he meant the kingdom of God is "within you." To get the kingdom of God in us is the best way for us to get into the kingdom of God.

In "The Battle Hymn of the Republic," Julia Ward Howe wrote:

> In the beauty of the lilies
> Christ was born across the sea,
> With a glory in his bosom
> That transfigures you and me;
> As he died to make men holy,
> Let us die to make men free,
> While God is marching on.

This song was written for the Union soldiers during the Civil War, and it is said that the effect produced was the equivalent of a reinforcement of a hundred thousand additional troops.

A glory in one's bosom transfigures all of those who have it. It changes people and circumstances. A glory gives one a vigorous, positive attitude of mind. It gives vitality of purpose. It prevents fatigue and assures victory. "A tired businessman is one whose business is not successful." A tired church worker is one who has insufficient interest in what he is doing. In athletics you never lose interest when you are ahead. You don't get tired when you are winning. If the work of the Lord is wearisome to you and you want to get rested, don't resign. Repent, and then speed up. Learn to work harder and more effectively if you want to get rested. We get battle fatigue mostly because we get behind, or because our burden has become too unwieldy for that which animates it. The answer is not a smaller load; it is greater power. It indicates the need to learn how to live under a higher voltage.

Someone said that he didn't want to possess a religion; he wanted a religion that would possess him. When God created man in his own image, he endowed him with a set of his attributes so that "every man carries within himself the very things that he seeks." If you seek great faith, look within yourself. God has already planted within your heart the seeds of faith, awaiting only for you to make them grow. If you need courage, seek it within. If you need greater strength, remember that God has given you the potentiality of omnipotence, but you yourself must bring that omnipotence to maturity.

It has been pointed out that everyone has two creators, God and himself. Dr. Alan Stockdale has reminded us that God left the world unfinished for man to work his skill upon. He left the electricity still in the cloud, the oil still in the earth. He left the rivers unbridged and the forests unfelled and the cities unbuilt. God gave to man the challenge of raw materials, not the ease of finished things. He left the pictures unpainted and the music unsung and the problems unsolved, that man might know the joys and glories of creation. "God supplies the quarries, but he does not carve the statues or build the cathedrals, except by the hand of man."

God has also left the world of men unfinished. That is, the creation of man was not something that was completed and done with in the Garden of Eden six thousand years ago. The creation of man is still going on, and you are the creator. You are presently creating the enthusiasms and the faith and the understanding and the devotion that will determine your future throughout eternity.

The greatest blessings of our lives come disguised in work clothes, demanding of us, like the stern Roman soldier, that we travel with him for that one hard mile. The ancient law gave the Roman soldier the right to compel anyone to carry his burdens for one mile. But Jesus didn't stop there. He said, "Whosoever shall compel thee to go a mile, go with him twain." (Matt. 5:41) Doing more than is expected of us is one of the best ways to get a glory. The glory takes the compulsion off our lives and fills our hearts with cheer. It releases an unheard of strength and an undreamed of satisfaction. A glory takes the frown from the face and the weariness from the body and makes the second mile a pleasure trip. A glory makes one wish that there were more hours in the day in which to do the work of the Lord. A glory translates duty into pleasure. It enables us to also say to the world, as Jesus did, "I have meat that ye know not of."

Scrubbing the decks of a river boat may be drudgery to some, but there is no drudgery when you've got a glory. To go a mile by compulsion may be so wearisome as to break down your strength. But to go two miles is a lot of fun when you've got a glory. Then is when we sing with its best meaning that great hymn which says—

We feel it a pleasure to serve thee
And love to obey thy command.

To fail to get a glory is to fail to make our part of the work of the Church a fascinating labor of love. Then we come short of the glory of which the Psalmist sang, "For thou hast made him a little lower than the angels and hast crowned him with honor and glory." It is our job to develop that glory with which we have already been crowned. It is a great thing to live with the kind of glory that makes everything glorious and helps us to do the work of the Lord better than it has ever been done before.

When we get a glory, it doesn't matter whether the weather is hot or cold or whether the assignment is great or small, for then obstacles and difficulties are of little consequence and we are able to say in every circumstance, "I got a glory."

The Jump School

SOME TIME ago in touring the East Central States Mission, I visited the paratrooper base at Fort Campbell, Kentucky. I watched the vigorous training of these young men who someday, with a heavy cargo of equipment and supplies on their backs, may jump from an American transport plane into the territory of an enemy of their country. Because it is thought that the life of a paratrooper requires great courage, stamina, and capacity for taking punishment, no one is taken in at Fort Campbell for training except volunteers. They want everyone who comes to Fort Campbell to know in advance that the training is tough and the career is dangerous. They call Fort Campbell "the jump school," and they don't want anyone there who is afraid or lazy or who can't take discipline or who doesn't want to be there.

To prepare themselves for jumping out of airplanes the paratroopers get experience and practice by jumping from a tall "jump tower" built for that purpose. They are loaded up with the equivalent of a gun, a supply of food, and a full load of gear, and then they jump from the tower. After they have fallen some twenty or thirty feet, a wire which runs from their harness to a trolley cable breaks their fall and scoots them to the ground a few hundred feet from the tower. As each man jumps he shouts his identification number to a man sitting in an observation booth on the ground. This observer grades each man's jump. After the jump the jumper goes to stand before his judge and have his performance rated. The judge tells him what was wrong with his jump. If necessary, he tells him in pretty

166

strong language, leaving nothing whatever to the imagination. If there is any fault to be found, or if the performance doesn't improve rapidly, the jumper is severely disciplined.

I saw one group doing a series of fifty "push-ups" as punishment for a poor jump. Incidentally, this furnishes a strong incentive to improve. Others were doing a similar number of "squat jumps" with nearly a hundred pounds of gear strapped to them. If you don't think that stimulates a better effort, just put yourself in that situation. Sometimes a man may fall from exhaustion, but that can't be helped. Their training is serious business. Lives depend upon jumps being made expertly, and mistakes, delays, or lack of effort are just not tolerated. If someone falls down or lies down on the job, his punishment is severe enough that he will not want to repeat the error if it can be avoided. These men don't expect leniency or softness. They knew their training was going to be tough before they volunteered, and they are prepared to take it. They don't expect or want it any other way.

It is reported that their discipline is even more severe during their hardening-up drills. They go on long marches, sometimes without food or water; they crawl through swamps and sleep in the mud. Their muscles are given a hard conditioning and their minds suitably toughened for a soldier who may have to endure the greatest hardships. If anyone should take exception to the severe "beating" he gets by way of discipline, he would immediately be thrown off the post in dishonor and thereby win the disgust of his fellow trainees.

To the paratroopers, hardship is all a part of the day's work. They know that severe discipline is absolutely necessary for the difficult job that they have to do. They know there will be no allowance made for weakness or incompetency if they find themselves in a death struggle

in the territory of a hard, powerful enemy. They are trained
to live by that code while still at Fort Campbell. They know
that no crisis can be postponed while they get toughened
up. Five of these men lost their lives in a training accident
the day before we arrived. They know that many will lose
their lives in the event the things happen that they are
preparing for. But that is part of the program which they
have already fully accepted.

The commanding general puts on his gear and makes
his jumps with his men. He took us into his office and
for thirty minutes told us of the objectives of Fort Campbell. He told us of the large number of American youth
whose bodies were soft and flabby and whose minds were
listless and apathetic. If we go to war we will confront a
ruthless and powerful foe, and we will need to have determined spirits and bodies of steel if freedom is to be
preserved. The general talked with us about our country
and what its freedom was worth to us. I found myself
feeling very proud of these young Americans who, though
they had been soft to begin with, had not sought ease or
personal advantage in discharging their military obligation,
but had volunteered for the most harsh discipline available.
I thought what a great benefit would come to all of us if
we had some comparable discipline to tone up our lives.
I felt only pride for these young men loaded down with
equipment till they could hardly walk, undergoing this
most rigorous punishment in the burning sun—all on a
volunteer basis and with a wonderful spirit. Even if it
cost them their lives they were ready.

I caught enough of their spirit that I felt an urge to
toughen myself up a little bit to do my assignment more
effectively. One look down from their jump tower and I
knew that I would need a lot of "hardening" of the spirit
before I would have courage enough to do even once what
they were doing every day.

And then I thought that maybe I ought to join some kind of "jump school" where the Lord could toughen me up a little bit for more effective service. I thought if these soldiers did their country's job like some of us sometimes do the work of the Lord, no foreign foe would have very much to fear.

They do not hesitate. When the plane gets to the Drop Zone and the jumper says "jump," that is when they jump. One hundred men must get out of an airplane in a few seconds. They are scared, but they jump just the same. One boy a little fearfully said to the jump sergeant, "If I hesitate give me a push." The jumper replied, "Don't you worry, kid. That's what I'm here for."

Then I thought about how we sometimes do our ward teaching and visit inactive elders. There is a lot of hesitating. We sometimes just do it when we feel like it, if we feel like it, and in the way that we feel like doing it. And we may not be doing a bit better job in ten years than we are now. This is so partly because nobody dares to correct us and help us with our problem for fear we will be offended at the correction. We need a jump school sergeant to give us a push occasionally. And while I suppose the jump school idea wouldn't work very well with a group of ward teachers, the jump school spirit would certainly help our efficiency and the dispatch with which we do our job.

The officers in charge of our tour also took us through the place where the parachutes were packed which the paratroopers wear in their jumps. The parachute has 88 square yards of fabric with 28 cords each 40 feet long. It must be very tightly packed in order to occupy a space as small as possible on the soldier's back. If improperly packed the chute may not open and a life may be lost. Those who pack the chutes also make jumps. They have a stimulating rule that every packer must jump in the chute that he himself packed. That is, the chute he is packing today may be the one that he will be jumping in tomorrow.

Then I wondered what effect it would have on us if we knew that the Lord was going to require us to jump in our own chutes. That is, suppose that our eternal lives depended upon our own leadership. This gets pretty close to the philosophy of Jesus that we reap as we sow. I wondered how I would like to trust my conversion to my own presentation. I suppose that if we pack a tangled chute we ourselves may get caught in it. Lucifer packed his own chute and he landed in hell. Judas made his jump in his own parachute of greed and he hanged himself.

I suppose that in one way or another, everyone jumps in his own chute. We have the chutes of our education, the chutes of our industry, the chutes of our faith. If we don't pack the right spirit into saving others, our own chute may not open. No one wants a greenhorn or an incompetent packing his chute. What could give us more satisfaction in our leadership activities than to be able to trust our own work, to know that we know our business, that we pack a good chute, that we always give good measure. Will we be satisfied with the reward mentioned by Jesus, who said, "With what measure ye meet, it shall be measured unto you again"? That philosophy might be a little tough on some of us.

When a paratrooper volunteers for rigid discipline, it is his own muscles that are being made strong and his own country that is being made secure. While we are building our mansions in heaven, it is well to keep in mind who will occupy them when they are finished, or who will benefit from the discipline we give ourselves. All of our building is really done for ourselves—at least it will be ours when it is completed.

Stradivarius said that he made his violins for eternity. It is reported that not one of the violins of Stradivarius has ever been known to come to pieces or break. Stradivarius never bothered to get a patent on his violins, for he knew that no other violinmaker would be so painstaking in putting superiority into his instruments. Every Stradivarius now in existence is worth several times its weight in gold. Stradivarius made violins, and then the violins made Stradivarius. He jumped in his own chute.

In our leadership development, we should make sure there is no want for thoroughness. We are also building for eternity. To do our best we need a little rigid jump school discipline. It will give our leadership an invigorating shot in the arm. Mostly we are not willing to prepare our own lives as Stradivarius prepared his violins, or as the paratrooper prepares his mind and his muscles. How seldom we organize our leadership qualities as carefully as the jumper packs his chute.

There is a great crowd of leaders always standing just outside the door of proficiency, never learning to do things quite as thoroughly as though their lives depended upon them, as indeed they do. Don't think that you will never hear from a half-finished job or a neglected or botched piece of work. Such work will never die and it will never be forgotten. It will bob up later on, sometimes at the most inopportune and unexpected moments, often to embarrass or mortify you when you least expect it. Like Banquo's ghost, it may rise to haunt you at exactly the wrong time. When we stand before the judgment we will not want to have our poorly done work exhibited even to ourselves. From the perspective of eternity, we will look back and be glad that we packed our chutes knowing that we ourselves were going to jump in them.

The life of every American citizen may depend upon the toughened muscles and disciplined minds of the paratroopers. It is very important that the proper preparation has been made. But eternal lives depend upon our effectiveness in the work of the Lord. That is not less important. I received a great thrill and spiritual uplift from my visit to Fort Campbell. It made me determined to increase my effort, and I found myself wishing that I could match these young soldiers in their spirit and effectiveness. I promised the Lord and myself before I left Fort Campbell that I would try to carry my own gear with a little more ability and enthusiasm. Maybe I can learn to "jump" with a little more courage and in better form. Maybe if I give myself a little of the jump school discipline I may be able to capture a little of the jump school spirit.

Leadership Development

THE *objective* of the Church is to get people into the celestial kingdom.

The *problem* involved is leadership. Mostly there is only one problem in the world, and it doesn't matter much whether the desired accomplishment lies in doing church work, building a business, or running an empire. The problem is always the same—Leadership.

The *solution* of the problem is leadership development through training. A trained man is always more effective than an untrained man. That applies whether he is a surgeon, a lawyer, a farmer, a basketball player, or a church worker.

There are six steps involved in this development process, as follows:

1. Selection

The first step in developing a leader is to get the man, the right man, in the right place. There are too many square pegs in round holes. There are too many people who don't like what they are doing. There are too many appointments made on the basis of convenience or expediency, without proper consideration of all of the factors involved. There are too many people loaded down with so many jobs that success is difficult in any. Faulty selection means a wasteful inefficiency, a high turnover in office, a general lowering of morale, less job satisfaction, and more work for everyone.

Anyone responsible for the appointment of personnel should carefully consider every available candidate. A complete list of all of those available is a great aid in selection. Businesses spend great amounts of time and money in aptitude testing, personal interviews, background studies, etc., in trying to upgrade their selection techniques.

Certainly the best man may not be the first man that comes to mind. He may not even be the man who is presently active. Wards and stakes are divided, partly for the purpose of furnishing activity. An effective selection process should include home visits to members whose abilities and backgrounds you are trying to discover. Every leader is a talent scout for the Church. Many of today's finest church workers were inactive a few years ago. There is something far more scarce and far more valuable than ability, and that is the ability to recognize ability. We need to look beyond the present. One of the qualities of an effective personnel officer is that he can recognize ability before it is evident to others. Everyone can recognize a leader if he is already wearing the blue ribbon.

Michelangelo made men out of stone. But before he became the great master, he learned to see the finished product in the raw material. He said—

> In every block of marble I see a statue;
> See it as plainly as though it stood before me,
> Shaped and perfect in attitude and action.
> I have only to hew away the rough walls
> Which imprison the lovely apparition
> To reveal it to other eyes, as mine already see it.

That is also our job. We must first learn to see the possibility and then to do the necessary things to bring it about.

It is a common mistake to think that only those presently in leadership positions have abilities. Jesus chose men like Peter and Joseph Smith, and then developed the potential within them. There is still a great wealth of ability lying dormant and inactive in people. There are a lot of wonderful leaders as yet unknown, even to themselves. In fact, it is often true that the last man to discover that he has ability is the man himself. But we can get many more people into the celestial kingdom if we give a little more thought to the selection of personnel and if we are a little more careful to get the right man in the right job, rather than the most obvious man or the man easiest to get. The same man should not be selected for three or four jobs.

2. Recruiting

There is a process that might be called recruiting, which can be a powerful aid in leadership development. Often people are placed in positions which they do not understand, and for which they are not prepared, or for which they have no heart. If one starts out in his assignment with the wrong attitude, or is not fully converted to his job, the objective may be defeated before it gets started. Anyone who does his work grudgingly does it poorly. What a wonderful difference it makes if an intelligent leader spends a little extra effort in recruiting.

During this process, full information should be given as to what the job entails. The time, preparation, labor, and opportunity involved should not be bypassed or understated. Conviction and enthusiasm in the worker can be built up and a solid foundation laid for his success during the recruiting interview. The prospective worker should fully understand the importance of his particular responsibility. This is the time for the recruiter to discover objections and bring unsolved problems out into the open where they can be dealt with effectively. This is the place to obtain a meeting of the minds.

In the recruiting process the "offer" and "acceptance" take place. It is certain that the acceptance should be firm and without too many reservations. If the candidate has any traits or attitudes that would make him unsuitable, or if he does not want the assignment, or if he cannot or will not give it the necessary time, he may not be the right man. But all these matters should be known and settled before the appointment is made. The following should be clear in his mind and a firm commitment made regarding each point:

1. He should fully understand and be enthusiastic about the opportunity.

2. He should understand that he is to assume full responsibility for the assignment.

3. He should be willing to spend adequate time in planning and preparation, and should be in attendance at all of his meetings.

4. He should understand that effectiveness in any church assignment is usually made up in large part of personal, individual work, and he should agree to do this work.

5. He should live the gospel. One cannot effectively teach what he does not adequately feel and live.

6. He should want to have this assignment. The Lord said, "If ye have desires to serve God, ye are called to the work." (D&C 4:3) If he doesn't want to do it, he can't do it. "Desire is the pilot of the soul."

7. It is a great help to a worker to know in advance that he will be expected to do his job well, and that he will have vigorous and expert supervision.

3. Induction

1. The candidate should be presented to members of his organization for their sustaining vote, and may be set apart to his office.

2. He should be made acquainted with the basic tools with which he is to work, such as:

    a. The handbook.

    b. Any teaching materials, manuals, teachers' supplements, etc.

    c. Access to libraries, maps, pictures, reference works, or other materials pertaining to his work.

3. He should be introduced to those who will train and supervise him. The nature of that relationship should be understood by both in advance.

4. Training

It has been said that training is a continuous process and properly goes in a circle, the formula for which is: I — D — O — C.

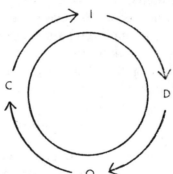

1. Instruct

2. Demonstrate

3. Observe

4. Correct

Every inductee should be properly instructed. But instruction is not enough. He must be shown how to do it. We seem to learn faster through the eyes than through the ears.

Everyone's work in the Church should be continuously observed as an aid to his improvement. It is far easier for one on the sidelines to see the errors of performance as a basis for giving assistance.

One of the most troublesome defects of supervision comes about because of our fear to give constructive aid. We are afraid the trainee will think we are being critical, and so we sometimes let him and the work fail, because we are not willing to run the risks involved. But if both the trainee and the trainer understand the training process before it begins, no unfavorable situation should arise. Training on the job is the backbone of business and military success; it is also the key to effective church work if it is expertly and frankly done.

5. Supervision

The old idea that the way to train someone was to throw him into the job and let him sink or swim by himself is generally discredited in our day. Business organizations, governments, and other enterprises have found that constant supervision for everyone can pay tremendous dividends. The one being supervised is helped in many ways: it gives his work importance and effectiveness and therefore gives him job satisfaction. These are of the greatest importance when the saving of souls is involved.

6. Motivation

It has been discovered that there are ways to make the fires of faith burn more brightly in human hearts. Everyone is more or less like a thermometer. His enthusiasm may be at 32 degrees below zero, or it may be at 212 degrees above zero, depending upon his motivation. Oscar Hammerstein said, "A heart can inspire other hearts with its fire." He said:

> Give me some men who are stout-hearted men,
> Who will fight for the right they adore;
> Start me with ten who are stout-hearted men,
> And I'll soon give you ten thousand more.

The Church started out with only six members. But knowledge, testimony and enthusiasm can be transmitted to others. The ability to motivate human personality in its spiritual aspects is certainly one of the most constructive abilities in the world.

The six steps mentioned above do not apply to newly-appointed personnel only. The formula is exactly the same if you are trying to discover where success is being short-circuited in those already in office.

Suppose you take each individual worker under your direction who is presently in office and go through these steps with each one personally:

1. Re-Select

Is he the best possible man for this particular job? If not, certainly a change must be made. It is unthinkable to allow the work of salvation to fail merely because the wrong man is in office. On the other hand, if he *is* the best man, but he is not getting adequate results, then we should—

2. Re-Recruit

Think of this re-recruiting process as a businessman would conduct it with an employee who had great possibilities but who was losing money for the firm. Why is the employee falling down? Does he understand exactly what is expected? Does he *want* to do the work? Has he any definite plans for improvement? Will he agree to do it in the future on a 100 per cent basis? There must be a meeting of the minds. We can't afford to lose money in our Father's business. Suppose the president of the firm said to a key employee, "Bill, we would love to have you keep this job, providing you can do it." It is of course unthinkable for him to be continued in office if he can't or won't get the desired results.

3. Re-Induct

Does he have the proper materials with which to work? If not, he should get them immediately, and we should know why he didn't get them before. Where is our organization falling down?

4. Re-Train

Training and re-training are the life of success. Someone said we must re-learn everything about every six months. Training and re-training are the processes by which understanding, skills, attitudes and habits are established and improved. Constant, effective re-training makes work productive and pleasant. When one is ahead of his job he loves it. When it is ahead of him he hates it. Thorough re-training will increase every accomplishment. It will increase satisfaction. It will reduce frustration, discouragement, turnover, and loss of time. It will also decrease the number of God's children who will lose their eternal exaltation.

5. Constant Supervision

Are you in constant contact with those under your direction? Do you know their weaknesses and strengths? Are you able and willing to give necessary help to bring about constant improvement?

6. Re-Motivate

It is human nature that people left to themselves sometimes run out of gas. They become discouraged. People sometimes get a kind of battle fatigue. Most of us need someone to stir up our faith, to recharge our enthusiasm and re-inspire our purpose. All of us need someone who is continuously interested in our accomplishment.

Many of the great business corporations report that their top leaders spend between 40 per cent and 60 per cent of their time working directly to instruct and motivate those under their direction. We should do more of it in the Church.

Our leadership should be constantly studied and worked at. By its proper development we may bring about the greatest power for good in the world, which is the ability to lead effectively.

The M Factors of
Leadership Development

W E CAN OFTEN be more effective
in our work if we think of our
ability in terms of its parts. That is, if we were going to
manufacture or repair an automobile, we would not think
of the automobile as just one thing, but as a collection of
many things all fitted together. Each part must first be
made effective before the whole can function properly.
It is the same with developing our leadership. Our total
ability is made up of many smaller abilities. As we perfect
the segments we improve the whole.

Life itself is made up of parts. These are the physical,
mental, spiritual and social departments of life. It is the
individual factors that make up and control our heredity,
environment, health, education, spiritual ability, etc.
Everything is made up of factors. An engineer speaks of
the "safety factor," meaning the ratio of maximum strength
to the probable maximum load. The doctor speaks of the
Rh factor in the blood. The scientist compounds the elements to make new products. A factor is an element or
part that gives the whole its characteristics. Our leadership ability also has its factors. If we overlook or fail to
develop one of the important elements of leadership the
whole may fall flat, like a cake when the baking powder
is omitted.

Some important sets of factors involved in leadership
ability are the "M Factors." They are the all-important
"motive factors." The dictionary describes motive as "an
inner drive," "an impulse," "a stimulating idea," or "inten-

tion" that causes a person to act. When these drives or intentions are absent or reduced in power in relation to the work to be done, accomplishment always slows down or stops. Our success depends upon the ratio of motive power to the maximum load to which it applied. Our achievement will therefore depend upon our ability to strengthen the right impulses and drives, both in ourselves and in others.

We use steam, electricity, gasoline or atomic energy to give power to machines. In a little different way we use stimulating ideas, natural instincts, inner drives, ambitions, objectives and desires to produce motive power in ourselves.

It is an unchanging law that a cause must precede every result. In occupational undertakings much time and money have been expended trying to determine what makes people respond as they do. Under certain conditions men work with great power and enthusiasm, and at other times effort drops to a minimum. Achievement ebbs and flows between these two extremes. The most successful leader is usually the one who can build up these motives and drives and then maintain them at their highest level.

One of the most common motives is to acquire wealth. People will work very hard for money. But they will work even harder for power. Generally they will work still harder to please someone they love, and they will work hardest of all for a cause in which they ardently believe. Pride of accomplishment is a powerful motive. People also work for comfort, security, prestige, a desire to excel or the privilege to serve. Amateur athletes can often be brought to work to the very limit of ability. The motive in one may be a desire to excel; another works for approval; another wants to win for the school. One of the greatest of the M factors comes from the consciousness of a great skill. We always love to do the things that we do exceedingly well.

The best coach or the most successful business or church leader is usually the one who can identify and most effectively develop and harness these M factors. To the degree that this can be done there will be a corresponding increase in accomplishment. In other words, success in the great science of leadership largely centers around the M factors. A great salesman finds out what the prospect's wants and needs are, and then he builds his stimulation around them. That is also true with every other accomplishment.

For example, until 1926, no woman had ever swum the English Channel. Then an American automobile company offered a red Buick convertible automobile and $2500 in cash to the first woman who would swim the Channel. There was a nineteen-year old American girl by the name of Gertrude Ederle who wanted an automobile. The challenge made a direct appeal to powerful motives. I suppose that no one really knows very much about motivation until he has a nineteen-year-old child who wants an automobile. As a result of this motivation, Gertrude Ederle decided to swim the English Channel.

But when she had gone only a part of the distance across this 21 miles of choppy, icy water, her strength gave out and she could not swim another stroke. While she was lying there, waiting to be taken out of the water, the image of this red Buick convertible automobile and all that it meant to her passed through her mind. As she held these thoughts and images in her consciousness her feelings were again aroused by the factors that had originally motivated her ambition. As these powerful drives again passed through the cells of her brain, they created in her an almost magic power which gave a great new surge of strength, and she never stopped again until she felt under her feet the solid earth of the other shore.

It is a well-known natural law that we can greatly multiply our strength by a highly-prized and firmly-held motive. Analyze your own successes and failures and see how unfailingly they are determined by these inner drives and motivating forces.

The science of crime detection is built around motive. The detective takes the result and works backward to find the motive. If the motive can be determined the criminal can usually be identified. On the other hand, the science of leadership is the science of crime detection in reverse. To reach an accomplishment leadership starts with a motive and works forward to a result. If the right motives can be established and sufficiently stimulated, almost any result can be guaranteed.

Consciously or unconsciously everyone is dependent upon his motives for every accomplishment. Motivation is the power by which we overcome what is probably the strongest negative influence in nature, inertia. Everything tends to remain "at rest." The stone lies inert upon the mountainside for a thousand years. The dictionary says to be "inert" is to lack the inherent power to move. To break this influence requires extra power. For example, it takes six times as much energy to set a flywheel in motion as it does to keep it going once momentum has been established. Powerful low gears are put in automobiles to overcome the dead weight of inertia. Motives serve the same purpose in human personality. The minds and spirits of people usually remain inert until motivating forces set them in motion.

To move someone is to provide a correct motive which is strong enough to produce action. Church leadership is supposed to help people develop the religious motives that will bring the greatest success and happiness. In the Church there is probably a greater variety of more power-ful motives than in any other field. It is our privilege to

select any worthwhile motive and use it to bring about
our own success and that of other people.

The first step in developing our motivation is to find
out what is holding us back. There is a reason for the
inactivity of every senior member of the Aaronic Priesthood. There is also a reason for every other inactivity, in
or out of the Church. But there is also a motive for activity, which, if properly applied, would overcome inactivity.
We must get the two together.

A large sales organization recently made a survey to
determine why salesmen failed. It was found that—

> 37% failed because of discouragement.
> 37% failed because of lack of industry.
> 12% failed because they would not follow instructions.
> 8% failed because of lack of knowledge.

All of these causes are preventable. All are forms of
inertia. They are all merely attitudes of mind which may
be overcome by a motive that has greater power than the
inertia. No one will work harder than his drives impel him,
and the impetus must come from within himself. There is
an old adage that says, "You can lead a horse to water, but
you cannot make him drink." But motivation finds a way
to make the horse thirsty so that he will drink of his own
accord. Jesus talked about people who hungered and
thirsted after righteousness. The mission of Jesus was to
help increase that hunger. That is also our mission.

There are some who hold the theory that there is no
such thing as laziness. We merely shrink from doing those
things which we don't know how to do, or don't have a
strong enough motive for doing. Sin also comes in this
category. We commit sins of omission because we lack
a strong, positive motive, and we are guilty of sins of commission because we have the wrong motives. But whether
the problem is sin or sloth, there are always motives strong

enough to break inertia if we can find them and know
how to apply them.

Think how completely the life of Saul of Tarsus was
changed when new ideas were put into his mind. Simon
Peter was transformed from a humble fisherman to a powerful apostle under the stimulation of the mind and program
of the Master. Worthy human motives may be given a
spiritual application and developed to have a far-reaching
religious significance. That is, treasures in heaven have
far greater value and consequently should be more sought
after than treasures here. A love that incites us to provide
for our family here has even greater power when applied
to our family needs for eternal life. Our bodies will be made
immortal, but so will our character qualities. Both go with
us beyond mortality, giving us a constant motive for self-
improvement. Religious motives have proven to be among
the most powerful causes of action known in the world.
Many people have been willing to give their lives for
their faith. While the fires were being lighted around the
stake at which the nineteen-year-old French peasant maid
Joan of Arc was to be burned alive, she was given a chance
to gain her freedom by denying what she believed in. In
choosing the fire above her freedom she said, "The world
can use these words. I know this now. Every man gives
his life for what he believes. Every woman gives her life
for what she believes. Sometimes people believe in little
or nothing, and yet they give their lives to that little or
nothing. One life is all we have and we live it as we believe
in living it and then it's gone. But to surrender what you
are and to live without belief is more terrible than dying—
even more terrible than dying young."

We need to learn to identify motives and be able to
make specific application of them in our own lives and
in the lives of others. Then great accomplishment is always
the result. For example, what is it that makes members

of the Church inactive in the face of the great blessings of the gospel? There are a great many factors involved. One man is inactive because he does not understand; another is inactive because he does not believe; another doesn't care; another can't make up his mind; another has a mental short circuit called procrastination. These causes are all forms of inertia. Like the stone on the mountainside, these people are "at rest," and will tend to remain at rest and lose their blessings, unless some motive power is brought to their rescue. The inert one needs a good low gear to help him establish momentum, and everyone needs some strong M factors to help him overcome this natural appetite for rest. It is the responsibility of leadership to help develop these motives which are the seeds of accomplishment.

The M factors are the antidotes for inertia. They are made up of education, stimulation, activity, righteous desire, faith, example. Jesus instructed and inspired twelve men, establishing powerful motives in their hearts. When once the motives were in force, the apostles could not be stopped by trouble, opposition, or even death itself. We have now been called to do this most stimulating work in the world, to teach and inspire and activate our Father's children to obey his commandments.

Think of some of the M factors of the gospel. Every principle has, attached to it, a blessing for obedience and a punishment for disobedience. As the Lord said to ancient Israel, "Behold I set before you this day a blessing and a curse; a blessing if ye obey the commandments of the Lord your God and a curse if ye will not obey . . . but turn aside out of the way." (Deut. 11:26-29) We need to get people to understand these blessings as well as the cursings. Think of the blessings for faith; the blessings for repentance; the blessings for baptism and the gift of the Holy Ghost. There is a blessing for paying tithing and for keeping the Word of Wisdom and for every other thing that God has commanded. And these blessings are far out of proportion to any other rewards that we know anything about. But at the same time we are working directly and entirely in our own interests.

We know the motive power that lies in a million dollar cash reward. But what about the motive power lying in the thought of living forever in the celestial kingdom? Or what is the value of saving your own soul? Or what would it profit you if you had even a hundred times a million dollars and lost the eternal association of your own family? The first soul that anyone should bring to God is his own soul. What greater or more personal motive could there be than this? The Lord has indicated that the most profitable way that we can invest our mortality is in bringing souls unto him. This carries blessings beyond our comprehension. But the motive power in us will be limited by our understanding of the importance of the blessing involved.

If you need some M factors to provide stimulation, think of the blessings that come from celestial marriage and vicarious work for the dead. Or think of how tremendously we are rewarded for maintaining the purity and integrity of our own lives. In fact, the scriptures are in one sense just a great collection of promissory notes, made out in our favor. Each one is attached to some gospel principle and the blessing is in force if the principle is lived. Every blessing is gauranteed by the Ruler of the universe himself. We may have as many as we please. The Lord has said, "I am bound when ye do what I say." Our responsibility in our own interests is to stamp the importance of the gospel principles in our understanding and put the appropriate motives in force to bring about any desired accomplishment.

An amateur athlete will work to the limit of his strength to win the approval of his coach. What will one of us do to win the approval of his God? A salesman devotes his life building motivation around some trivial material need. What kind of motivation are we developing around the needs of eternal life? How much M factor is there in the sure promise of eternal progression? Does it stimulate our industry to know that we may someday become even as God? But "he who would move the world must first move himself." We therefore need to plant a little deeper in our hearts and minds the great ideas and spirit of the gospel. There are no more powerful stimulants. They will make every accomplishment not only easy but delightful.

The Management Team

ONCE EACH YEAR the Harvard Graduate School of Business sponsors a national business conference attended by prominent businessmen from all over America and abroad. Participating on the program are some of the world's top executives and administrators, as well as Harvard's own business experts who devote their lives to the study and development of successful business principles and procedures. The general theme for one of these recent conferences was "Releasing the Full Potential of the Management Team." Subsequently a book was published entitled *The Management Team* in which have been recorded many of the ideas brought out in the conference, designed to help leaders make their business more effective and profitable.

This is noted here only because it is one example of the many studies that are being made and the great amount of research that is going on in educational institutions and business organizations to discover more effective business procedures. These ideas are made available to every one who may be interested. Those of us who are charged with administrative responsibility in the Church might well take advantage of the specialized knowledge thus made available.

Success as we find it in different fields has much in common. Procedures in one area may be adapted and used in another. In fact, most successful individuals and most successful organizations borrow generously from the profitable researches and experiences of others. Certainly the Church has much to contribute to business, but it is also true that business, with its knowledge of efficient operation, has much to contribute to the Church. The fact that one business or church organization may be extremely effective and a similar organization equally ineffective indicates the importance of acquiring the best available methods and skills. It is often far easier to learn to make an effective application of proven administrative procedures and techniques than to "break our own trail" in every undertaking.

The concepts of administration that one business firm might think of as elementary though absolutely essential may be hardly understood at all in some less successful firm where the leadership is not so advanced. Many business experts are now being sent out by their companies to study the successful procedures of others, just as in times past we have sent our doctors and engineers to take advantage of the most up-to-date methods of world leaders in these fields. Why shouldn't we take that same kind of interest in improving our church leadership abilities?

One of the chief characteristics of leadership is management. The dictionary says that one of the early uses of the word "management" was applied to handling horses and meant "to train them in their paces." It also means the "art of administration," "supervision," "direction." It implies a skillful operation of the all-important executive function. It is the ability "to influence people favorably" to get them to do the right things. Effectiveness in church leadership is also made up largely of management. Each group of leaders might be properly thought of as a team with a captain, a coach and individual players. Their ability to work together is all-important. It might help us to think of a ward or stake organization as a team. In each organization there is the chief executive officer with properly designated assistants. They are responsible for the training and performance of other members. They are the ones to put the workers "through their paces." They must shoulder the responsibility for the accomplishment of the team. President Grant once said to a stake president just before setting him apart, "Brother Jones, you will be held responsible for the welfare of this stake." The management skill of the stake president will largely determine how well the responsibility of others will be carried out.

There is a ward team and a Sunday School team and a Primary team. However, there are no one-man teams in the Church. Time was when out on the frontier men lived and worked by themselves, but that is no longer true. The shift of emphasis means a change in the kind of skills we need to develop. Abilities must be created in the art of all working toward a common objective. This means that we must be properly organized, that each one must have his own set of job specifications. He must know exactly what he is expected to do and be committed to effective performance. He must have the necessary skills to carry out his part of the program. A well-trained team is one in which the team is stronger as a unit than the combined efforts of all of its individual members. Each is stimulated, assisted and complemented by all of the others.

In the 72nd Section of the *Doctrine and Covenants* is the following: "It is required of the Lord at the hand of every steward to render an account of his stewardship both in time and eternity." The Lord also said, "Wherefore now let every man learn his duty, and to act in the office in which he is appointed in all diligence. He that is slothful shall not be counted worthy to stand, and he that learns not his duty and shows himself not approved shall not be counted worthy to stand." (D&C 107:99-100)

It is the responsibility of the chief administrator to organize, delegate, supervise, administer and be responsible for the organization's general welfare. He must also train the leaders under him in the same qualities that he himself must possess. Therefore, when a leader increases his management abilities everyone is better off, for good management increases the total output of the organization. The manager's responsibility is to raise objectives of members of the team, increase their incentives, provoke effective thinking and incite them to appropriate activity. He must hold others responsible for their stewardship, just as the Lord will hold him.

The fact that we understand that inefficiency in our business ventures may cause a great financial loss helps us to understand the greater possible losses that may take place in the work of the Lord if we, the leaders, are ineffective. From the point of view of an efficiency expert, think of the consequences of the fact expressed by the Lord that "strait is the gate and narrow the way that leadeth unto life, and few there be that find it." This indicates our need to be more businesslike in the conduct of our Father's business.

We need to see more clearly the reasons for success and failure. We can learn most rapidly by keeping constantly before ourselves the contrast of good and evil, right and wrong, efficiency and inefficiency.

Every doctor and every leader must be an expert diagnostician. We need to be able to tell when a patient is sick, or when a church organization has poor management, and what to do about it. An organization is sick when its statistics are low, when many of its young people are being married outside of the temple, when church members do not attend Sacrament Meeting or pay tithing or do their ward teaching as they should, or when a comparatively small percentage of the Aaronic Priesthood boys receive an individual award. Other symptoms show themselves in various ways. Sometimes those in charge of the Aaronic Priesthood do not even know how many boys they have in their charge, or the number of awards they are earning. Sometimes the percentage of awards takes a severe drop and that fact is never even discovered. Such a situation would be disastrous in financial affairs. Is it less serious in the work of the Lord? If we conducted our business as we do our church work, what would be the result?

One leader of boys owned a herd of purebred cattle. He knew exactly how many cattle he had and exactly where each one of them was, what they were eating and what their daily growth was. He was very businesslike with his cattle. But he knew very little about the boys under his care. It wasn't that he lacked ability; his problem went far deeper than that—he lacked interest. The other leaders under his direction were largely following his example. They had no objectives or plans that would compare in effectiveness to those used in fattening their cattle. Some of the leaders were not even aware that improvement was necessary so far as the boys were concerned.

At their leadership meeting, 67 percent of those who should have been present were unaccounted for. Only 21 percent of those who were present possessed a handbook. Consequently they did not know the program. They had not "learned their duty." They were not "acting in the office in which they were appointed in all diligence." And the Lord has said, "These shall not be counted worthy to stand." That is a pretty serious situation, because when the leader "shows himself unworthy to stand" the rest of the members of the team run the risk of losing their blessings also, for no member of the team can go far ahead of the leader. All of these problems arise because of the lack of effective management.

How different is the picture of another group where last year over 80 per cent of their Aaronic Priesthood boys received an individual award. The rest of their activities were in proportion.

When in a stake with 6,000 members you raise the percentage of activity ten points, you save an additional

600 people. Such is the opportunity of effective management.

It is always more satisfying to do good church work than to do irresponsible church work. But it is also much easier. When there is a high percentage of activity you have the advantage of the "power of majorities" working for you; you also have the spirit of enthusiasm. Nothing succeeds like success. But work is also more pleasant when you are working at the top of your potentiality.

It may be that both effective and ineffective groups believe the gospel. They both may compare favorably in living it. But goodness is not enough in leadership; there must also be strength. It is not enough for a topnotch leader to be a "saint"; he must also be an administrator. It is not enough for a leader to qualify for the celestial kingdom; he must also see to it that the members of his organization qualify. His work will never be a complete success while one soul is left unsaved. It is not enough to believe in leadership; we must be able to produce its fruits in others. And we should train ourselves to take advantage of the best information from every available source.

Creating a Favorable Atmosphere for Success

THE ATMOSPHERE in which we expect to produce success should never be taken for granted or overlooked. Every living and growing thing does best where the climate, soil, and atmospheric conditions are most suited to its needs. This truth also applies in the field of human accomplishment.

For example, a great general does not take his army into the decisive battle in a demoralized, rebellious condition, if he can help it. His soldiers should feel that the cause is their own. They should understand exactly what is expected of them. They should be well drilled and have a feeling of confidence in themselves, their leaders, and in each other. They should be well fed and well uniformed. This all contributes to their ability as soldiers and helps to produce that fighting spirit that is a sign of high morale. There should be a spontaneous, buoyant enthusiasm among them. One soldier with high morale may accomplish more than ten who are demoralized or have a burdensome feeling of depression. This is probably even more true of success in church work than in the army. In the army there are such factors as compulsion, fear of punishment, etc., not present in church motivation.

But in or out of church work, there are some situations in which effectiveness will readily thrive and grow and some others in which it cannot survive. We should know what these favorable conditions are in the work of the Church so that we can do whatever is necessary to bring them about.

All group success requires a mutuality of understanding. There should be common objectives and cooperative effort, where all are working together with mutual respect and common interests. Because people have various degrees of progressiveness and understanding, it is certain that there will be differences in their ideas, diligence and methods. This points out the need for coordination and guidance. Certainly there will be mistakes and errors in judgment. There will be times when assignments will not be carried out. And while errors cannot be permitted to go unnoticed, there are ways by which they can be handled without the kind of condemnation that leads to friction, lack of confidence or loss of prestige which result in an unfavorable climate.

It seems that almost no one becomes inactive in the Church because he does not believe the doctrines of the Church. He usually leaves church activity because of some feeling of offense or misunderstanding or because he was not properly recognized or appreciated. He may feel that he is not receiving the personal help that he should have done or that he was not making sufficient personal growth. In other words, he feels the climate to be unfavorable.

The technical part of a problem may be difficult, but the really important part of our job, or any job, is usually our morale, or group attitude. Failure almost always begins with an unfavorable atmosphere, and that has to do primarily with people failing to work effectively and agreeably together. Fairness, understanding, integrity and tact in people are just as necessary in qualifying us for success as are technical ability and skill.

A farmer's success is often determined by the kind of seed bed in which his crops are planted. No farmer ever got very far who planted his seeds on the sidewalk. That is also true in church work. It is well known that everything else being equal, the man who enjoys his work and likes his associates will always be more successful than the one who dislikes his assignment. It has been said that "no profit comes where there is no pleasure taken." If then, the maximum of accomplishment is to be attained, there must be a maximum of satisfaction and enjoyment coming from people working together. Their relationships must be easy and pleasant, even though their backgrounds and the importance of their responsibility may be very different.

All people like appropriate recognition. When a leader becomes a boss, wears his authority on his sleeve, and seems to be more conscious of his prerogatives than of his responsibilities, the junior members of the team sense it quickly, and often an unfavorable climate begins to develop. Soon thereafter the temperature begins to fall and we see symptoms of declining morale. Members of the team drop out one by one until the organization loses its capacity to do effective work.

Sometimes we try to solve the problems of ineffective work or poor morale in a church organization by releasing people and starting over on a clean slate. But already great harm has been done by the destructive dislocation that has taken place. This might have been avoided if more thought had previously been given to this art of creating and maintaining a favorable atmosphere for success. Even when we start over with new people, the conditions which produced the poor morale in the first place may still be present and will reproduce the same attitudes in the new workers.

All workers like to have a sense of belonging. It always helps the general atmosphere when each has an appropriate part in the planning and helps to determine objectives, etc. The climate also becomes more favorable when each worker is thoroughly instructed in his job and and its importance, and when he acquires the knowledge, attitudes, skills and habits that bring high accomplishment and the resulting satisfactions.

Usually the biggest single factor in the creation of a favorable atmosphere is the executive himself, who by his own example, attitude and friendly interest influences the spirit of his workers. An executive who lacks professional skill or who procrastinates and alibis will not rate very high as a leader. If he himself falls down, either because he can't or won't provide the necessary leadership that goes with success, he soon loses his hold on the members of his organization.

Some time ago a stake president said that the last seven people that he had asked to serve in the stake had all declined. If you could feel the spirit of this particular stake you would easily understand the reason. The statistics representing their accomplishment were very low. Leadership on every level seemed irresponsible and lethargic. At an officers and teachers' meeting a very small percentage of those who were supposed to be present were in attendance. The leaders seemed inefficient. They hadn't the faintest idea where their absent people were or why they were not present. There was an attitude in the air that the work they were doing was not very important. They knew no one would check up on them or even be aware of their absenteeism. They seemed to have been given the idea that it was an easy, unimportant job that they could do if they wanted to when they got around to it. This attitude is very bad for morale.

Former President Hadley of Yale University said that the most important thing that anyone ever gets out of college is the college spirit. Everyone likes to feel a spirit of friendliness and know that he has a job important enough to be checked up on, and while he wants to feel that there is kindness and understanding toward him, yet he wants to know that he must be responsible for accomplishment by his own efforts; otherwise he will lose morale. The one in charge must have the ability to guarantee accomplishment in those under his direction. There is no particular virtue in commanding people to work, especially when morale is low. If conditions are unsuitable, proper growth just does not take place.

Ernie Pyle, the late war correspondent, said that nine-tenths of morale is made up of pride in your outfit and confidence in your leaders. What a wonderful situation we have in the Church for pride in our outfit. We work in the organization that has been set up by the Creator himself. It has as its aim the most important accomplishment ever undertaken upon the earth. It is the work in which God spends his entire time and its purpose is to bring to pass the immortality and eternal life of man. What a thrilling idea!

But even that may not be enough to bring about high morale. Even these factors are not important to morale if we don't understand them. To get these important facts over to the workers is the responsibility of leadership.

It is, however, the "confidence in your leaders" part of the formula where morale is most likely to break down in the Church. Workers frequently lose confidence in their leaders either for some real or imagined reason. When that happens, no matter what the reason, morale begins to worsen. When we think of our superiors we ask ourselves more or less automatically, "What does he contribute to make me better in my job?" When the leader does not make us better, the spirit of success is diminished.

We want to be on the team that has prestige and effectiveness, where all work together for a common cause with a common goal. We want to feel in our associates the ability to win a few victories. We want to enjoy the consciousness of good work. Robert Louis Stevenson said, "I know what pleasure is for I have done good work." That is one of the main factors of morale. It does little good to receive praise when the members of the team themselves know the praise is not merited. Then the spirit may become even more distressing because they know the praise is insincere.

The subject of how to produce high morale is one of the biggest problems of leadership. It can only be solved by constant study, thoughtfulness and experience. But the first step is to know that if we are to have a successful organization, we must have a good seed bed. We must produce favorable conditions for the synthesis of ideas and the solution of problems and the building of men. A favorable climate facilitates the transformation of ordinary individuals into an extraordinary team with a high spirit and a great power of accomplishment.

A good atmosphere should not be taken for granted merely because we work in the Church. Neither should morale be allowed to grow by itself. It must be developed and should include a real sense of devotion to God. Our need for God is our greatest need, and the first and greatest commandment has been built around it. But the second greatest need in human beings is built around our relationships with each other, and how we solve these relations will largely determine our success.

Effective Communication

IN THE WORK of the Church it
is necessary that a large group
of people with different backgrounds, different objectives,
different ambitions, different motivations, and different
personalities work harmoniously together. The fact that
people also differ in their understanding and ability tends
toward a very great variation in perspective. Because success depends in so large a part on a complete understanding
between us, one of the primary conditions of success is
communication. That is the process by which understanding is brought about.

Ralph Cordiner, the president of General Electric,
has written a very interesting little book entitled *New
Frontiers for Professional Managers*. He has indicated that
40 percent of all of the time of the officials of General
Electric is spent in communication, in helping junior members of the organization to understand the objectives,
methods, resources, ideals, etc., of General Electric.

One person may be overly timid or have an under-
developed opinion of his own abilities. He must be encouraged. The person working next to him may be overly
ambitious and have a superabundance of eagerness. He
may need to be restrained. One person may expect and
need detailed instruction and authority from those above
him. He does not like to move without orders. Someone
else may desire a little more freedom to use his own
initiative and go forward on his own power. Some others
may be held back because they do not have the necessary
understanding or skill to go forward. These must be taught.

Success, like salvation, is an individual matter and can best be brought about by individual attention.

In any given assignment, everybody needs to know certain things. He wants to know exactly what is expected of him, what the limits of his authority and duties are. If adequate communication does not take place, accomplishment is greatly diminished. The junior members of the team want to know that their superior officers understand their problems and are capable of giving help whenever needed.

In many effective business organizations, there has been published a set of job specifications which defines as carefully as possible the various duties of each particular assignment. Until the objectives, duties and spirit of an assignment have been properly explained, sufficiently understood and accepted, real progress is very difficult.

Communication is not a one-way street. Many of the best ideas of any organization come from the "man on the ground" who is actually doing the job. If he is not consulted, plans are likely to be inadequate or actually harmful. Without good communication "up," there cannot be good communication "down." And thereby management loses much of its strength. There should always be a large flow of ideas and suggestions from the lower levels to the higher levels, and vice versa; otherwise, an administration is inadequate, no matter how elaborate the system of management may be. Even differences of opinion frankly expressed can be very helpful. Some periods of "constructive conflict" are often good for communication as they may help to clear the atmosphere and enable the leadership to know how to plan for needs and training. Effective communication should make every possible effort to have an adequate meeting of the minds of all of those involved.

There may be some "ivory tower executives" in business or in church work who are not conversant either with their people or with the practical aspects of the problems to be solved by those under their direction. These put the organization at a great disadvantage. Or when the leader attempts to be too much of an authoritarian and gives orders, he shuts off information and destroys his own lines of communication. Fighting with a blindfold is not the best way to achieve. A prominent political leader after an unsuccessful election said, "I did not communicate successfully." That is also one of our most distressing difficulties. When members of the team feel that their opinions are not wanted, or are not listened to, it either kills a source of valuable information or the communication goes underground to smolder and fester in bad relations, which makes future success more difficult.

The discussion of goals and plans should also go up as well as down the ladder. Most people work harder and better if they have been a part of the planning and if the goals are known and have been accepted by all concerned. Goals should be regularly re-examined. There should be constant search for means to weigh accomplishment and improve performance. Detailed planning, constant interrogation and full communication both up and down can lead to a better coordination and more efficient operation.

One of the most important contributions ever made to success came from football when someone invented the huddle. Here the members of the team get their heads together and decide on a program. The huddle is also one of the most effective devices for the benefit of church leadership that has ever been discovered.

When plans and results are checked and communicated regularly, it is possible to eliminate mistakes more rapidly and increase good will. No one succeeds by himself. We are all in the boat together. All must succeed or no one can succeed. This is one of the major problems that has confronted industry. It has been difficult for everyone engaged in a particular enterprise to understand that we are all dependent upon each other. This means labor, capital, management, etc. All have a common denominator whether we realize it or not. The common denominator should be our interest in keeping the ship afloat, because we are all on it together. After we make sure that the ship will not sink, then we can discuss details about who will be captain, first mate, etc., and what our various responsibilities and benefits will be.

In the Church, even more than in industry, we ought to understand one vital fact about the ship, and that is that you can't sink just one-half of it. You can't be just "half safe." You can't sink the officers' quarters and let the crew continue on as if nothing had happened. You can't sink the crew and let the officers proceed with their cruise undisturbed. You can't sink the Primary without hurting the priesthood. You can't injure the bishop without hurting every member of the ward. The story is told of two Irish laborers who were on shipboard. One rushed up to the other and shouted, "The ship is sinking." The other one shouted back, "Let 'er sink. She ain't ours."

In the organization of the Church we all go up or down together. The Sunday School superintendent can't be successful if the teachers are untrained. The leader's success is dependent upon his associates, and their success depends upon him. It is the leader's obligation to solicit ideas as well as to give ideas. It is also his job to be able to resolve conflicts and help to find a common goal which can and will be accepted by all and to which everyone will dedicate himself. We do the work of the Church by common consent. It is "one for all and all for one." No one can say to any other, "I have no need of thee."

The leader has the personal obligation to know at all times how well every worker is carrying out his responsibility. He should know in what particular each worker is making his greatest possible contribution and where and how he could do better.

There is a vast literature on effective and proven communication in various fields with which we should be familiar as church leaders. Some of the various subdivisions under which we might classify effective communication are as follows:

1. The force of example in the leader is probably the most effective single means of communication. Example is one of the strongest powers in the world, and the world's best method of communication.

2. A good handbook, describing the program, job specifications, objectives, methods, etc., is also indispensable.

3. Then there are conferences, seminars, training courses, council meetings, luncheons, socials, etc.

4. One of the greatest means for effective communication is the personal interview. All success is individual. No one's problems are exactly like the problems of anyone else. In a personal interview, individual differences may be resolved, deficiencies may be supplied, personal errors may be corrected, objectives may be defined, thinking may be clarified, and personal motivation given in exactly the right amount. This can be done more adequately in a personal interview than in any other way. It has been said that even the chairman of the board should get out of his chair and spend some of his time personally lifting up the standards of those under his direction. In every instance there should be a relationship favorable to informal discussion and personalized communication. The chief executive who regularly works in the field sets the pattern for other executives. This develops their personal knowledge and intimate relationship, and is very helpful to effective administration. The workers are then welded into a team.

They no longer remain merely as a group of one-man operations bound loosely together.

5. Communication can also come from manuals, bulletins, letters, pamphlets, graphs, performance charts, reports, and a thousand and one ways of written and oral management communication.

6. There is also group counselling or other discussions on an informal group face-to-face basis. This may also be effectively done through social occasions.

7. The telephone can sometimes add much to communication, to let someone know he was missed or to give assignments or to check on performance, etc.

But certainly, without good communication all effective team work is impossible. For how can one perform effectively if he lacks essential information, or if his efforts are not coordinated with others? If any joint enterprise is to be successful, the responsibility and the degree of authority must be spelled out in clear, unmistakable terms. Then not only will the individual to whom responsibility is delegated know the extent of his responsibility and the limits of his authority, but others in the organization will also have a clear understanding of team objectives and team play; otherwise their progress will be retarded.

There should also be a constant flow of statistical information from the workers to the leader to enable him to measure performance and direct activity. There should also be a constant flow of motivation, reports of accomplishment and other stimulating communication from the leader to the various members of the organization.

One of the barriers to communication is the failure of the leader or others to listen intelligently. Often we listen only with our ears, not with our understanding or our hearts. We don't always try to put ourselves in the other man's place or see his problem as he sees it. Consequently we do not always understand what the issue may mean to him. When a junior or senior officer knows that the communication is not getting through, then discouragement often sets in and success becomes more difficult. Therefore, we should have means of measuring the effectiveness of our communication.

A teacher gives a written examination to determine how much information has gotten through to the students. There are other means, such as questions, reports, group discussions, questionnaires, planning meetings, etc., to determine if the communication is really communicating.

We also need to know if the explanation has explained and if the motivation has motivated. Communication procedure must be repeated hundreds of times. There is a tendency to feel that if we have done our communication a few times everyone else ought to know about it more or less automatically. For example, here is a bishop who during his tenure of office may have fifty different sets of Aaronic Priesthood presidencies. He may do a thorough job of communication and training so far as one presidency is concerned and then tend to think that all the others should in some mysterious way inherit that information. The exact reverse of that is true. Those receiving the communication actually only remember a very small part of what they hear. Sometimes we don't remember any of it. Therefore necessary communication should be gone over time and time again even with the same people, to make sure that everyone understands, for only when we understand are we in a position to make progress.

But in all great leadership, there must always be clear and distinct lines of communication. These lines of communication must always be open and in use.

Delegation of Responsibility

GENERAL LUCIUS D. CLAY, Chairman of the Board of Directors of Continental Canning Company, recently delivered an address before the Harvard National Business Conference, entitled, "The Art of Delegation." This is one of the most important subjects in all the fields of administration and executive responsibility, and General Clay made excellent suggestions about how it should be done.

The earliest military commanders, realizing their inability to be at all places on the battle field at the same time, appointed deputy commanders and assigned them specific missions each, to guide and conduct some part of the battle. It is self-evident that in such an assignment, the deputy commander must know what is expected of him. He must know what his authority and responsibilities are. He must know that he must answer to the general for how he uses his authority.

The same procedure is necessary in any undertaking which requires the services of more than one man. No executive can handle all of the problems arising in business, military operations or church work. Therefore, his chief duty is to divide up and parcel out this responsibility and then see to it that each carries out his assignment. The number of jobs that need to be done are so many and the number of items an executive can handle personally are so few that delegation or what has been called "coordinated decentralization" must take place if the job is to be done.

One of the classic examples of delegation is recorded in the Bible, and took place in the early part of the history of the children of Israel. Moses was working from dawn till dark trying to do all the work himself, listening to the troubles and complaints of his people. But many people were standing around in groups waiting to be heard. This caused dissension and murmuring among them. Jethro, the father-in-law of Moses, observing the confusion said, "The thing that thou doest is not good." Then he advised Moses to select able men and make them rulers of thousands, rulers of hundreds, rulers of fifties and rulers of tens, and let them judge and teach the people. That is, under the direction of Moses, they were to bear the burden of leadership. Moses accepted the counsel of Jethro and placed parcels of his authority upon others. When a problem arose, it was solved if possible on the lowest level. More important problems rose to a higher level, but only those issues which could not be handled by anyone else came up to Moses.

In our day, as in the days of Moses, all the authority in the Church is vested in the President of the Church, but he cannot do all of the work of the Church. So like Moses, he must delegate some of his authority and responsibility to other officers, including stake presidents, bishops, etc. Neither can they do all of the work which comes to them under their delegation, and so they in turn divide it up and delegate parts of their authority and responsibility to others working under their direction. When this process is properly done every worker in the Church has a specific responsibility and a specific authority to cover it.

The idea of delegation is, of course, absolutely necessary, and the effectiveness with which the delegation is made and received greatly influences all of our success. The delegation of responsibility decentralizes management; it develops leadership on every level of responsibility; it gives everyone an opportunity to serve. It is the best and only way to get the job done.

Since most problems can be solved on the lowest rung of the supervisory ladder, every effort should be made to resolve grievances and do the work of the Church as near its source as possible, so that only the vital problems come through to the President of the Church.

There are some leaders who go through the motions of delegation, but then hug to themselves the essence of the job. This means that for all practical purposes no delegation was made in the real sense of the word. That is, it is not real delegation if the bishop gives certain responsibilities to his counselors and then, because he may feel that he can do the job better himself, suspends the delegation whenever an important matter comes up. In that way the counselor never knows what his real authority is or whether the bishop may have already superceded him, nor is there any way for him to get the development of his office. Nor is it real delegation when the work is handed out but the credit kept. Successful delegation cannot just partly delegate, nor can it give authority with one hand and then take it away with the other. Responsibility can be learned only when it is fully given.

One of the pitfalls of delegation is the belief by some leaders that to have a job well done he must do it himself. How are other leaders going to be developed? It is the job of the leader to make those under his direction better executives than he himself is, and prepare not one but many who can take over his responsibility if he were no longer available. On the tombstone of Andrew Carnegie is written the following: "Here lies a man who knew how to enlist in his service better men than himself."

A good leader does not attempt to solve every problem personally, for as long as the top man is solving all of the problems, those down the line are usually unwilling to take the initiative and therefore never develop themselves. The one delegating authority can, by question and suggestion, teach the one to whom the authority has been delegated, how to arrive at the proper solution.

Theodore Roosevelt once said that the best executive is the one who has sense enough to pick good men to do what he wants done and self-restraint enough to keep from meddling with them while they do it.

On the other hand, delegation is not abdication. A leader does not lose his authority nor his responsibility when he delegates it. He must still remain primarily responsible. And he must guarantee the success of the one to whom the responsibility is delegated. He cannot delegate and then turn his back on what occurs afterward. He must inspect; he must train; he must encourage; he must supervise the one to whom the responsibility has been given. No one can delegate away his responsibility. He delegates his responsibility without losing it. Delegation without control is irresponsibility. Nor has there been any real delegation if the responsibility has not been fully accepted. Incompetence or unwillingness of an individual to accept responsibility should not go undiscovered or uncorrected. Rather, such unwillingness should be immediately known to the one who still holds the primary responsibility.

But just as delegation is not abdication, neither does the acceptance of responsibility mean usurpation. Each must work within the limits of church policy and the authority given to him. He must also work under the direction of him to whom he is responsible. Each executive in the chain must know his job and be able to subdivide and delegate effectively. He must know the individual to whom he is giving authority and be sure that the assignment comes within the individual's capacity and that he can and will devote the time to carry out the assignment properly.

One of the most important hurdles in proper delegation is to select the right man to whom the responsibility is to be given. Men in any responsible position should be selected largely because of their worthiness and their specific ability to do that job better than anyone else can do it. We might have examples in some political situations where someone is given a job as a matter of patronage or payment of a debt. Men in these jobs may be rotated from one position to another without regard to their fitness or specific skills. But success is more adequately served if men are selected because their particular qualifications fit the desired accomplishment. We don't pick out men to be doctors, lawyers, salesmen, teachers, or janitors, merely because we like them; at the end of one term, we don't put them all back in the pool and draw straws again to see who practices medicine and who becomes the teacher. The salesman or the janitor may be just as good as the doctor, but they may not get along as well in the operating room with a complicated brain surgery.

Neither is it very reasonable to take an expert Scout man who is doing splendid work and transfer him to some department for which he is not fitted or for which he has no interest. It is a matter of common knowledge that men and women do not and cannot change their interests and their inclinations to fit many jobs in quick succession. It is true that people in the Church should have broad interests, but knowledge, skills, attitudes, habits, and enthusiasm cannot be transferred as readily as a hat from one head to another. In church delegation and responsibility, we are dealing with the all-important matter of getting people into the celestial kingdom, and we need men who are highly skilled in particular functions. Then each man should be effectively trained and adequately supervised, and his particular interest developed in him to a high pitch. Even if the very best man is obtained for each specific job, he should still not be abandoned after the delegation and allowed to go his own individual way. It is still the responsibility of the executive to check performance and supply adequate supervision and control.

Effective delegation should clearly outline areas of responsibility. It should help to establish the principle aims and objectives. It should make sure that the one to whom the delegation is made is not only qualified but that he fully accepts the responsibility. The importance of acceptance cannot be overemphasized. If there is full acceptance then the delegation should be made without reservation. The leader should delegate the whole job with all of its satisfactions, prestige, and spiritual significance. This offers a challenge worthy of the highest dedication to both the one making and the one accepting the delegation.

The art of delegation involves some of the greatest administrative skills. We ought to give it constant, complete and continual study and then back up our study with practice.

Control

IN ANY EFFECTIVE organization there must be good morale, adequate communication and responsible delegation of authority. But there must also be effective control. The dictionary says that control is "to exercise authority over, to direct, restrain, etc." A comptroller is one who "governs" or "manages." A comptroller is also a device for controlling the speed, power and direction of a ship, automobile or an airplane. Power, great and small, must always have controls.

The administrator should know at all times the degree of success or lack of success in the work of every individual under his supervision, but he must also be able to exercise direction and control. Weakness, sin or malfeasance in office must not remain uncorrected. The leader should do everything in his power to keep workers from failing, but if failure appears inevitable and replacement appears to be in the general interest, then it must be done quickly.

The Lord said to Nephi, "It is better that one man should perish than that a nation should dwindle and perish in unbelief." That truth has many latter-day applications. Sometimes someone is left in office who has inadequate ambition, or insufficient training, and consequently we may expect a low grade of accomplishment. This is always to the eternal detriment of other people. To allow the failings and shortcomings of one person to cause preventable injury to others should not be allowed to take place.

For example, some time ago the general superintendent of the Sunday School, through the members of the General Board, called to the attention of one superintendent of one of the stakes that a relatively small number of their officers and teachers subscribed to *The Instructor,* the teaching magazine of the Church. The general officers of the Sunday School suggested that in their opinion it was not possible for any teacher to do his best work without this helpful and excellent teaching aid. And the stake superintendent was requested to see to it that a personal interview was conducted with each Sunday School teacher to make sure that everyone subscribed to and studied *The Instructor.* At the stake Sunday School convention a report was made on these personal visits. A ward superintendent reported that one of his teachers claimed that he had subscribed to *The Instructor* for three years, but he had never opened one single copy. He felt that this ought to entitle him to a subscription immunity for the future.

It was my privilege to visit the class of this particular teacher who felt that he did not need this expert help. I had not been in his class for more than two or three minutes before I was absolutely certain that he had been telling the truth when he said he had not opened an *Instructor.* But it was equally evident that he had not opened the lesson manual. Neither had he had a very intimate relationship with the scriptures. He took up the entire period telling his students about his war experiences, and they were badly told, with no point, and in very poor taste.

You can't get bread out of an empty cupboard, and you can't get ideas out of an empty head. This man was drafted into the army. He was forced to have some war experiences. He apparently had had very few spiritual experiences. Authority had been delegated to him to teach Sunday School, and he was failing miserably. In my opinion he was guilty of the grossest kind of malfeasance in office. It is almost always true that those who need help most, want it least and those who need it least want it most. Certainly those who lack even the consciousness of their need should not be abandoned by those who have charge of their work. Poor teaching by itself is bad enough. But the thing that disturbed me most in this case, and the thing which seems to be a dozen times more serious than the poor teaching, is the fact that even though the warning signals were flashing everywhere, yet this teacher had been provided with absolutely no supervision or control. So far as could be discovered, no member of the ward superintendency, bishopric, or the stake board had ever made one visit to his class or made any attempt to find out the kind of work he was doing. If they had made a visit and done nothing about it, then more than ever there would be reasons to be disturbed.

If we say this teacher was incompetent, what will we say about ward and stake officers who indulged in this loose, irresponsible supervision? Not only had they made no effort at correction, but they were not even aware of what was going on. For three years this man had been allowed to impose his ignorance, sloth, and bad taste on the minds of little children. These children were being deprived of their right to hear the principles of the gospel discussed in an inspirational, uplifting way each Sunday morning. Instead, this man, filled to overflowing with the sins of omission, occupied the time in perverting their minds with irreligious thoughts.

To teach the gospel is the duty of the Sunday School, and those in charge must accept the responsibility. In this case that duty had been neglected, and there was a complete absence of any attempt at improvement or control. Rather, this misguided man was allowed to go his individual way, trampling upon the standards of the Church as well as the spiritual interests of a class of immortal souls. In addition, he was adding to his own sins the sin of flagrant malfeasance in the most important office in the world. It must have been about one such of whom Jesus said, "He who offends one of these little ones, it were better that a millstone were tied about his neck and he be drowned in the depths of the sea."

It is the responsibility of the one who has delegated the authority to see that the assignment is understood, accepted and fully performed. The Lord says in the 101st Section, 93rd verse of the *Doctrine and Covenants* that "all men must be left without excuse." That applies to those who fail to *hear*, but it also applies to those who fail to *teach*, or *supervise* or exert proper *control*. We expect that great judgment will be visited upon those who reject the word of the Lord by failing to hear, but those who fail to teach must also bear their share of responsibility, including the prospective condemnation of Paul who said, "Woe is me if I preach not the gospel."

But more important still, what about the condemnation of those who fail to bear the responsibility for proper administration and control? The Lord has said that where much is given, much will be required. Since those who have the administrative responsibility may be among those who have been given the most, how can they escape the great responsibility of their office, especially where there is little real evidence of good faith in their assigned task of supervision?

Even where there is some attempt at supervision, it has little value if it is done in a loose, inefficient manner. The responsibility for the development of leaders and for the coordination, supervision and control of those in office is a very great one. Where authority is delegated without any machinery for control, a harmful irresponsibility may develop to constitute a serious breach of trust. A "hit or miss," "go as you please" operation in any department in the Church should not be permitted. Such procedure invites and encourages inferior performance, and administrative officials thereby lay themselves open to a serious charge of irresponsibility in their stewardship.

We might think about control under several headings:

1. To exercise effective control, the one having primary responsibility should have expert knowledge of how the job should be done so that he can be of help to those working under his direction.

2. He should ascertain that each worker is making his maximum contribution. There should be serious efforts made to measure accomplishment so that there will be a proper basis for judging improvement.

3. There should be constant supervision and continuous training, including a substantial amount of personal observation by someone who knows his business.

4. There should always be effective communication. The subordinate can be led to discuss his objectives and the degree of success he feels he is having in their attainment. If the worker is not reaching the objectives, embarrassing questions or remarks need not be asked nor made. Ordinarily the worker himself will be aware of his deficiency. If the relationship is right, he will not only explain his own failure but he will also point out some of the reasons for it. He himself can be led to suggest changes and solicit help. Out of the discussion with him a decision can be reached as to what may be done to bring about improvement.

A control that is largely stimulated by the man being controlled has many advantages. He participates in the formulation of plans, and he likes the objectives because he had a part in formulating them. He is stimulated rather than depressed by the control. A man will work hardest to achieve his own objectives. He may be led to bring up his own problems rather than to have someone else call them to his attention. It is out of these discussions that effective control may be brought about. The one doing the supervising serves as an expert helper as well as a substitute conscience, making suggestions that might improve performance. One teacher said, "I felt that he was cooperating with me, not telling me what to do." The leader may be the captain or the coach, though not necessarily the dominating personality.

But every worker at every level must be expected to show satisfactory results. If he does not show suitable progress and cannot or will not be trained to do so, then it may be advisable to relieve him of his responsibility. We must get the job done, and we must agree to be judged by our fruits. We must also agree to give and receive the desired supervision. When this is understood in advance, then the brash may be restrained without having their confidence destroyed. The timid may be drawn out and encouraged to make their own decisions. Credit should be given to those who deserve it. Some leaders even assume to take the blame for those who are unsuccessful unless repeated failure has demonstrated their unworthiness to be continued in office.

An executive, and particularly a top executive, must have time at his disposal. He must not be so tied down with details that he is unable to attend to the duties of his office.

This lack of time is probably the cause of one of our greatest weaknesses in the Church. The administrative officers are sometimes so heavily loaded down with details that it is difficult if not impossible to attend to the important problems of administration. This potential cause of failure should be carefully avoided.

Men in Step

THE GREATEST invention of all time is said to have taken place 2500 years ago at Platea when an obscure Greek perfected the process of marching men in step. When it was found that the efforts of a large group of people having different motives and different personalities could be organized and coordinated to function as one, that day civilization began.

Certainly throughout all of human history this quality of unity or harmonious joint action has proven to be one of the most important elements in any accomplishment. When men are not able to unite and work together, then those going in one direction tend to neutralize the efforts of those going in the opposite direction, and the result is confusion and failure. It doesn't matter very much whether the desired accomplishment lies in the field of sports, business or church work, the ability to make a united effort toward a common goal is usually the acid test of superiority.

So important is this quality that God has described the presidency of heaven as being "one." They are one in purpose, one in understanding and one in method. Now the Lord has set up his organization upon the earth to bring about the exaltation of his children. He has staffed this organization with workers and has given to each a definite assignment to fill. And one of the most important requirements of the Lord is that we should be one, even as he and his Father are one. That is a great idea. Our success will largely depend upon our ability to work harmoniously together as the Lord has directed.

To achieve this unity is by itself an almost certain guarantee of success. But this is a requirement that we should not take too lightly, for it is difficult for some people to learn to work together. This is true no matter how important the undertaking may be. Sometimes we resemble a team of horses without a driver; sometimes we resemble a balky team; sometimes we resemble a divided team, each pulling in a different direction. This confusion is not necessarily brought about because those concerned are not capable or because they do not believe in the doctrines of the Church; it is more likely that they have just never learned how to coordinate their efforts and work as one.

There are several reasons for this. It is natural that questions will come up where there will be a difference of opinion. Proper procedure indicates that these differences should be fully discussed. If all available information is obtained and carefully considered, it may be that there will be a unanimous decision. But there may be occasions when the vote may not be unanimous. Then comes the test which will often determine our success.

Just after the United States had declared war on Germany in 1917, Elihu Root made a speech in Chicago which might be of great help in our church work. He said: "The declaration of war between the United States and Germany completely changed the relations of all the inhabitants of this country to the subject of peace and war. Before the declaration everybody had a right to discuss in private and in public the question of whether the United States should carry on war against Germany. But now that war has been declared, it becomes the duty of every American citizen to stop discussion and go to work. The question is no longer before us. It has already been amply discussed and carefully decided. It now becomes the responsibility of every citizen, no matter what his previous position may have been, to proceed immediately to do everything in his power to enable the government of his country to succeed in the war upon which it has entered. . . . A nation which declares war and then goes on discussing whether it ought to have declared war or not is impotent, paralyzed, imbecilic and earns the contempt of mankind and the certainty of humiliating defeat and subjection to foreign control. A democracy which cannot accept its own decisions made in accordance with its own laws but must keep on endlessly discussing the questions already decided, has failed in the fundamental requirements of self-government. . . .From this time on arguments against the war in which the country is engaged are enemy arguments. Their spirit is the spirit of rebellion against the government and the laws of the United States. . . . It is impossible to resist the conclusion that the greater part of those who do not desist in their opposition are at heart traitors to the United States. . . . You may be opposed to raising an army in one way, and I may be opposed to raising it in another way, and so long as the question is undecided we are entitled to try and get our own views adopted. . . . But now the president and the duly elected Congress, after having listened to your views and mine, have decided the question and that should be the end of discussion and every loyal citizen of this country should from this minute on do his utmost to bring about his country's success."

What would you think of a member of a group or a council in the Church who, after a decision had been made, continued his opposition or withdrew his support because his viewpoint was not adopted? That has been the downfall of many men in and out of the Church since the beginning of time.

Jesus pointed out another reason for lack of united effort. It comes from the fact that people naturally have different interests. Jesus illustrated this disharmony in a group of men in his day. Each had some excuse. One had his own business to attend to; one was going to be married. Every one had something different on his mind and was therefore incapable of uniting in the general interest. Consequently the good the Lord intended could not be brought about.

Here is another reason for lack of unity. In any undertaking, including church work, we have leaders appointed to give us direction and to keep us going at the right speed at the right time. It is their responsibility to try to unify effort and control results. But we frequently fail to respond to their direction. A recent government survey showed that 84 per cent of a certain group of paid workers did not work effectively if the boss was not constantly present. That is, many people can work only by compulsion. This is an interesting but very dangerous characteristic in us. Isn't it amazing that a group of students will pay money to go to school and then try everything they know to get out of doing the work! That is why we need truant officers and roll books and examinations. Sometimes we behave in about that same way even when working for our own eternal salvation.

Another reason for lack of unity is that we have never learned obedience. We are disobedient for many reasons. Sometimes it is because we do not fully understand a situation. For example, Naaman, the captain of the host of the king of Syria, was told by the Prophet Elisha to wash in the Jordan seven times and he should be clean. (2 K. 5:10) But Naaman said, "Are not the rivers of my own country better than the waters of Israel?" Sometimes, like Naaman, we argue or rationalize ourselves out of our blessings. For instance, the Lord has told us to be baptized by immersion for the remission of sins. Then somebody immediately argues that sprinkling should do just as well. Or why should one be baptized at all? But the Lord has said, "He that believeth and is baptized shall be saved,

and he that believeth not shall be damned." That sounds
pretty authoritative and pretty final, and we had better
let it go at that.

What a wonderful thing it would be if we accepted
the word of the Lord in all things at its face value and
then just did what he said and did it when it should be
done. We could make an application of this principle to
our planning meetings, our industry and our obedience
to the principles of the gospel.

Recently one of the popular ministers of the world
published an autobiography in which he apologized for
a book he had written a number of years ago when he
opposed one of the principles of the gospel. Greater experience and more mature thought had caused him to
change his mind. But the thousands of copies of his book
with its false philosophy could not be taken out of cir-
culation. They still continue to lead people astray, bringing
confusion and disobedience into their lives. Now he has
convinced himself that he was wrong. But the damage has
been done and can never be corrected. But that is not all.
As long as this man puts his trust in his own opinions
instead of the word of the Lord he will probably continue
to go off on other tangents in the future. Let's not allow
ourselves to make any of this kind of mistake. How much
better it is just to trust in God and march in step with him
and his program.

Sometimes the Lord must get pretty weary of our
discord and confusion, because so many trust in their own
ignorance and prejudices. To obey is still better than
sacrifice, and it is also a lot safer.

We pay money to see a great athletic team in which
the players have learned to synchronize their efforts and
play for the team. Then each player submerges individual
wishes in seeking the welfare of his group. Each feels that
the team and the cause are bigger and more important

than the individual. We do not enjoy the game when each player is trying to show how capable he is individually; we would not think much of a player who would not obey the signals. The thing that we do want to see is team performance where every play is properly coordinated and effectively executed. It is certain that that is just what the Lord wants to see in us. No football team would ever accomplish much if every member carried his own book of rules and called his own signals and did his own scoring, with each having his own objectives in mind and his own independent procedures for accomplishment.

For these and many more reasons, it is a far wiser procedure for us to coordinate our efforts and march in step with the Lord and the program of the Church in every detail. This invention of "men in step" is a great one, and we should use it more, especially when the Lord is calling the signals.

In the Church as in football or the army, it is necessary for every man to know his assignment and to carry it out on his own responsibility. The commander-in-chief may not be able to take the time to persuade everyone personally that the course outlined is the proper one. But if the army could not move until every private had given his personal approval on every detail of procedure, the army would never get very far, as there would be about as many opinions as there were individuals involved. The effective church organization, like the effective army, must as a fundamental success requirement first learn unity and obedience, to march in step not only with their feet but with their hearts, their wills, their purposes, their minds and their abilities. In some of the wards and stakes we have not adequately learned this great lesson.

In the work of salvation, God is the directing power, and our own exaltation depends upon our effective execution. How much better it would be if we always placed our trust in him and accepted the program wholeheartedly. We may not always understand the whys and wherefores. It may appear to some that civil marriage is about as good as temple marriage. Or we may think that the observance of the Sabbath Day or the payment of tithing is not very important, or that a little irresponsibility in our assignment won't make much difference, or that making our reports is not important. Then when we find out our mistake the wrong has already been done, and no matter how sorry we may be, there is not much that can be done about it. But in addition, when we are out of harmony we contribute to the discord and confusion of other people, for it is far more difficult for others to march in step if we are breaking the rhythm. That applies to every activity in the Church.

A number of years ago the Church adopted the welfare program, and a plan of procedure was taken to all the wards and stakes. But some of the leaders insisted on calling their own signals and making their own rules. One person did not follow instructions because someone else was not following instructions. And even after twenty years have passed, some haven't yet progressed far enough to learn the program. They have also done themselves great damage by being out of step. These may be wonderful men personally; they have just not learned a fundamental lesson of success. For each to make his own rules would soon completely destroy the effectiveness of any army or football team or business. But when we throw our influence toward retarding the work of the Lord we are also robbing ourselves of our blessings and destroying our leadership.

Here is another place where we need to march in step. Jesus initiated a program of individual work, illustrated by the parable of the lost sheep. The Church has tried many times to establish this program in the wards and stakes. For example, if the plan of personal visits could be the united action of the proper leaders and workers, a great awakening could immediately be brought about all over the Church. Some respond wonderfully; others make a feeble effort; and some do almost nothing at all.

It is the old story as told by Jesus. One person can't follow directions for one reason and another falls down for a different reason. Some think they have more urgent things to do. Others don't want to be bothered. Some don't understand; some don't remember; some don't care. Some insist on playing according to their own rules at their own pleasure. Consequently accomplishment runs up and down the scale from the top to the bottom. Seeing this situation we can easily imagine why Jesus said, "If ye are not one, ye art not mine." We can imagine the kind of person he had in mind.

We have been invited to march in step with God. Our united effort would guarantee a maximum of accomplishment. What a thrilling idea it is to cooperate, to harmonize our minds and efforts with him to bring about his purposes. Think what would happen in any ward if all efforts were perfectly synchronized to do his will. We would multiply our ability and accomplishment many times. We would then also have his spirit; we would all be going in the right direction at the right time. "In unity there is strength." If each unit responded as one man, nothing would be impossible. To think would be to act. To plan would be to accomplish. There would be no time lag of days or months or years between the impulse and the accomplishment. When the Lord spoke, we would hear. When the President of the Church gave a direction we would carry it out.

To be "in step" is one of the greatest devices of success. But it is also one of the most important commandments of God.

Mind the Light

IN NEW YORK harbor between Manhattan and Staten Island is a sunken shoal called Robin's Reef. A small lighthouse stands there to warn of hidden dangers to those who go by sea. For many years the keeper of the Robin's Reef lighthouse has been a woman, now an elderly widow, by the name of Mrs. Jacob Walker. Mrs. Walker was recently interviewed by some newspaper men. She told them the story of her life. It is a story of inspiration and devotion which shines out like the beams of the beacon which she has so long minded.

She said: "I was a young girl living at Sandy Hook, New Jersey, when I first met Jacob Walker. He was the keeper of the Sandy Hook lighthouse. He took me there as his bride and we were very happy. Some years later we were transferred to the lighthouse at Robin's Reef. After four years my husband caught a cold while tending the light. The cold turned to pneumonia and they took him to a hospital on Staten Island. I remained behind to look after the light. A few nights later I saw a rowboat coming through the darkness. Something told me the message it was bringing. We buried my husband two days later on the hillside of Staten Island not too far away to be seen from the lighthouse. Every morning since then when the sun comes up, I stand at the porthole and look out across the water toward Jacob's grave. Sometimes the hill is green, sometimes it is brown, sometimes it is white with snow. But I always get a message from him. It is the same thing I heard him say more often than anything else in life. It is always the same, just three words: 'Mind the light.'"

That is a very short message, but it has an important meaning. The significance of its message is in some ways comparable to that other three word message wherein Jesus said, "Come follow me." Or it might be compared to the message that comes down to us from the morning of creation when God himself spoke a four word command saying, "Let there be light." With each new rising of the sun we might try to imagine what it must have been like to feel the oppression of that brooding, unbroken, unrelenting pre-creation darkness, and then picture to ourselves the contrast when in the forward march of progress God first said, "Let there be light."

But ever since that first day of creation so long ago, darkness in one form or another has continued to be the central problem of the world. In the beginning, "God saw the light and pronounced it good," and "God divided the light from the darkness," and he turned the faces of men toward the light. But men have often turned about and have loved darkness rather than light. In Dickens' *Christmas Carol*, Scrooge, the central figure, sat in the darkness of his money-changing counting house and said, "Darkness is cheap; therefore I like it." But Scrooge was mistaken. Darkness has never been cheap. Darkness is the most expensive thing in the world—the one commodity that is always in the greatest and most constant oversupply.

With awful meaning, Isaiah looked down across the centuries to our day and said, "Darkness shall cover the earth and gross darkness the minds of the people." The darkness that covers the minds of men is oppressive and stifling. We feel its offensiveness in the words of the Lord's fateful pronouncement about our own day, "The world lieth in sin and groaneth in darkness." (D&C 84:49)

It is one of the most startling and thought-provoking paradoxes of our day of wonders and enlightenment that men are still walking in darkness as at noonday. (D&C 95:6) Thus we bring upon ourselves the fate mentioned by John the Beloved, who said, "If a man walk in the night he stumbleth because there is no light in him." (John 11:10)

As disturbing as the darkness itself may be, it is still more disturbing to try to look behind the scenes and understand the reasons for the blackout which we bring upon ourselves. No less an authority than the Master himself has said that men "love darkness rather than light because their deeds are evil." (D&C 10:21) Some receive not the light because they perceive it not. (D&C 45:29) They not only lack vision; they also lack interest. We sometimes voluntarily turn our faces the other way, even though we know that that which doth not edify is not of God but of darkness. (D&C 50:23)

The one supreme gift that the inhabitants of our world need more than any other is the gift of light. The one line in all of sacred literature which should most concern us is the one wherein God said, "Let there be light." That is not only our greatest need, it is also his fondest wish for his children.

In various periods of the history of our world a renewal of that edict has been given, bringing light again into a darkened world. Speaking of this renewal in our own time, the Lord said, "And when the times of the gentiles have come in, a light shall break forth among them that sit in darkness and it shall be the fullness of my gospel." (D&C 45:28) And God will judge all men according to the use they make of the light which is available. (D&C 82:3) God has made it abundantly clear that the rejection of light is the greatest of all sins, and for those who have great light and knowledge "and altogether turneth therefrom there is no forgiveness, neither in this world, neither in the world to come." It naturally follows that the greatest opportunity provided for man in this world is to join with creation in the program of bringing about God's first and probably most important decree of "Let there be light."

The bounds of darkness must be pushed back. The lighted frontiers must be extended in breadth and increased in intensity. The need of the world for more light "minders" and more light "carriers" is very great. Mrs. Jacob Walker spent her life directing the saving beams of her lighthouse beacons out across the dark waters of Robin's Reef. She was always faithful to her trust. She could always be depended upon. Each morning as the sun came up and God's day was renewed in the world, she stood at her post by the porthole and received her charge anew, "Mind the light."

Those who "mind the light" must always have foremost in their hearts the interests of others. Mrs. Walker translated that interest into service as the shafts of light reached out across the dark waters to bring safety to those who sailed within reach of the hazards of Robin's Reef.

The philosophy of light has always been one of the most important philosophies of our world. For behind the light there is God and goodness and safety and happiness for man. "God is the light and the life of the world, your Redeemer, your Lord and your God." It is he who enlighteneth every man that cometh into the world that harkeneth to the voice of the spirit. (D&C 84:46) He is in the sun and the light of the sun and the power thereof by which it was made. (D&C 88:7) It is that light that "enlighteneth your eyes . . . and quickeneth your understanding, which light proceedeth forth from the presence of God to fill the immensity of space—The light which is in all things, which is the law by which all things are governed, even the power of God." (D&C 88:11-13) The same light that draws the stars across the sky pumps your blood and activates your brain. It lights the shoals of Robin's Reef and inspires the faithfulness of Mrs. Jacob Walker. It enlightens every man in the things of God. It offers the greatest employment in the universe, which is to be "minders" and "bearers" of light.

The duty of light bearers is to "chase darkness from among men." (D&C 50:25) The greatest need of men is greater light. Just before his death, Bill Porter, known to many as O. Henry, said, "Pull up the shades. I don't want to go home in the dark." O. Henry concluded his life's story in a New York hospital with this challenging statement which might well be the burden of the cry of church leadership. The last phrase spoken by Goethe was, "More light." That is the life work of leaders and teachers. The best way to have more light is to see that our own lives are always increasing in brightness. The Lord has said, "He that receiveth light and continueth in God receiveth more light and that light groweth brighter and brighter until the perfect day." (D&C 50:24) "Whereas every man whose spirit receiveth not the light is under condemnation." (D&C 93:32)

The spirit lived in light before it came here. Not to recognize it and love it here may mean "outer darkness" hereafter. Our entrance into this world is as a reward of faithfulness in our former state, and our position in the world to come is now being determined by how we mind the light which we have been given.

To be an effective "minder" one must himself have a quality of spiritual phosphorescence. We must not only be reflectors, but our own souls must be aglow from the depths inside of us. We need to keep a light in our eyes and a light in our minds. We must have lighted and enlightened souls. Jesus said, "Let your light so shine before men that others, seeing your good works, may glorify your Father which is in heaven."

Sometimes the light flickers uncertainly in our human lives. When we waver in our duty the light grows dim.

The Lord said, "If you keep not my commandments the love of the father shall not continue with you; therefore ye shall walk in darkness." (D&C 95:12)

Jesus was the chief light giver of the world. He lights our lives and sends us out to light others. We are both givers and receivers of light.

> I met a stranger in the night
> Whose lamp had ceased to shine.
> I paused and let him light
> His lamp, from mine.
>
> A tempest sprang up later on
> And blew the world about
> And when the wind was gone
> My light was out.
>
> Then back again the stranger came;
> His light was glowing fine.
> He held again the precious flame
> And lighted mine.

Our light does not grow less even if it kindles the flame for thousands. It was said that the light of an unknown continent burned within Columbus. The light of the eternal continent burns within us, and we must not hide it under a bushel. Jesus bids us put our light high on a candle stick that it may serve as the beacon for everyone to see. The Lord has established his own lighthouses and selected lighthouse keepers to "mind the light" and send it out to those who walk in darkness and danger.

> There's a call comes ringing o'er the restless wave,
> Send the light.
> There are souls to rescue, there are souls to save,
> Send the light.
>
> We have heard the Macedonian call today,
> Send the light. Send the light.
> And the golden offering at the cross we lay,
> Send the light. Send the light.

Let us pray that grace may everywhere abound,
Send the light. Send the light.
And a Christ-like spirit everywhere be found;
Send the light. Send the light.

Let us not grow weary in the work of love,
Send the light.
Let us gather jewels for a crown above,
Send the light.

Send the light, the blessed gospel light,
Let it shine from shore to shore;
Send the light and let its radiant beam
Light the world forever more.

Those who radiate light also generate warmth. Warmth is a manifestation of light. The two greatest of all the commandments have to do with warmth in human hearts. The warmth we radiate to others will also light their lives.

Tyndale, sitting in his cold dungeon prison, asked that warm clothing be sent him, "For," said he, "these I have are very thin." Then he asked for a lighted lamp and a Bible. Said he, "It is so dreary sitting alone in the dark."

How dreary might it be sitting alone in the darkness of eternity. Now is the time to get our lamps lighted and with our Bible begin our journey toward the city of eternal light. And each day for a brief period we might pause and stand at our own portholes while we receive anew from God our charge, "Mind the light."

The Miracle of Personality

No DISCUSSION of leadership development would be complete which did not give consideration to the personality of the leader. The most inspiring and the most important thing in the world is a great human personality. The masterpiece of all of creation is a human being at its best. Yet probably the thing that we know less about than almost any other thing is our own individual selves. If you ask a man about science, invention or history he will answer you. But if you ask him to write out an analysis of himself, to tell you about his mind and soul qualities, you will not get a very good answer. Self-analysis, self-control and self-improvement are very difficult. We not only have trouble correcting our faults; we even have trouble discovering them. But the best way to build leadership is through effective personality development.

The dictionary defines personality as the qualities of being a particular person. Your personality is what distinguishes you from others. What we are forms our habit patterns, develops our character qualities and determines our physical, mental and spiritual behavior. It has been estimated that as high as 85 per cent of all success depends upon personality.

Personality is very complex. In nature there are 102 known elements including nitrogen, hydrogen, iron, carbon, oxygen, etc. These are nature's building blocks, out of which, in the right combinations and proportions, nature fashions all of the material things of the world. For example, an ocean is made up of two parts of hydrogen and one of oxygen. Every other material thing has its own formula, depending on its own particular combination of elements. Then it has been said that in human personality there are 51 elements. There are kindness, faith, spirituality, industry, devotion, courage, ambition and integrity. Put these together in the right combinations and proportions and you have what someone has called a magnificent human being.

The personality of each leader might also be expressed as a formula. That is, what is it that makes President David O. McKay what he is? It is his great devotion to God, his untiring efforts to serve, his ability to do, his warm friendliness, his absolute fairness, his kindly personal interest in others, his unwavering integrity, his love of truth. Put these elements together in the right proportions and you have David O. McKay. Now think what made Napoleon Bonaparte what he was. Napoleon also had some great qualities, but they were mixed with ruthlessness, self-seeking, ignorance and disregard of the rights of others. The result was that he was exiled by his own countrymen at age 46.

The thing we need to know is how we can use this power of personality in our own leadership. That is, how can these good qualities be developed to bring us to our peak of effectiveness, and how can we eliminate those qualities which tear us down? Socrates said, "Know thyself." It is very important that we be expert in the process of self-diagnosis. It is also important for us to study personality in others. If we can identify a harmful trait in someone else, we can more easily eliminate a like trait from our own personality. When we love good qualities we can more easily reproduce them in ourselves. Probably the greatest power in the world is the power of example. We learn to walk, to talk and to eat by watching someone else. Most of our manners, morals, habits, attitudes and personality qualities are acquired through the power of example. Even Jesus said, "The Son can do nothing of

himself but what he seeth the Father do." (John 5:19)
We can hardly realize the tremendous influence that the
example of personality can have upon another.

It has been written that "we reap as we sow," but that
is only part of the fact. Mostly we reap as others have sown
for us. We reap as our parents have sown; we reap as our
teachers have sown; we reap as our associates have sown.
Walt Whitman said, "A child went forth and became what
he saw." Certainly we become what we love and think
about and do. This emphasizes the importance of reading
good literature, thinking good thoughts and having good
leaders and good associates. The influences that are most
strongly impressed upon us come from people, and we
absorb those qualities most readily that we see clearly and
that have a strong attraction for our minds.

For example, Louis Fischer wrote a book portraying
the life of the Indian patriot, Mohandas K. Gandhi. This
little brown man weighed 112 pounds. He went around
four-fifths naked; he lived in a mud hut without electric
lights, running water or telephone. He didn't own an automobile. He never sought or ever held a public office. He
was without political post, academic distinction, scientific
achievement or artistic gift. He had no armies, no diplomats,
no property. Yet men with great governments and powerful
armies behind them paid him homage.

The great British government soon discovered that it
could not rule India against Gandhi, and it could not rule
India without Gandhi. Gandhi became as near "India"
as anyone or anything could be. By the sheer power of
developing his personality, Gandhi raised himself to be
the unquestioned leader of 500 million people and became
the greatest power in India and probably in the world.
Gandhi's followers renamed him The Mahatma, meaning
The Great Soul. Louis Fischer calls this phenomenon by
which a man with small beginnings can raise himself to

great heights of accomplishment, "The miracle of personality." This miracle is made more important by the fact that each of us may perform it for himself.

Gandhi started his life under some very real handicaps. He regarded himself as a coward. He was afraid of the dark. He had a damaging inferiority complex. He had an uncontrollable temper. He had some very serious sex problems. Because of these disadvantages with which he started life, he worked to the end of his days at age 78 to remake himself. At one time he called himself "a self remade man."

For those who are looking for a good phrase with startling possibilities, "a self remade man" is one of the best. Personal improvement is absolutely necessary for great accomplishment. It is impossible to rise higher as a leader than we rise as a person.

Gandhi believed in *being*, not in *having* nor in *seeming*. He believed that the discord between deed and creed lies at the root of innumerable wrongs in our civilization. He believed this discord to be the weakness of churches, states, parties and persons. Gandhi felt that to believe a thing and not to practice it was dishonest and gave institutions and men split personalities, whereas he believed that the personality of every successful man should be well-integrated and balanced.

Gandhi never trifled. He practiced severe self-discipline all of his days. With Gandhi, to believe was to act. There was no pretense. Face-saving was to him an unintelligible concept. When he had decided something was good he forced himself to follow through and translate every thought into action.

Gandhi's mother taught him that eating meat was wrong, inasmuch as it necessitated the destruction of other life. And so young Gandhi took a pledge to his mother to remain a strict vegetarian throughout his life. Many years after Gandhi's mother had died, Gandhi himself was very ill and not expected to live. His physicians tried to persuade him to drink a little beef broth to save his life. But Gandhi said, "Even for life itself we may not do certain things. There is only one course open to me, to die but never to break my pledge."

Just imagine what it would mean in the world if all of the present-day leaders of nations had that kind of integrity, where their word could absolutely be depended upon and where trust and confidence were the foundation of every relationship. In the matter of trustworthiness Gandhi excelled. Everyone understood that Gandhi was absolutely honest, that he could be trusted, that his motives were right. When Gandhi said something everyone knew that that was exactly what he meant. Millions trusted Gandhi; millions obeyed him; multitudes counted themselves his followers. But strangely enough, only a few ever attempted to do as he did. Gandhi's greatness lay in doing what everybody could but does not do.

One of the greatest ambitions of Gandhi's life was to free India. But he felt that before he could free India from the British he must free himself from the weaknesses that held him down. Man at his best must be in perfect control of himself. Gandhi determined to make himself an effective instrument of negotiation for India's welfare. How well he succeeded is known to everyone. It is Mr. Fischer's opinion that not since Socrates has the world seen Gandhi's equal for absolute self-control and composure. He was thought by some to be the world's most Christ-like person, and yet he was not a Christian.

Gandhi went on long fasts for discipline. He reasoned that if he could not curb his passion for food, how could he handle the more difficult of life's situations? He said, "How can I control others if I cannot control myself?"

Gandhi realized early in his life that integrity and

manhood are among the most important instruments of power. This gave him a great advantage in his dealings with others. Gandhi said, "I cannot conceive of a greater loss to a man than the loss of his self-respect." Even while fighting England for India's independence, Gandhi had the constant respect and trust of British leaders. His motto was, "Harmony in adversity; love despite differences."

There came a time during the Second World War when the fate of England was in the balance, and she could not spare even a single soldier for the defense of India. Many prominent Indian leaders were in favor of throwing out British rule while England was helpless. But Gandhi said, "No! We will not steal even our independence." Gandhi would have given his life at any moment in exchange for his country's freedom, but he did not want independence if it could not be had honorably.

Gandhi believed that ideas and reason, fairness and understanding were superior to force as instruments of negotiation. This he practiced, even when he had absolute power to do as he pleased. How inspiring is the spirit of a truly great man. By way of contrast, there are men living today who would not hesitate one instant to use any means at their command to enslave everyone in the world if they thought they could.

Gandhi's tremendous personal power often remained unused. He said, "We cannot learn discipline by compulsion." He never retaliated. His reason told him that the policy of "an eye for an eye" if carried out would eventually make everybody blind. Gandhi did not attempt to be clever. He once declared, "I have never had recourse to cunning in all of my life." His mind and emotions were almost as completely exposed to public view as was his nearly-naked body.

Then came that fateful day, July 30, 1948. At 5:05 p.m. Gandhi was hurrying to the village prayer ground.

In the front row of the congregated worshippers sat one Nathuran Godse, clutching a pistol in his pocket. As the two men almost touched each other, Godse fired three bullets into the body of the Mahatma. At Godse's trial he said he bore no ill will to Gandhi. He said, "Before I fired the shots I actually wished him well and bowed to him in reverence." In response to Godse's obeisance, Gandhi touched his palms together, smiled and blessed him. At that moment Godse pulled the trigger and Gandhi's mortal life was ended. But even in death, this little brown man was engaged in the act of blessing people and doing good.

A few minutes after Gandhi's death, Prime Minister Nehru went on the radio and said, "The light has gone out of our lives and there is darkness everywhere, for our beloved leader, the father of our nation, is no more."

What a great power of leadership can be built up within ourselves, if we merely develop to their highest denomination these great God-given qualities.

Now what are the traits that we need to carry on our own particular part of the work of the Lord? The Lord himself has said, "And faith, hope, charity and love, with an eye single to the glory of God qualify him for the work." (D&C 4:5) He said, "Remember faith, virtue, knowledge, temperance, patience, brotherly kindness, Godliness, charity, humility, diligence." (D&C 4:6)

What a thrilling thought, that we can build these qualities (specified by the Lord) into our own personalities in their most productive combination. Have you ever thought about the fact that man is the only part of creation favored with a personality? We think of the body as going with us throughout eternity. But how often do we remember that the personality is also immortal and will go with us forever? You would not like to be resurrected with an inferior body. But how would you like to have an inferior personality? God has placed these potential talents and abilities in the human soul for us to develop to their highest possibility. That is the process by which we may have a maximum of joy. That is the process by which we may render a maximum of service. That is also the process by which we may become even as God.

Lord Bulwer-Lytton said: "What men need is not only talent but purpose; not only the power to achieve but the will to labor." That is the key to our own personality development, and each of us must accept complete responsibility therefor. We know what the Lord would have us do. We need only to put our personality qualities in full force to make any accomplishment possible.

A great philosopher once said, "Shun no effort to make yourself remarkable in some talent." This is the process by which we perform the greatest miracle in the world, "The Miracle of Personality."

> The human will, that force unseen,
> That offspring of the human soul
> Can hew a way to any goal
> Though walls of granite intervene.
>
> Be not impatient in delay
> But wait, as one who understands.
> When spirit rises and commands
> The gods are ready to obey.

"Operation Andrew"

A T THE VERY beginning of the
Savior's ministry, John the
Baptist was at Bethabara beyond Jordan, and when he saw
Jesus he said, "Behold the lamb of God who taketh away
the sins of the world." Two of John's disciples heard him
and followed Jesus. One of the two was Andrew, Simon
Peter's brother. As soon as Andrew had satisfied himself
about the divine mission of Jesus, he hurried to tell Peter,
and the record says of Andrew, "He first findeth his own
brother, Simon, and sayeth unto him, We have found the
Messias . . . And he brought him unto Jesus." (John
1:41-42)

We are familiar with the tremendous impact that
Jesus had upon the life of Simon Peter and of the great
work which Peter did as a consequence. But I like to
remember that Peter didn't find Jesus by himself. *He was
brought to Jesus by his brother Andrew.* It is interesting
to speculate on what might have been the result if Peter
had been left to himself and not put on the track by his
brother.

Someone has appropriately called this process of discovery and intermediary contact "Operation Andrew."
This service becomes more significant when we remember
that the Savior himself was the great mediator between
God and man. It was his mission to bring us to God. This
personal work is certainly one of the most important areas
for us to develop effectiveness in our church leadership.

There are many other people who would never have
found themselves nor their place in the world if others
had not been their discoverers. If you wish you may call

245

this process "the missionary approach" or "personal work," but I would like to call it "Operation Andrew" in honor of this great church worker who led Simon Peter to the Master. Andrew set the pattern for our most constructive method of bringing others to Jesus. We are not only our brother's keeper; we are also responsible for his discovery, his development and his exaltation.

One of the strongest powers known in the world is the influence of individual personal attention. Many lives besides Peter's have been greatly changed by it. This individual work was the basis of one of the most instructive of the teachings of Jesus. In the parable of the lost sheep, Jesus pointed out with obvious good common sense that a good shepherd should give each of his flock this individual, personal service. That is, not all of the work can be done in the corral on a "flock" basis. There must be many individual trips made out into the mountains to visit those with a tendency to stray away. So far as I know, the most effective way to bring them back is by personal, individual attention to their needs.

The medical patient feels better because of a visit from the doctor. Even the mentally ill can often be cured without medicine or surgery by the psychiatrist who understands the influence that one personality can have upon another under the right circumstances. For many other situations there is just no substitute for individual contact. A great personality can exercise a creative, vitalizing, regenerating power in the lives of others. Every expert salesman, teacher, doctor, missionary and church leader knows that almost any activity flourishes under the personal touch and withers when it is withdrawn.

Skill in personal, individual relationships is the foundation of conversion, training, supervision and motivation in the Church. All personal welfare work depends upon it, and it is the very heart of our public relations. Sometimes entire lives are changed by a single contact, and probably every person in the Church owes much of his success, just as Peter did, to the friendly, thoughtful assistance of someone else. Charles Kingsley was once asked the secret of his radiant, useful life, and he replied, "I had a friend." Such is the effect of one personality upon another.

Each of us is probably most appreciative of certain experiences in his own life. When I was seven years old we had a kindly ward teacher who used to come and talk with our family about the principles of the gospel. I can still feel the stimulation that I then received from that wonderful man. There is a new and expressive term, born of our nuclear age, called "fall-out." An atomic explosion occurs and impregnates the air with little radioactive particles. Then as this air mass is shifted around by the wind these particles fall to the earth like an unseen, unfelt rain and may greatly affect everything with which they come in contact. In a way I suppose that every human spirit is radioactive. There is a spiritual fall-out from a great personality which falls unseen upon us. The New Testament tells of a woman in the crowd who received virtue from touching the garment of Jesus. I felt a similar benefit of being touched by the presence of our ward teacher. Even at age seven, I could feel virtue radiating from this humble, devoted servant of the Lord, and I knew then that I was absorbing some of his spiritual radioactivity. How much I owe to him for the direction he gave to my life at this early age!

Another great blessing from personal contact with a great man came to me when I was ten, when one Sunday I met the stake president. I just happened to get in the aisle at the right time as he came along. He stopped and shook my hand and asked me what my name was. Then he asked me what my father's name was, and he said that he knew my father. I suppose that this interview lasted a total of one minute, but something wonderful happened to me in that brief period as I felt his warm, friendly interest and sensed his deep spiritual strength. I decided immediately that someday I would like to represent in my person some of the qualities that I could feel in him. I have felt that same influence from others over and over again throughout my life to the present time.

I share this experience with you because it is also your experience. You have also been greatly uplifted by the stimulation of others. It is also probable that every day you inspire someone else. You may change someone's entire course in life without even knowing it. This help doesn't need to be put into words. When you love someone very much, you don't need to tell them; they will feel your love. In the same way if you have some great quality of spirituality or faith you don't need to spell it out for people; they will understand without words. Thomas Curtis Clark has written up our common experience as follows:

> I saw him once: he stood a moment there;
> He spoke a word that laid his spirit bare;
> He clasped my hand, then passed beyond my ken—
> But what I was, I shall not be, again.

One of our greatest opportunities in leadership is to develop and use this great power that God has given to human personality. One of the parables so strongly recommended by Jesus had to do with leaving the ninety and nine to help the one that was lost. If we were to bring this parable up to date statistically and apply it to our own church work, we might find that there were only forty in the sheepfold each Sunday morning and sixty absentees in need of special attention.

When Jesus repeated over and over to Peter, "Feed my sheep," he certainly did not mean to feed just those that were safe in the sheepfold where the feeding could be done on a mass basis in one manger. One of the greatest opportunities to feed the flock of Jesus is to do "the outside work" with those who don't show up very often at the corral. We need to learn our way around in the mountains a little better.

The organization known as Alcoholics Anonymous can teach us some valuable lessons. When they find someone in trouble they don't just invite him to come to church, nor do they merely write him a postcard or say a prayer in his behalf. They go in person, and they go now, and they go charged with a helpful purpose, and they go with a program. And when they get there they don't talk about the weather or the election, and they don't talk in a disinterested, halfhearted, unfriendly way. And they don't quit until they get their job done, and then they go back again and again until the one in trouble is back on his feet. Success is accumulative. Each time you put a little more wood on the fire you raise the level of accomplishment.

An effective contact with another personality is not only one of the most beneficial experiences; it is also one of the most pleasant. Isolation or banishment from our kind is the greatest punishment. The shipwrecked Enoch Arden was forced to live by himself for eleven years. Tennyson said, "He had no want for sustenance." He could satisfy every important material need. But Tennyson said, "What he fain would see he could not see: a kindly human face or ever hear a kindly human voice."

Many have made shipwrecks of their faith and live in more or less spiritual isolation. Their need for warm, friendly, personal help may be as great as that of Enoch Arden or some friendless alcoholic. Here is our greatest opportunity. It is also our greatest tragedy that we are not always on the job. Nero fiddled while Rome burned. The soldiers diced while Jesus died. The apostles slept while Jesus suffered. And we sometimes indulge our "verbal

Christianity" while our brothers and sisters lose the celestial kingdom.

Wherever a great man goes other men will be made better. In the late fall I walked by a dry alfalfa field. The irrigation water had been carried by means of a head ditch past the dry field to nourish more valuable crops. But in two or three places the water had broken over the bank and run down through the dry field. Wherever these "fingers of moisture" had reached out into the field, the alfalfa could be seen standing eight or ten inches higher than that which had not received the water. That is exactly what happens when the personality of a good man makes a contact with other people for whom he has leadership responsibility.

For example, I know an Aaronic Priesthood adviser with nineteen deacons, every single one of whom has qualified for an individual award in each of the past three years. Last year the adviser made 268 personal visits to these boys in their homes. He talked to them and their parents in an interesting way about their eternal salvation. Through "Operation Andrew" he is bringing them to Jesus.

It may be argued that this personal work takes time. But is there a better way? If our work is worth doing, it is worth doing right. And this is the only way to give each the exact help that fits his need. If a doctor has a dozen patients he gives each one a separate diagnosis and treatment. He does not make a mass prescription for broken legs, ruptured appendix and weak hearts. A good doctor meets his patient on an individual basis and often. He knows he can't always do a very good job through the mail or over the telephone or by mental telepathy. Neither does he merely say a prayer for the one in trouble. Rather, he puts on his hat and goes in person. That is the spirit of a great church worker.

One might listen to a great preacher from now till the cows come home and not be greatly affected. But a personal, individual, professional interest, tailor-made to fit each particular situation, will solve almost every problem. That is especially true if the solution is transmitted through an understanding, friendly, radioactive personality. The influence thus produced is too powerful to be resisted. And when this radio beam is directed toward getting men and women into the celestial kingdom, it can become the most productive force known in the world. Salvation itself is an individual matter and can best be handled on an individual basis. That is the best way to solve personal problems and develop spirituality in the lives of people.

Individual work is not only the best way to give help—in many cases it is the only way the exact assistance can be given when it is needed, where it is needed, and in the right way. There would be many thousands more members of the Church who would qualify for their blessings if we could just master the technique of personal work referred to by Jesus in the parable of the lost sheep.

Not only should the message be interesting, but the messenger should be interesting also. The highest function of a teacher is not always to impart knowledge; it is to make people happy, promote friendliness, produce spirituality and faith. It also serves its purpose in recharging the spirit. Very little learning takes place until the student and the teacher reach a common ground where a desire to learn is present. It should not be forgotten that the visit should always be made in the personal, individual interest of the one being visited. If he has a grievance, help him to unload it. If he has something that is bothering him, help him get it out of his system.

A good psychiatrist listens and asks questions and understands, until the patient empties himself. Then he is ready to learn. The psychiatrist doesn't try to win too many arguments. His job is to extract the poison that is causing the patient distress. Only then is he in a position to give help. That is sometimes a part of an effective Operation Andrew.

Almost every life has disappointments and sins and complexes, and only after the steam has been blown off or the sin purged is the soul in a position to let the sunlight get in. Many times a sympathetic ear and a friendly heart have lightened a soul so that he could be brought unto Jesus, whereas if an opportunity had not been given to air grievances and hurt feelings they may have continued to fester until cure was impossible.

What a great power for good we hold in our hands if we take advantage of our opportunities for individual work. "Operation Andrew" is one of the most helpful methods of religious accomplishment. It can be used effectively by every member of the Church.

The "P" Formula for Success

M UCH OF SUCCESS is in being able to follow directions. We may succeed by formula. Science is merely a collection of success formulas. The sick patient follows the prescription of the doctor. A good businessman usually has definite standards and rules to direct him to his goal. An aviator carries a compass. A dressmaker follows a pattern. A good cook works from a book of recipes. If she follows the directions on page three of the cook book she gets one kind of cake; when she goes by the recipe on page four she gets a different kind of cake, because she follows a different set of directions. Success in church work, or in any other field, can be greatly increased when we have and will follow a proven success pattern or formula.

When Alexander the Great finished his job of conquering the world he wanted to become an orator like his teacher Aristotle. Accordingly, Aristotle wrote out for him the sixteen laws determining success in oratory. They are still available. If you want to become a great orator, just do these sixteen things. Success is as simple as that. If you do certain other things you will become a great farmer, or a great teacher, or a great church worker. If the formula is right and you follow it strictly you can't miss. But the formula is no good unless it is followed. A woman, after hearing the music of a great violinist, said, "I would give half of my life to be able to play like that." The violinist replied, "Madam, that is exactly what I have given." And that is exactly what everyone else must give. Nothing is more common than someone who is willing "to give half his life" but will not follow the formula. The formula for becoming a great violinist prescribes among other things that one must take some violin lessons. No formula can produce a master violinist that does not include violin lessons.

We can also measure success and determine its effectiveness or volume. In ordinary situations we get the volume of a thing by multiplying its dimensions. That procedure may not only help us to determine, but to increase, the total volume of our leadership. Suppose we think of leadership as coming in the six dimensions given below. They make up the "P" formula for success in church work.

First, we should learn to follow the formula. Second, we should appraise our performance under each of the headings. Then we just multiply together our personal scores under each P. By this process we will get a figure representing our total leadership accomplishment. The formula is:

$$P \times P \times P \times P \times P \times P = P.P.$$

That is,

Planning x Preparation x Personal Work x Persistence x Presentation x Personality = A Perfect Performance

Now suppose that you give yourself a rating of between zero and ten under each P. For example, suppose that last year you rated 3 in each item. Three multiplied together 6 times gives you a total score of 729. Then suppose that this year you increase your effectiveness 33⅓ per cent to a total of 4. Then multiply your six 4's together and you find an amazing thing. While you have increased each of the dimensions by only 33⅓ per cent, the total has been increased over 500 per cent. That is, if you make your personality more effective it automatically increases the quality of your presentation, personal work, preparation, planning, etc. It is the same with each of the other items. So if you want to increase your leadership success, all you need to do is to increase your goal under each "P." That is, set your total goal for next year at whatever you would like it to be. Then you can figure backward to determine what your rating will need to be under each "P." Write it down in the space provided below. Then all you need to do is to develop your P's to reach the score you have set for yourself.

	Planning x	Prep-aration x	Personal Work x	Per-sistence x	Pres-entation x	Personality =	Score
Last Year	3	3	3	3	3	3	= 729
This Year	4	4	4	4	4	4	= 4,096
Your Goal	..	..	..	..	..	..	=

We should, of course, be certain that none of these important "P's" are missing, for success in or out of church work is not like a cafeteria where you take what you please and leave out what you don't want. In church work, you don't say, "I will take the welfare program and temple marriage, but I won't take repentance, ward teaching or sacrament meeting." In the Church and in success you take the whole program. It is like making a run in baseball —you must touch all of the bases or nothing counts. They don't give any credit for the runs that die on third base. It is about the same with success. If you leave out planning, for example, you are like the baseball player who wants to score but never gets on first base.

See for yourself what happens under the formula when you have a zero under one heading. That is, suppose you get a score of 4 in everything except the presentation, in which you get a zero. Then the arithmetic is as follows:

$$4 \times 4 = 16 \times 4 = 64 \times 4 = 256 \times 0 = 0 \times 4 = 0$$

If you get zero any place in the formula you get zero for the final score. That is about what happens with our success. Recently I heard two men being discussed for church appointment. Of the first they said, "He is a fine man. He knows the gospel thoroughly. *But* he is undependable." Of the second man they said, "He is a wonderful person. Everyone likes him. *But* he won't prepare his lessons. He is a good man, *but* he isn't organized and he won't plan." Both were disqualified for service by one negative factor. The Republicans praise the Democrats by saying, "They are good people—*but*"—It is the "buts" that we need to look out for. It is the "buts" that get us into trouble. No one can hope for a maximum of success until he can dispose of his "buts," as "one vice will overcome ten virtues."

But if you will just do these things superbly well with no "buts" you will be a great success in church work. Suppose we think about them individually.

I — Planning

The highest paid man in the army is the planner. The architect lays out on paper every detail of his building before any work is started. The First Presidency and the Quorum of the Twelve spend all day Thursday in the temple planning and thinking and discussing. No stake presidency will ever get far without regular, well-directed planning meetings. No bishopric can get the maximum number of people into the celestial kingdom without planning. If the elders' quorum program isn't going over or an auxiliary is falling down, check on the planning. If you want to have a good deacons' quorum, teach the leaders how to plan and organize and coordinate their ideas and efforts.

Just suppose, for example, that I am a deacons' quorum adviser, and I invite the presidency to my home on Thursday night (when my wife makes lemonade), and help them to develop their ability in this valuable skill called planning. That is, we learn how to arrange the best possible program for next week's meeting. We make up a written agenda. The work is organized and the officers are prepared to carry it out. Then they are able to conduct the quorum's affairs with confidence and dignity. Every week they think their problems through in advance; they consider every eventuality and get the right answers to every problem. Each member of the presidency makes his contribution, and the ideas of each are tested by the whole. They retain in their plan all that is good and eliminate all that is bad. They learn how quorum meetings can be made more effective. If their record of activity is low they find out why and decide what can be done about it. What outside work should be done during the week? How can the quorum members be helped individually? A part of an idea given expression by one member of the presidency may be improved by number two and matured by number three. It is then put in force by the unit. "Three heads working together are often much better than three heads working separately."

All success depends on planning. The real church leader who knows, or will take the time to learn, how to plan and organize his work effectively has a big head start toward his objective—success.

II — Preparation

Preparation for effective church work should be a combination of mental preparation, physical preparation, spiritual preparation and emotional preparation. The first law of preparation is that everything worthwhile is brought about by labor. There must be industry and study and drill before we get full possession of success.

Many people are not ready for success. They have not earned success. Success must be deserved and paid for. We need to develop a mental hunger for success. We need to get excited about success. Most of all we must be prepared for success. People who are unprepared for success don't get much out of church because they haven't much to get it in. For every accomplishment there must be adequate preparation. One great teacher spends eight hours in preparation for each hour of class work; another spends five minutes. Their accomplishment is usually in proportion.

III — Personal Work

One of the most valuable secrets of success in church work, the one thing that can be done that will bring almost miraculous results, is to do sufficient effective, personal, individual work with those for whom we have responsibility. The best worker is the one who gets the most and the best work done. And the most important problems can only be best solved on a personal, individual, face-to-face basis. Someone said that if you want to get the milk out of a bucket into a dozen milk bottles, the best way to accomplish it is not to throw the bucket at the bottles; you will accomplish the job more quickly and satisfactorily if you take each bottle and fill it one at a time. That is also the most effective way to get the Spirit of the gospel into people.

IV — Persistence

Many people are licked before they start because they lack stick-to-it-iveness. We always fail if we lose interest and quit too quickly. The easiest thing in the world is to quit. It doesn't matter what you are going to quit. It doesn't require faith, knowledge, character or ambition to quit. In fact you can quit quicker if you lack all of these. There are some people who, when their first enterprises miscarry, lose heart and throw in the sponge. People who lack persistence tire easily. They are unable to supply their own motivation. Such people are always starting and stopping without finishing what is started. It is easy to become a spiritual ne'er-do-well, one who is always jumping from one thing to another without taking time to do anything well. Success is pretty difficult without a good supply of persistence.

Calvin Coolidge said: "Nothing in the world can take the place of persistence. Talent will not; nothing is more common than unsuccessful men with talent. Genius will not; unrewarded genius is almost a proverb. Education will not; the world is full of educated derelicts. Persistence and determination alone are omnipotent."

V — Presentation

Skills come largely from drill. A great actor or a great speaker or a great musician is constantly perfecting his presentation by practice, drill, study, correction and then more practice. The way to learn to skate is to put your skates on and get out on the ice. The way to become a good basketball player is practice. The way to become effective in church work is to get on the job. "If you will do the work you shall have the power." That means practice. We can learn to make an interesting and effective presentation of our ideas by making interesting and effective presentations over and over again.

We need to know the principles of the gospel, but we also need to be able to present them effectively. We need to know about content, arrangement and delivery. We need enrichment material. We need sequence, logic, study, reason and persuasion. This we get by doing. Skill is not something that comes by wishing. "There is no excellence without labor."

VI — Personality

The sixth "P" is personality. That is what we are. The eight most important words in the language are, "And God created man in his own image." Not only are we created in the image of God, but each of us has been endowed with a set of the attributes of divinity, the development of which is one of the purposes for which we live. We don't just work to acquire; we also work to become. One of our most important leadership requirements is to *be* a great human being.

Suppose that we learn to be *personality chemists* so that we can analyze ourselves under the microscope. What personality elements do we lack and what should be done about them?

We have heard of the "ABC's of success." Here is a post graduate course of six "P's." Multiply them together and we have our success score. If you would like enough more P's to equal Aristotle's sixteen, here they are: There is prayer, and priesthood, power, purity, perfection, punctuality, practice, persuasion, push and praise.

Thomas A. Edison had a great formula made almost entirely of one "P." It was perspiration. He said success was 99 per cent perspiration and 1 per cent inspiration. It is thought that those proportions are still in pretty good order. Edison's formula is still right up to date, as it is pretty difficult for one to be *inspiring* without being *perspiring.*

Not all great words begin with P. For example, L U C K is a great word which does not begin with P, but notice how it is improved if you put a P in front of it. It then becomes P L U C K.

If you want to develop your leadership just watch your P's. The three R's are wonderful, but with the six P's you can't miss.

Planning

THE FOUNDATION of all success is planning. The planner is the one who thinks, devises strategy and blueprints accomplishment. Battles are won in the tent of the general. The same principle holds true in every other field. The architect lays out on paper every detail of the building before construction is started. Henry Ford once said that the difference between the old Model T and the new Lincoln was planning.

Planning is even more important in church work where the welfare of immortal souls is at stake. Planning is the mother of almost every other ability. If we want to increase our effectiveness in church work and help to get more people into the celestial kingdom, the best place to start is to learn how to plan our program, organize our thoughts, effectively direct our efforts and utilize our time. These are all born of planning, and we learn to do by doing.

Following is a simple formula that will not only help us to plan but will also help us to carry our program through to completion. This formula was given by James G. Harboard, a general of World War I and former chairman of the board of the Radio Corporation of America. He said that before anyone under his direction attempted to carry out any mission he must do four things:

1. Make a written statement of objectives.
2. Make a written inventory of all available resources.
   (List all possibilities for reinforcement.)
3. Make a written inventory of the resources of the enemy.
   (List all reasons why the mission may not succeed.)
4. Prepare a written plan, explaining exactly how he intends to use his resources to overcome the resources of the enemy and accomplish the objective.

We clarify our thoughts when we write them out. We also impress them deeper into our minds when we keep them constantly before us in visual form. Writing makes more certain that we will finish our thinking before we start action. Most unwritten plans are not plans at all; they are only ideas. They are like certain New Years' resolutions: indefinite, incomplete and soon forgotten. If we write our resolutions and set up a definite timetable with a deadline for its accomplishment, success can be made easy and certain.

Defects are more easily recognized and eliminated when plans are in writing. Many excellent ideas will pop into our minds while the plan is being made. A written plan may be checked by the "general" who has supervision of our work, and thereby we may get the advantage of his expert suggestions. A plan should represent the thinking of the team. If written, a plan can be more easily understood by the others concerned; it can also be referred to regularly, and it prevents forgetfulness.

The greatest sin of a military commander is to lose the battle. That is also the besetting sin of church workers. When the Lord gives us the responsibility of saving souls he wants us to succeed. To fail is a sin, not only for itself alone, but for what it is a sign of. It may be a sign of sloth, ignorance, indifference, disobedience or procrastination in us. Generals sometimes give the effect of invulnerability by never allowing an exception to success to occur. We can become invulnerable if we effectively plan our work and then thoroughly carry out our plans.

1. The Objective

A good place to start to plan is to set up a definite objective. We should know where we want to go before we get started. Success is made much easier by a definite objective. For example, an athlete can jump higher if he lays a bamboo pole horizontally across measured uprights and then tries to jump over it, than if he merely jumps up in the air. It is impossible to increase efficiency without some accurate measurement of progress made. Progress should be regularly checked, timed, measured and counted.

When once the goal has been established, we can work backward to success. For example, I know a farmer in Idaho who last year grew 500 sacks of potatoes to the acre. A neighbor on the same kind of land grew 150 sacks. What makes the difference? And what can he do about it? The farmer with 150 sacks per acre must first find out the reasons for his lower yield. It may be bad seed, a poorly prepared seed bed, lack of fertilizer, improper care, or it may be disease. If we know why we have failed, and if we have a definite goal, then we are in a position to tell what is necessary to bring about the results we desire.

2. Your Resources

We must know what we have to work with. A good general has an accurate inventory of tanks, guns, oil, men and food supply. The Idaho farmer has soil, fertilizer, irrigation water, seed, labor, climate, etc. A good church worker has the gospel, the spirit of the Lord, the program of the Church, his associate officers and teachers, the members of his organization, their parents, friends, etc. He has his own time, resourcefulness, initiative and enthusiasm. He has his ability to train, supervise and motivate, and a hundred other abilities that the average man never really uses.

3. The Resources of the Enemy

Abraham Lincoln said that when he was preparing for a debate he spent one-fourth of his time thinking about what he was going to say and three-fourths of his time thinking about what his opponent was going to say. When you go into battle the more you know about the enemy the better. The enemy of the Idaho farmer was whatever caused his poor yield. If a church worker is going to plan to increase his effectiveness, he must know why he previously fell down.

It is one of the great secrets of success to be able to put our finger on our real enemies. What is preventing a bigger yield for the Idaho farmer? Or what is holding us back personally? That is, who is it that keeps me ignorant and poor and unsuccessful? It is sometimes a little difficult to get an accurate point of view about an enemy who is so close to us. Our faults, like our blessings, mostly come in disguise. Some men go through their entire lives without ever finding out where their failure is coming from. Some never even know that they are failing. It is so easy not to be conscious of weakness or to put the blame in the wrong place. The natural tendency to make this mistake makes planning very difficult.

Who is it that is holding our particular church organization back? Most likely it is not enemies from the outside. What about the leaders themselves? Who is it that keeps us from following the program of the Church? Who causes us to make decisions that are not clear-cut and have objectives that are weakly held? It is well to keep in mind that "he who aims at nothing is sure to hit." It may be that because of our own inertia, irregularity, irresponsibility, lack of motivation, lack of determination, or shortage of some specific skill to put our job over that we ourselves are holding back the work of the Lord.

A church worker once complained to me about his lack of progress. I asked him what his trouble was. He said, "I haven't the faintest idea." Not only did he not know, but he wasn't interested enough or thoughtful enough to try to find out. How do you think God would feel about such weakness? Is that our situation? Do we regularly check up on ourselves? If we are failing do we know why and where? We ought to know. It is our business to know. The Lord expects us to know. He says, "It is required of the Lord at the hand of every steward to render an account of his stewardship both in time and in eternity." (D&C 72:3) We can't render a very accurate account if we don't know the facts.

We must be able to identify, isolate and overcome the enemies of the work of the Lord. We must also be aware of our strengths and how to increase them. Elbert Hubbard once said that "The secret of success is constancy of purpose." That infers a master plan and constant effort over a long period. Disraeli said about the same thing, that "genius is the power to make continuous effort." Someone else said that "success is the power to visualize the objective." How is that possible for one who has no objective?

4. A Written Plan

When one knows where he wants to go, what his resources are, and what will tend to hold him back, only then is he in a position to decide on strategy and set up a road map and a timetable for success. That is planning.

Exactly how are you going to use your resources to overcome the resources of the enemy to accomplish the objective? We must increase our ability. We can't grow in the work of the Church unless we grow as individuals. We must keep the score on ourselves. Everyone recognizes the folly of giving his son an assignment and then failing to check up. That failure is a dozen times worse if you do it with yourself. Can you clearly visualize the objective and at the same time keep your own statistics in constant view? This objective or image of success can be so strongly fixed in your mind that it will actually help to bring it about.

Never allow an exception to success to occur. Think of the importance of your work. It is inconceivable that you should allow yourself to fail God. Figure what you need to do to accomplish your objective. What is your plan for learning the program? What is your plan for getting your fellow officers and teachers to know the program? What is your program for getting the parents working for you instead of against you? How are you going to get the members of your organization organized and trained and motivated? How are you going to get everyone coordinated and following the program of the Church? How are you going to eliminate those weaknesses which caused you to fall down last year? What skills and attitudes and habits must be developed to bring about an accomplishment that would please God?

We must succeed in the work of the Lord. Failure is weakness. All success is comparatively simple once we have an objective and a plan backed up by sufficient determination and industry.

Preparation

ONE OF THE most beautiful, wonderful, useful, effective words in our language is the word "preparation." The habit of being prepared has brought more success, been responsible for more happiness, done more good, and saved more souls than any other single thing. The most productive workers, the most pleasant friends, the most useful citizens and the best church leaders are those who are always fully prepared. Almost all of life is made up of preparation. How well we prepare determines almost every success. We prepare for school; we prepare for marriage; we prepare for our life's work; we prepare for life itself; we prepare for death. "The future belongs to him who prepares for it." That not only applies to the future but to the present. It also applies to our eternal exaltation in the celestial kingdom.

Probably the word that brings about the most tragedy in our lives is the word "unprepared." The word "unprepared" is tragic because it implies that the failure was preventable. Try to picture the needless embarrassment and disappointment of the five foolish virgins with no oil in their lamps. Their foolishness was their neglect. Every day we see the tragedies of young men with untrained minds and unschooled spirits. The benefit is available, but they "receive not the gift."

Recently I attended an important church meeting to which a hundred leaders had been invited. To begin with, those who were in charge of the meeting were late in arriving. The room in which the meeting was to be held was in complete disorder, indicating that no advance interest had been taken. The chairs had not been arranged. The room had not been aired out. There were no flowers, song books or other evidences that the leaders had given any thought whatever to this important occasion. The meeting itself was not organized, and therefore largely failed in its purpose. But the leaders were in as great a disarray as the room.

Lack of preparation is significant for many reasons. It is usually the cause of failure, but it is even more important for what it is a sign of in people. It shows apathy and sloth in visible form and pictures the unwillingness of the people concerned to assume their proper responsibility. Jesus said, "Where there is no vision the people perish." And if we cannot even see the little things lying immediately before our eyes, how can we hope to see the great things lying off in the distant future?

When Jesus appeared upon this continent after his resurrection, the people were unprepared to receive him. For many years, prophets had told them of his coming to redeem the world. This would be the greatest event ever to take place upon this earth, and would happen but once in the entire history of the world. But when he came, they were not ready. They were even unprepared to learn. Jesus said to them, "I perceive that ye are weak and that ye cannot understand the words which I am commanded of the Father to speak unto you at this time. Therefore, go ye unto your homes and ponder the things which I have said, and ask of the Father, in my name, that ye may understand, and prepare your minds for the morrow and I will come unto you again." (3 Nephi 17:2-3)

It was not enough that Jesus had given his life for them, but now he must wait while they prepare their minds even to understand his message. People were unprepared in the days of Noah; they were unprepared in Jerusalem; they were unprepared upon the western continent. We are unprepared now. And we will still be unprepared when he comes again in glory in the clouds of heaven.

Preparation is the most important part of our lives. It is the most prominent teaching of the Lord. Jesus himself lived upon the earth only thirty-three years, thirty of which were spent in preparation. If you want that percentage figure, it is over 90 per cent. That is a good figure to start with. The scripture is filled with such admonition as: "Prepare ye the way of the Lord." "Prepare yourselves for that which is to come." "Prepare my people for that great day." "Prepare your hearts." The greatest need of our lives is for adequate preparation.

The dictionary says that preparation is "to set in order," "to make things ready," "to put together according to a plan or formula." That applies to our thought and minds and our lives. We need to practice it every day and in everyday things. We have an entire life in which to put our lives together according to a divine formula, and yet with a lifetime to prepare, many people are not ready when the time arrives. The vast majority of all of those who have lived or who will live upon the earth, will present themselves before God at the time of judgment, unprepared to enter the celestial kingdom.

Every one of us has the ability to be saved. What a wonderful improvement we can bring about in our lives if we just acquire the habit of being prepared, of always getting things thoroughly organized and arranged in advance.

Napoleon said that providence was on the side of the army with the strongest battalions. Napoleon knew the tremendous military advantage that came to those who were trained and organized and thoroughly prepared in advance. Certainly the Lord is on the side of those who are prepared, those who have trained themselves to be valiant, industrious and faithful. They are the ones who have their minds made up and their hearts determined. The Lord is on the side of those who have prepared themselves physically, mentally, emotionally and spiritually. The grand prizes in life go to those who are ready for them.

Walter Hagen, one of the greatest of all of the golf champions, was once asked about the secret of his success. He said that early in his career he discovered that he could not "outplay" his opponents in the tournament unless he "outworked" them during training. He won his many championships because he drilled hour after hour. He practiced every stroke until it was perfect. Then in the tournament, he was prepared.

Why shouldn't we follow that same course in our church work and in our lives generally? Certainly they are more important than a golf championship. Or what better way is there to develop leadership than by thorough preparation, constant study and intensive drill? If it was profitable for Walter Hagen to prepare thoroughly for a golf tournament, certainly it is profitable for us to prepare for the celestial kingdom and the work of the Lord.

Another great champion said that he owed more credit for his success to the habilt of "always being ready" than to all of his natural abilities combined. We think we would jump at the chance to improve our abilities; that is the purpose of preparation. Certainly preparation is our most wonderful opportunity. Yet how seldom we really take advantage of it. Think how infrequently we find a young man or woman who is really willing to prepare for his life's work. A little education is all most people want —a little smattering of books and they are ready for business. That is also generally true of those who work with human souls in "our Father's business." Mostly, we are unprepared.

One of the greatest of all the paradoxes is that almost everyone wants to improve his circumstances, but almost no one wants to improve himself. And yet our personal preparation is the key of all success; it is the key to happiness; it is the way we multiply our abilities; it is the way to please God. Only by effective preparation can we make full use of our God-given talents. If we lack for anything, it is not for ability, but for thoroughness in our preparation.

When we are not preparing to succeed we are automatically preparing to fail. When we stop getting better we stop being good. Someone once asked Admiral Farragut if he was prepared for defeat. He said, "I certainly am not. I am prepared for victory." When we are not preparing for victory we are automatically preparing for defeat. "Victory comes by design; defeat comes by default." The Lord wants you for important service in the Church. "Many are called but few are chosen, and why are they not chosen?" Because their minds have been set on other things and they are not prepared. If we are not prepared, why aren't we? And what are we going to do about it? There is not much time left. Abraham Lincoln said, "I'll prepare now and take my chances when the opportunity arrives." Lincoln began building his character when he was a child, and even then, he was hardly ready when the need came.

Just suppose the Lord should come today. How much oil do *we* have in *our* lamps? Will we be any better off in a year or ten years? Each of us is preparing for something. Is it failure or success? And in what degree? All of the principles of the gospel were given to prepare us for the celestial kingdom. No principle of the gospel was given to get us ready for the lower kingdoms. We qualify for the lower kingdoms by default. Those who will inherit the lower kingdoms are those who are not prepared for the higher.

It is something to think about, that the vast majority of the children of our Father in Heaven will go to one of

the lesser kingdoms where they had no intention or desire
to go, merely because they were not prepared for the better
place. Spiritual achievement does not depend primarily
upon the number of our brain cells or our heredity or our
environment, but rather upon our preparation.

Success in life is so tremendously important that no
one can afford to take hold of it with only the tips of his
fingers. We need to grasp it securely with both hands. We
are preparing for the highest possible career. We need to
think ahead and plan ahead so that we will be ready when
the time comes.

We might classify preparation under some of its
subheadings:

1. Physical Preparation

In any undertaking such as a church meeting, think
how much can be added by a thorough physical preparation. The surroundings can be made attractive, the meet-
inghouse itself can be made clean, tidy and orderly, the
chairs, song books, etc., can be properly placed. Flowers
and other evidences of thoughtfulness will uplift the spirit.
They will help to make every occasion a great occasion.
The Lord's house is a house of order, but not only should
his house be orderly, but our lives should be orderly.
Order, like other good things, comes by effort, and we
should expend whatever amount is necessary to bring
that order about.

2. Mental Preparation

Almost all of the satisfactions in life come from the
way we ourselves think. We have heard of a negative
mind; we have heard of a morose mind; we have heard of
a depraved mind; we have heard of a damned mind. All
are the result of a particular kind of preparation. If some-

day we would like to have a celestial mind, we must start preparing now.

I know a great Sunday School teacher who never goes before a Sunday School class without spending an average of eight hours in preparation. What a thrilling experience to be his student! There are others who spend very little time, and their accomplishment is usually in proportion. As teachers and speakers read and think and organize and pray, ideas can be made to take on new beauty, maturity and importance. It is not fair to take the time of people when one has little or nothing to give them.

3. Emotional Preparation

Everyone knows the importance of having his piano tuned before the concert. We see to it that the automobile engine is functioning harmoniously before the long journey is begun. It is also important to have the human spirit tuned and the mind harmonious. We can get the spirit of the gospel through preparation. We not only need positive, active minds, but we also need hearts and emotions to match. We need a rich spiritual and intellectual background for our emotions.

I know a bishop who goes to the church Sunday morning an hour before anyone else arrives. The beautiful grounds and the house of worship furnish an effective atmosphere for meditation, reflection and emotional conditioning.

Jesus told the people on this continent to go home and "Prepare your minds." We need minds that are peaceful and quiet and unconfused. If we are not prepared to understand, certainly we are not prepared to teach.

We also need to "prepare our hearts" and our feelings. Every occasion should be made a great occasion to give our spirits a background for accomplishment. We must be prepared in all ways The slogan of the Boy Scout organization says, "Be prepared." The Lord also says, "Be prepared." It is doubtful that two more important words could be found in all our language.

We ought to stamp these words into our minds and see to it that they are practiced every day of our lives. The Lord will probably be very pleased with what we do during the "tournament" if, like the champion golfer, we do our utmost during the "preparation." But we ought to make sure that when he comes again, or when we stand before the judgment, we are not like the unprepared Nephites or the foolish virgins and have to ask him to wait while we get prepared.

The Prodigal Who Stayed Home

O NE OF THE best-known teachings of Jesus is the parable
of the prodigal son. This parable has to do with a young
man who left his home and wasted his inheritance in riotous
living. When the substance had been used up, he found
himself unable to provide for his own needs. Then when
want began to make things uncomfortable, he left the "far
country" and made a beeline for home, the source of his
former supply.

The record does not tell us about the later life of this
young man. If he really learned his lesson and made a permanent change in what he thought and how he spent his
time, then it was little enough to kill the fatted calf in his
honor. However, we don't always change our habits of
thinking and living that quickly. The law of averages in
human nature suggests that some "returned prodigals"
would have taken the necessary time to restock their for-
tunes and would then have taken off again in some other
direction. And no matter how many times he strays away,
he expects that "a prodigal son welcome" will always be
handed out after every fresh dereliction.

But merely to get back home does not always solve
such a problem. The difficulty to begin with was not in the
"far country," but in the prodigal, and it was at home where
he had formed the inclinations that led him away in the
first place. We have a tendency to excuse our actions during
our periods of trouble or crisis. Yet the crisis does not cause
the trouble; it only reveals it.

For example, we tend to close our eyes to a man's un-
becoming actions when he is drunk. We feel that when he

is under the influence of liquor he is not really responsible. We say he is a fine person "when he is sober." But it was while he was sober that he committed his greatest wrong, for it was while he was sober that he decided to get drunk. His drunken behavior only calls attention to his weakness and paves the way for more questionable conduct to follow.

That is, sins, like everything else, have offspring. The prodigal seemed like a pretty good boy when he decided to leave home. The waste and the harlots and riotous living came like a chain, all linked up together, and they came later. One evil trait may give birth to a whole company of evil. Sins usually do not come singly, but in chains or clusters or family groups. Weaknesses and sins feed upon themselves. Failure today is the best prediction of failure tomorrow. It is a psychological principle that the mind tends to follow the track of a thought. Subsequent thoughts and activities walk in the footsteps of the one that breaks the trail. Each repetition makes the path of least resistance easier to follow.

The safest plan is not to let the "problem" get too much of a head start to begin with. The only sure way for us to keep out of trouble is to keep the trouble out of us. Changing our location doesn't usually do the job unless we change ourselves. Being away from home did not "make" the prodigal. It only showed him what he had become. Returning home would not necessarily change his prodigality unless he determined to change himself. We must recognize not only the evil consequences of sin, but we must recognize in ourselves those traits that breed the trouble. This is very difficult, for faults in ourselves have little resemblance in our eyes to the same faults as they appear in others.

Our big concern, of course, should be, what can we do about it? A physician learns medicine by comparing the diseased and healthy bodies of others. Everyone and everything teaches an alert physician. Even death itself makes its contribution. We can best learn to live successfully by a similar process of comparison.

The Lord went to great pains to provide us with opposites. All around us we can see good and evil side by side. The parables of Jesus are themselves comparisons. It is the contrast that makes the lesson easy. We more readily understand the comparative merits of the Levite and the good Samaritan when we see them together. It is the same with the wise and the foolish virgins. The experience of the prodigal son may serve as a looking glass to show us how to adjust and adorn our own lives. A thoughtful consideration of his experiences may be the inoculation that will produce an immunity in us and prevent us from contracting the disease which caused him so great a loss.

This parable may teach us many things. Each may get from it the particular ideas best suited for his personal requirements. There are parents into whose minds it will stamp a little deeper the loving and forgiving spirit of the prodigal's father. Other parents might give thought to the conditions in the home that produced the prodigality in the first place. The older brother teaches us something on both sides. His loyalty and industry are in sharp contrast to that of his younger brother. The older brother had served for many years and "never at any time transgressed the commandments of his father." That indicates great merit. However, there are some who would place demerits on his account because he apparently lacked something in charity and tolerance, though we can understand the feeling he might naturally have toward his brother whose attitudes were so radically different from his own. We may incorporate into our lives whatever qualities we wish, and leave out those traits that we feel would not become us.

But the prodigal himself is the central figure of the parable and merits our special consideration. Everyone has likenesses and differences when compared to the ideal. Upon a close examination we may find that we ourselves bear some rather striking resemblances to the unfortunate young man that we call the "prodigal son." The chief characteristic of the prodigal son was that he was a waster. That is the meaning of "prodigal." He wanted to do as he pleased. That is a common weakness. That inclination too much indulged is usually a symptom telling us that serious trouble is coming up.

If an ounce of prevention is worth a pound of cure, then it makes good sense for us to check our symptoms before the disease gets too far advanced. One of our most important guarantees of balance is to develop the ability to do "the right thing" instead of allowing ourselves endlessly to do as we please. The prodigal son "came to himself" only when he was brought to his knees by circumstances beyond his control. Very often we accept direction only when it is forced upon us. Think how wasteful and even resentful we sometimes are when advised against evil tendencies by parents, friends, leaders and even God. Think of how many wasteful experiences we could have avoided if we had been willing to take the proper counsel. Someone has said that as cheap as good advice is, we ought to use more of it. We often resemble in too many ways the prodigal son. He not only wasted his money; he also wasted his time and the time of the people; he wasted his educational opportunities; he wasted character, both his own and that of his rioting companions. He wasted the respect of those people who might have been his sincere friends. He wasted the abilities and the profitable employment that might have been his.

Some people can only learn by actual experience, but sometimes we don't profit very much even from our actual experience. Sometimes our success is unable to survive our experience. It is a very wasteful and destructive habit to insist always on having every experience personally, for as wonderful as repentance is, it is not a very good substitute for wise, original direction. It is pretty hard, for example, to repent of "wasted substance." William James once said that the Lord may forgive us our sins, but our brain cells and our nervous system never do. Those pathways through the mind are pretty difficult to hide from future thoughts going in that direction, and at a later date we may find ourselves making the trip again even though we thought we learned better after the first experience. In any event, the greatest beneficiary of an experience is not always the one who has it. To him, the lesson often comes too late or leaves him so badly weakened by the consequences that he has lost the power to take advantage of the lesson. The wisest doctors never insist on having all of the diseases personally. There are better ways of learning. We can learn certain lessons from the prodigal son and relieve ourselves of the necessity of having the experience ourselves. We can have his lesson without his loss; we may have his experience without the risk. We may have the advantage without paying the penalty.

The sin of prodigality has many destructive branches. We should not only avoid this particular experience which we see before us, but we should realize that everyone stumbles in a different place. It would require the lives of prodigals to make even our vicarious experience complete. We should not wait for someone to spell out every wasteful lesson for us. God has given us reasoning and a conscience and commandments to save us from our experience.

Waste, a by-product of vice, is a disorder in our lives from which we should save ourselves, as we should from the vices themselves. It is pretty difficult to eliminate the waste and retain the trait that causes it, just as it is pretty hard to save ourselves from the results of cancer while we nourish the disease. Surgery is a helpful part of medicine, but it is also a helpful part of religion—and a good time to operate is before the patient gets too sick.

The traits that cause us to waste our time do not stop there. Neither do all wasters go to a "far country." By far the largest number of prodigals never leave home. Prodigality of the particular intensity told of in the parable is like a high fever. The patient either dies or the fever burns itself out in a comparatively short time. The money that supported the fever of our friend was soon exhausted, and he was thereby largely deprived of his power to waste any more substance so long as his supply was not replenished. He is therefore forced to do something about it. This is not always true of the prodigals who stay home. Their wastefulness may not be so spectacular, and yet be more serious in the long run because it lasts longer. The prodigality that is like a high fever is one thing, but the prodigality that is like leprosy is something else.

But whether waste is at home or abroad, acute or chronic, it is one of the greatest of all sins. We waste time; we waste opportunities; we waste wealth; we waste health; we waste self-respect. We even waste eternal life. The laws of God say that we may have any blessing that we are willing to live for! God cannot give us more. He has put his greatest gift within our easy reach. But through the besetting sins of waste in the forms of idleness, ignorance, indecision, inertia, procrastination, lethargy, and sloth, we throw away the very blessings of the celestial kingdom, sometimes without even knowing they are gone.

Most of us, whether we regard ourselves as prodigals or not, waste enough hours in ten years to get a doctor's degree at any university. Carlyle said, "For one to die who might have been wise and was not, this I call tragedy." A lost hour is not just wasted time; it is wasted power, wasted character, wasted future happiness. Many of us are no wiser at thirty than we were at twenty; no more dependable at forty than at thirty; we generate no more ambition at fifty than we did at forty; and our godliness may be no greater at sixty than at fifty. The end of life, therefore, may find us no nearer the celestial kingdom than the beginning.

Thus man, the great masterpiece of creation, endowed with all of the attributes of God, ordained to have dominion over all the earth, fails to get control even of himself and his own destinies and thus wastes "our Father's substance." Like a sixteen-cylinder motor, we sometimes only have one cylinder firing while we waste fifteen. The great wastelands of the earth can only inadequately symbolize those greater wastelands of the human mind and spirit. The greatest waste there is in the world is not the devastation that goes with war, nor is it the cost that goes with crime, nor is it the erosion of our soil, nor the depletion of our natural resources. It is not even all of these put together. The greatest waste there is in the world is that human beings, you and I, the children of God, live so far below the level of our possibilities.

Life is very short at best. We have to crowd things into it. But we make life shorter still by waste. We have wasted a part of our opportunity when we fail to grow. We should not let next year find us with no more abilities than we had this year. Instead of having many years of experience, we sometimes have just one year's experience, repeated over and over. We need to plow new ground. We need to learn more, and do more, and be more.

The other day I rode for seven hours on an airplane carrying 67 passengers. Almost everyone spent those seven hours idly looking out of the airplane windows or listlessly thumbing through magazines. Socrates said, "He is idle who might be better employed." That statement has a particular significance to us who waste our time while men and women are losing their blessings.

Recently I attended what was to me a very stimulating religious meeting. But there were some who apparently were not stimulated. Some were dozing; very few were taking notes. The one who offered the benediction prayed, "Bless us with retentive memories." That is a prayer that will probably never be answered until we ourselves do something about it, including taking a little more interest, and possibly a few notes. The very best ideas may escape us or soon be forgotten. In either case they are wasted. It has been said that "the forgotten man is the man who forgets himself and his opportunities."

The prodigal son did as he pleased to his downfall. So do the idler, the disobedient, the ignorant and the lazy. One of Shakespeare's characters said, "I wasted time and now doth time waste me." That is the law.

Benjamin Franklin said:

If time be of all things most precious, wasting time must be the greatest prodigality. Since lost time is never found again, what we call "time enough" always proves "little enough." Let us then be up and doing to a purpose; so that by diligence we shall do more with less perplexity.

Producers and Consumers

THE PROFESSIONAL approach to accomplishment is first to determine the problem. Aristotle once said that "we never really know a thing until we know it by its causes." Every success has a cause; every failure has a cause. Indigestion has a cause; overweight has a cause. Spirituality has a cause. There are causes for enthusiasm and there are causes for dedication. If we can find the causes of success we can reproduce them. If we can find the causes of failure we can eliminate them.

The causes for most things, both good and bad, are usually right under our noses. They are often so close to us that we don't see them clearly. One of the causes for success that fits about any accomplishment is just good old-fashioned industry. It might be said about industry what James M. Barrie once said about charm: "If you have it nothing else matters much, and if you don't have it—well, nothing else matters much either."

Next only to my belief in God, I believe in industry. Industry and the resulting activities underlie all spiritual success, just as surely as they underlie all other success. James said that even "faith without works is dead." As important as faith is, and as powerful as it may become in our lives, it can't survive when separated from works. Isolate faith from its appropriate task and it always dies. There is no such thing as "preserved faith," apart from works. Nor is faith alone in this regard. Almost everything else also dies without works. We ought to give this important success factor the greatest priority in the development of our religion and its leadership.

We don't rate a man very highly in material affairs who is merely a consumer to be supported and cared for by someone else. Not only does deterioration immediately begin to take place in the presence of inactivity, but it is economically unsound for one group of people to support another group in idleness. Our economy is based on producers. Civilization itself is put in serious jeopardy when too many people insist that the world owes them a living.

It is exactly the same in our spiritual affairs. It is spiritually unsound for one group of the members of the Church to do the work of the Church while another group spends its time in inactivity. The people who believe that the world owes them a living have their counterpart in the Church. Apparently some feel that God owes them an eternal life. Such people must at last be doomed to disappointment, for the basic law of the Lord is "the law of the harvest," that "whatsoever a man soweth, that shall he also reap." It is not expected that this law will soon be changed; it is the basic law of time and of eternity.

I have a friend who has been very successful in teaching industry and enterprise to his sons. He helps to provide them with the means and the incentives of production. Then the "harvest" is up to them. When his boys were small he started each out with a calf or some chickens or a small plot of ground. They soon understood the law and were able to put it to good use. Each was an agent unto himself, limited only by the restrictions which he himself imposed. As each developed his ambition, ability and industry, the harvest was increased accordingly. Any deficits in the worker would be reflected in the crop. God is the author of this law, and it is applied to all impartially. It is not a bribe, nor a gift; it is a consequence and applies to the increase of our lands or to our eternal exaltation. God gives us the raw materials of intellect, opportunity and will. We may refine and develop and use them to suit ourselves. The benefits of the resulting harvest will be left in our hands.

We know that if we do not plant we will not be able to reap. Or if we plant thorns we will reap thorns. It is the same law which applies to this enterprise wherein each is permitted to work out his own salvation. No one else can work it out for us. No one can do our learning or our growing for us. No one can develop spirituality for someone else. Because some do not want to work, the Church is overflowing with people who, in a religious sense, are merely consumers. That is, instead of teaching, they are content in being taught. Instead of learning to pray, they are satisfied with being prayed for. Instead of blessing other people, their interest is only in receiving blessings. They insist on their right to receive inspiration. Yet they disregard their obligation to give inspiration. They want miracles and wonders but are not willing to perform their most simple duties. They merely want their prayers answered fully and on time.

Some time ago a group of people prayed for rain. One man remarked that if the Lord took as long in complying with their request as they had taken to comply with his, the rain would be far too late to do them any good. The opinion has been expressed that too many people think of God as a sort of cosmic bellboy whose responsibility is to respond when the button is pushed.

A little boy once explained that the reason he didn't say his prayers every night was because "there were some nights when he didn't want anything." Too many of us pattern our spiritual lives a little too literally after the lilies of the field. "We toil not, neither do we spin." Our appetites are too much the appetites of consumers, not enough the appetites of producers.

When the members of a Sunday School class were once asked to name the parables they liked the best, one little boy said that he liked the one about the man who loafs and fishes. We hope this is not an example of the truth that as the twig is bent so the tree will grow. However, this is a reflection of a very common inclination in the Church.

In our material affairs necessity pushes us from behind, but in our religious affairs where this pressure is absent, we consciously or subconsciously drift toward becoming mere consumers.

George Bernard Shaw had a pretty good idea when he said that we "have no more right to consume happiness without producing it than we do to consume wealth without producing it." This kind of reasoning is pretty well understood and accepted in economics, but it is not so well understood and not so generally accepted in our spiritual affairs. Most people of necessity go to their day's work on their own power, but too many of us in the Church have to be lured or coaxed or reminded to attend to the affairs of eternal life.

The Lord has told us to go to the house of prayer on the Sabbath Day and offer our oblations unto the Most High. But before we go, some of us first like to find out who the speaker is going to be and what the program is. Then we decide whether or not the service will be sufficiently rewarding for us to attend. Even then we often hear the remark, "I didn't get much out of the meeting." It does not frequently occur to us to ask ourselves how much we put into the meeting.

The spirituality of a mere consumer in the Church tends to become like Bruce Barton's story or the Dead Sea. The Dead Sea is "dead" because it merely receives; it gives nothing. The Dead Sea is one of the most brackish bodies of water in the world. No fishes swim in its waters; no vegetation borders its shores. Every day for itself and in its environment, it lives up to its name, the Dead Sea. It is a different story with the Sea of Galilee. The Sea of Galilee is a delightful fresh-water lake, because it gives as well as receives. Fish abound in its waters; singing birds skim over its surface; vegetation is nourished around its edges. The Sea of Galilee is a fine example for us to pattern our lives after.

Someone once complained that Christianity was just give, give, give. His friend said, "What a wonderful definition of the religion of Jesus." God is a producer. He "created" the heavens and the earth. He "created" the great miracle of human life. He "moved" upon the face of the waters. He has a program of activity, and he is its center. He wants us to be like him, to stand on our own feet and work our own way. "God helps those who help themselves." God loves producers.

It is the function of leadership that the Lord has authorized upon the earth to see to it that every member makes the maximum contribution of which he is capable, for that is the means by which the maximum development comes. Responsible leadership must hold itself accountable for every member under its direction. It is to ferret out the stowaways and to teach them the thrill of working their own passage. The greatest pleasures do not come from a free ride or from bread that is not earned. It is not a pleasant thing to be a one-way receiver of charity. Rather, the greatest leadership is that which develops the most extensive and constructive activity. It thereby confers the greatest benefits.

"He who gets ten men to work is greater than he that does the work of ten men." If one does the work of ten men he is merely a good worker, but if one can get that many into the proper activity, he is building men.

The Church, in one way, is like a giant gymnasium where we develop our spirituality by our own exercise. The young man who only sits in the gymnasium in a comfortable chair, looking at the equipment and watching the exercises of others, never develops very much, either in muscles or endurance. An ambitious father may do all of the prescribed exercises for his son, but as long as the son merely sits and watches, it is pretty difficult to help him. If the son doesn't want to be a weakling, he ought to get hold of the weights and pulleys himself.

It is not unusual for fathers who are "producers" to have sons who are non-producers. There are many well-meaning fathers who try to do the occupational as well as the spiritual exercises for their sons, while the boys themselves are content merely to watch the process. But as these non-producers sit on their cushions of advantage, they go to sleep and their powers decline. No matter what their observations may have been, those who take no exercise will probably come out of the gymnasium as weak and unprepared for the hard struggle of life as they were when they went in.

One father said that he had worked his way through college, and now he was working his son's way through. Too many people are trying to work someone else's passage to the celestial kingdom. Most such experiments must in the end have unsatisfactory results. It is like one giving his son $100,000 to start him out in life only to find that because of the gift, he never does start.

No leadership is maximum which gives the willing church worker three or four jobs and leaves others sitting on the sidelines in idleness. It is one of the primary responsibilities of leadership to discover and develop new talent continually. Overloading some only because we have not uncovered the abilities of others, injures those on both sides of the activity. To bring out the best in everyone, everyone must have his own work to do. You can't develop people by talking to them about their blessings. Spirituality is an experience that each must have for himself. It is

like a Thanksgiving dinner; hearing about it is not nearly
as satisfactory as a personal experience.

The gospel is not just a set of ideas; it is also a set of
feelings and activities. One of our biggest national worries
is unemployment. That is also the biggest of our spiritual
worries. The welfare program stipulates that so far as lies
within our power we ought to let no one stay unemployed
for even one week. Why then should religious leadership
allow large numbers of people to remain spiritually unemployed and religiously idle for many years at a time?
Everyone in the Church should be a producer. It is not
a sound principle for one group of people to support
another group in idleness.

Punctuality

A MONG the wonderful personality and character qualities
that all leaders should strive to develop, there are some that
set their possessors apart for special distinction. One of
these is that sure and steady quality of always being on
time. This perfectly wonderful habit called punctuality
can be a most valuable part of character. It is our guarantee
that we will always be in our proper place exactly when
we should be there. This quality is all the more important
because it is found in comparatively few people. For some
reason punctuality is not usually thought of by most people
as one of the major virtues. We think it doesn't matter
very much if we default a little in our appointments. What
difference does it make if we fall down in our punctuality?

But punctuality is very important. It is a quality that
is closely related to dependability and faithfulness and
determination. The late Cornelius Vanderbilt once said,
"Want of punctuality is an unpardonable sin." Another
great man said, "I could never think well of a man's intellectual or moral character if he was habitually unfaithful to
his appointments."

George Washington once made an appointment to
buy a span of horses at three o'clock. The would-be seller
showed up at 3:01. But General Washington was no longer
interested in the span of horses nor the man who was not
faithful to his word. The amount of time involved may
be great or small, but the difference is only one of degree;
the principle remains the same. Technically the appointment is cancelled if one of the parties defaults by being
late, but the inconvenience and discourtesy can never be

cancelled. President Washington had a habit of inviting
new members of Congress to dine with him. Occasionally
someone would arrive late and be mortified to find the
President eating. Washington once said, "My cook never
asks if the guests have arrived, but only if the hour has
arrived." Experienced senators who knew the President
never arrived late for any appointment with Washington.

When the secretary of George Washington tried to
excuse his lateness by saying that his watch was slow
Washington replied, "Then you must get a new watch or
I another secretary." Isn't it quite likely that God may
feel about that same way about us when we continuously
and habitually violate this first law of order which is
punctuality?

If it is bad form to be late for an appointment with
the President of the United States, it is bad form to be
late for an appointment with anyone else. But what about
the impropriety of being late for an appointment with the
Lord? The Lord is the greatest of all believers in punctuality. In fact he is the author of punctuality. He has a billion
planets whirling through space in different directions and
at different speeds, but each one is exactly on time. If one
planet were a half minute late there might be very serious
consequences. But God, who is the author of order, is in
the habit of having his creations in exactly the right places
at exactly the right time. Then how do you think he must
feel when his greatest masterpiece, created in his own
image, shows a high degree of irresponsibility and unde-
pendability in keeping his most simple appointments? It
is far safer to foretell the exact minute that a planet will
conclude a billion mile orbit than it is to tell whether or not
Brother Jones will be on time to his priesthood meeting.

Some time ago I attended a very important ward leadership meeting to which the bishop had invited all officers,
advisers and presidencies of the Aaronic Priesthood. A

number of people had been asked to make extensive preparation for the meeting. Most of the boys and leaders arrived five or ten minues before the scheduled hour. The appropriate thing, of course, would have been for the bishop to have been there ahead of everybody else, not only to make sure that everything was in readiness, but to be on hand to greet his workers and invited guests as they arrived. This would also have helped to establish the right spirit for this important occasion.

The meeting had been called for eight a.m. The very latest the bishop should have arrived was fifteen minutes early, but he was not fifteen minutes early—neither was he one minute early. Eight-fifteen came and still no bishop. Everyone was kept waiting, and no one likes to be kept waiting. The stake committee had been asked to conduct a program of leadership training, and of course they were disturbed, knowing that because of lack of time their well-planned program would now have to be discarded or so severely shortened that it would largely lose its effectiveness.

At 8:20 the bishop arrived. Every one was in his place. But the bishop took the time to go around the room and shake hands with everybody and inquire about their families, etc., apparently not even aware of the confusion he had caused and was causing. Because he had made no preparation for the meeting it was then necessary to get song books, a song leader, etc., which took a few minutes more. At about 8:30 he was ready to begin. He made no apologies or excuses, as though he was not aware of any offense.

To waste thirty minutes of one person's time is very bad taste, but to waste thirty minutes for each of many people multiplies the offense. But in addition it throws the program out of gear and means that its full purpose will not be accomplished. Who has the right to do this, especially when the goals to be accomplished have to do with the work of the Lord?

After the opening song the bishop asked a deacon's quorum president to lead in prayer. This young twelve-year-old leader asked God to bless the bishop and help him to do his work well. What a wonderful prayer this would have been if the Lord could have answered it. But how can God help one who is not willing to do some of the most simple and obvious things for himself? God can forgive us our sins, but who can forgive us our confusion or our disregard of the trust imposed in us? Or who can forgive us our lack of punctuality, or our lack of interest, or the bad example we set for others? It is impossible to isolate ourselves and say that the evil we sponsor shall not spread to others. Men's lives are as thoroughly blended with each other as is the air they breath. The evil of bad example and a bad attitude sometimes spreads as rapidly as disease.

Punctuality is not only important for itself alone, but it is also important for what it is a sign of. Lack of punctuality shows lack of consideration for others. It shows a lack of responsibility. It often indicates a lack of interest in the work of the Lord. This bad habit is often responsible for loss of the spirit of the work and the spirit of accomplishment. There also follows in the wake of lack of punctuality a long train of other evils as "no sin comes single." The single fault of being unpunctual is closely connected with unpreparedness, disinterest, lethargy, sloth and the rest of the family of failure. This one fault, with its family connections, is often sufficient to destroy success.

Unpunctual people sometimes have a good excuse. But Benjamin Franklin once said, "I have generally found that a man who is good at excuses is usually good at nothing else."

One of our greatest and most important problems is found in this fault of tardiness. It reaches out in many directions. I know of a young man who was not baptized until he was eleven; he was two years late being ordained a deacon; he did not receive the Melchizedek Priesthood in time to get married as he should. All of his children were born and one had died before he finally got around to going to the temple. He always had the very best of intentions, but the good was not accomplished because he was always behind schedule. He was usually late for school; he was never prepared for the examination when it came. In all probability he will not be ready when the call comes for him to go and stand before God.

There is a saying that some people have three hands: a right hand, a left hand and a little behind hand. These people are usually behind in their responsibilities and unpunctual in all of their other duties. They are behind in their faith and behind in their works. The trait of being unpunctual is a very bad habit, amounting sometimes to a serious personality perversion, and it always leaves behind it a trail of confusion and failure.

This trait was given a very prominent place in the attention and teachings of Jesus. One of his most instructive parables describes some foolish virgins. They were the ones who did not have their lamps trimmed and burning on time; consequently by the time they got to the marriage feast the doors were locked and they were not admitted. There probably wasn't anything wrong with these particular women, except that they were just plain tardy. Five virgins were on time and five were late—that is still about the going ratio. That is also the reason why a lot of other people miss their opportunities and objectives, for by the time they get there the door of opportunity has been closed.

Often we are like one of Lincoln's generals who was always getting ready but was never quite able to do anything in its proper time. Lincoln said, "He will be ready to fight a magnificent battle when there is no enemy to fight." And that is often the pattern we follow in working out our salvation. We very often proceed as though we had forever to get ready. But opportunity and responsibility sometimes come "like a thief in the night," and too many times find us in the foolish virgins' category.

"We can't postpone a crisis while we prepare for it." "Hell is truth seen too late." When we go to stand before God in the judgment there will not be one person *then* who will have any question as to what he ought to have done. But the judgment is not the place to go and say, "I am sorry. I will do better next time." If we are not ready then, the door of the celestial kingdom will be closed against us. Then it will be forever too late. Then "the summer will be past, the harvest will be ended and our souls not saved." "Too little and too late" will be the sad story of exaltation forever lost for many of God's children.

What a tragedy to see people who are always just about ready to do something, but continuously failing because they were not on time. Experience that comes too late or decisions made after the crisis has passed are never worth very much. Procrastination, indecision, lethargy, lack of standards, lack of deadlines, develop in us this ugly and wasteful habit of unpunctuality.

Solomon said there is a time to be born and a time to die. And there is a time for everything in between. There is a time to do ward teaching, a time to do our planning, pay our tithing and improve our abilities. Think how wonderful it is to do business with someone who always pays his bills on time without being coaxed, reminded, begged or threatened. Probably the Lord feels the same way in his dealings with us. Every one of us has 24 hours in each day. And one of the most important things we need to learn in life is to do things properly, and on time.

We should add to our list of personality traits to be developed this bright and shining virtue called *punctuality*. Lord Nelson said, "I have always been a quarter of an hour before my time, and it has made a man of me." Another famous general said, "To this quality of punctuality I owe my extraordinarily rapid promotions in the army." He said, "If I had to mount guard at ten I was always ready at nine, and never did any man wait one minute for me."

What an accomplishment it would be if we could live all our lives on that basis, especially as it applies to the work of the Lord. The Lord doesn't have to wait for the planets or the seasons or day and night. The birds fly south at the right time; the squirrel isn't always in trouble because he didn't think to get his nuts stored up on time. Why shouldn't we train ourselves to be as effective and dependable as a squirrel? Then the Lord would never have to wait on us to get our ward teaching done or our reports in or our bills paid. The Lord must get a little weary when required to wait almost an entire lifetime for one of his children to get around to giving up some bad habit or to become the kind of person that God can give his blessings to *now*. We should not keep God waiting month after month and year after year until we are frightened into some pitiful form of last minute, deathbed repentance.

Time is the substance of which our lives are made. To waste our own time is an indulgence we cannot afford. But to waste the time of others is a sin to which we have no right. It is also a discourtesy to God which we should avoid. Certainly it must make him feel very happy when we get to our meetings fifteen minutes early and have all of our greetings taken care of and are ready to begin "his business" at the appointed time. Some people excuse themselves in being late because they know others will be

late and the meeting will not start on time. That is no
excuse, and it only helps to build this ugly habit.

Punctuality is the father of many wonderful traits
and abilities. It is one of the greatest of all the virtues. It
is also one of the least expensive to develop. Why not
acquire *now* that sure and steady quality of always being
where we should be, and always being there on time? To
do our duty when it should be done is one of the cardinal
virtues of leadership.

The Razor's Edge

A FEW YEARS ago Daryl F. Zanuck made a four million dollar movie out of W. Somerset Maugham's book, *The Razor's Edge*. The point of the book has to do with the idea that the line that separates failure from success is as fine as a razor's edge.

One of the best illustrations of this truth was demonstrated in the filming of the picture itself. There were eight principal actors and eight stand-ins. That is, each principal had a substitute to do the hard, grueling, tiresome work. After the film was finished *Life* magazine published the pictures of the eight principals on one page and the eight stand-ins on the opposite page. The stand-in for Tyrone Power, for example, was Thomas Noonan, a close associate. They had gone to high school together. They were about the same size, equally intelligent; they were dressed about the same and were very similar in appearance. As close a similarity as possible existed between each principal and his stand-in. But in one way they were not similar. The combined salaries received by the eight principals for filming this picture amounted to $480,000, and the combined salaries for the eight stand-ins amounted to $6,534. The principals were just a little bit better, but they received seventy-five times as much compensation.

We see this principle illustrated all around us every day. In sports, for example, to be just a small fraction better may make one a champion. For example, in the big leagues, a .350 batter may receive $3,000 a month. A .250 batter may get $300 a month. The champion gets on first base three and a half times in ten tries; the .250 batter gets on first base two and a half times in ten tries. The champion is successful just once more often in ten tries. The second man may actually be the better hitter, but can't run quite so fast. That is, there are enough photo finishes at first base to indicate that the better man may be only one-half step faster once in ten tries. The margin of difference is as small as "a razor's edge," and yet what a tremendous difference it makes in the result.

Exactly this same principle is continually operating in all success, including church work and life generally. We frequently see two men with abilities so nearly equal that we cannot tell the difference, yet one becomes a star and the other becomes a stand-in. One is just a little more thougthful, a little more constant, a little more punctual, a little more loyal, a little more faithful, a little more industrious. He spends a few minutes more time in lesson preparation, and a little more time on his planning. But what a tremendous difference in the consequences!

Someone has pointed out the magic that can be found in a mere 10 per cent. An ordinary man stands 72 inches high. Subtract 10 per cent and you have a little man five feet five inches tall, but if you add 10 per cent you have a giant. Comparable changes take place when you subtract or add 10 per cent to your diligence or your perseverance or your enthusiasm. It makes the difference between a peewee and a giant. As a result of this principle, we discover one of the greatest secrets of leadership success. The outstanding leader is the one who does his best and then adds 10 per cent. He is the one who aims 10 per cent higher and works 10 per cent harder and stays at it 10 per cent longer.

On the walls of the Library of Congress is written, "He aims too low who aims beneath the stars." If this is true of ordinary success, what would we say of a low aim when the celestial kingdom is at stake for many people?

The slightest success then becomes tremendously important. Think what would happen if each of us raised his objective 10 per cent or 20 per cent. Think what the result would be in eternity.

> It doesn't take a man of giant mold
> To cast a giant shadow on the wall;
> But he who in our daily sight
> Seems but a figure mean and small,
> Outlined in fame's illusive light
> May cast a silhouette sublime
> Across the canvas of our time.

Suppose we just miss the celestial kingdom by the margin of a razor's edge. That may not be much difference, but how important that difference may be throughout eternity. We all achieve about what we aim for; therefore we have the statement that "not failure but low aim is crime."

On October 6, 1955, a United Airlines plane crashed into the top of Medicine Bow Mountain in Wyoming, and sixty-five people lost their lives. The pilot was flying at 12,000 feet. If he had been flying at 12,055 feet the greatest air disaster in American history to that date could have been averted, and the lives of sixty-five people would have been saved. What a difference a few more feet in altitude would have made to these people and their families.

It is the same with our success. Often we fly just high enough to miss the treetops. We try to do just enough to get by, and that is about all most of us ever do get, whereas just a little more effort, a little more determination would put us in the big leagues of success in our leadership.

The Duke of Wellington once said to some French soldiers that British soldiers were not braver than French soldiers; they were only brave for five minutes longer. And Jim Corbett, the former heavyweight champion prize fighter of the world, said that the secret of success in the prize ring was the ability to stay one more round.

One of the greatest lessons of success taught by the Master was to go the extra mile, to do the little more, to do it with a little more faith, a little more energy, a little more go-at-it-iveness and a little more stick-to-it-iveness, a little more devotion, and behold you have changed yourself from a stand-in to a star. The results are tremendous, though the difference may be as fine as the razor's edge.

A Religion of Action

Sɪʀ Wɪʟғᴏʀᴅ Gʀᴇɴғᴇʟʟ once made an appeal for "a religion of action, not diction." This is a common need. There is a great tendency among us to become what someone has called "Bible Christians." That is where the religion is mostly in the Bible and not very much in us. What we need is some new kind of Urim and Thummim to help us translate our creed into deed, our information into know-how, our faith into works. We need to know how to get the religion out of the Bible and accomplishment out of the handbooks and into us.

For one who studies, it is not at all difficult to *understand* the principles of the gospel. But our big problem is that of *translation* and *application*. Our works seem to lag too far behind our words. We need the ability to live the gospel as well as we understand it. We need to learn to work as well as we pray. We need to develop the power to get our church work done as well as to talk about it.

The work of the Lord does not consist in merely giving out information; it is rather to arouse desire and produce activity. The purpose of the gospel is not only to discuss repentance but to bring about a reformation of life; not just to teach the meaning of faith, but to produce faith in the lives of people. Those bearing the priesthood are not expected merely to understand the available power of God, but to manifest that power in their lives by doing the Lord's will and the Lord's work effectively. It may be that we spend too large a portion of our time merely discussing religion and too little time in actual performance. It is our responsibility actually to develop in people's lives the attitudes and activities that will get them into the celestial kingdom.

Sermons should be concerned not only with subjects to be explained, but with a way of life to be lived. It is so easy to preach about moral courage without making anyone morally courageous. It is easy to deliver a discourse on faith without creating faith in people's lives. We may teach that man has the power to decide his own eternal destiny without getting anyone then and there to make that momentous decision.

Socrates, the ancient Grecian philosopher, is remembered not because he claimed to be a great teacher; he merely tried to get people to *do* those things which they already knew. The discord between deed and creed is responsible for innumerable wrongs in our civilization. It gives both institutions and men split personalities. It is estimated that there are 999 men who *believe* in honesty for every honest man. Therefore, instead of merely teaching honesty, Socrates tried to get men to *be* honest. How is it possible for one to say that he believes honesty who is not honest? Or how can anyone believe in religion if he fails to manifest it in his life? Only those who are valiant will inherit the celestial kingdom. That means "a religion of action."

The practical aspects of this situation have been pointed out by one who said that it may not be important whether or not a man has been through college, provided the college has been through the man. Similarly, to get a man into the Church has many benefits, but to get the Church into the man is our ultimate aim. This can best be done by the appropriate activity.

Some people ask God to direct their footsteps, and then they fail to move their feet. What good does it do to ask God to direct our efforts if we then turn off our engines? How much is accomplished when we sustain the President

of the Church with our uplifted hands, if we fail to sustain
him with our industry and our courage?

History records many periods of "apostasy from the
faith." But we should not overlook those tendencies to
personal, individual apostasies of works or apostasies of
effort. We sometimes have periods of apostasy from works
at the very time we are trying to cling to our faith. But
when we have a period of inactivity the spirit of accomplishment tends to become limp and apathetic. Then, like
the beat of a weak heart, our religion gets so faint that its
pulse can hardly be counted.

Think of the activity the Lord has provided for us.
Every boy has the opportunity to hold the priesthood and
function therein at age twelve. Beginning with the deacons,
each quorum has its own officers and conducts its own
activities on a scale of its own choice. The Lord has given
to each group a certain part of the work of the Church.
A deacon has his own responsibilities. When he is ordained
a teacher his field of service is enlarged. He is then entitled
to be a ward teacher, "to watch over the Church," "to
strengthen the members," "to see that there is no iniquity
in the Church." When he becomes a priest his duties are
again increased. He may now baptize for the remission
of sins in the name of the Lord. He may administer to the
sacrament and accept a larger field for preaching the gospel. As he grows in faith other opportunities are given to
him. Every worthy man and boy above age twelve may
bear the priesthood and share in a divine ministry of activity. Think of our advantage as compared with some other
groups where no one has any divine authority, and only
one or two people have most of the activity.

We need to stir up our enthusiasm and make sure that
we are "doers of the word" in its fullest sense. We need
to do more than merely *believe* in that light "that lighteth
every man that cometh into the world." We need to get

it actually started in someone and keep it going until their lives are made luminous.

We should have a religion of action, but we should also be men of action. Alexander the Great said, "What Aristotle is in the world of thought I will be in the world of action," and that formula made him the conqueror of the world by the time he was 26 years of age, and it will make us anything we wish to be, including a conqueror of our own weakness and winners of the celestial kingdom.

A violinist of great distinction once acquired a valuable Stradivarius, but this violin had been in the private collection of a wealthy family and for many years had lain unused on a velvet pad. The violinist said, "The violin is asleep, and I must play it until I wake it up and bring it to its proper form. It will have to learn its own power and beauty all over again."

Disuse is harmful to a violin; it is also harmful to a child of God. We should wake ourselves up by use. We can only get full possession of our potentiality by proper activity.

Jesus said, "If ye know these things, happy are ye if ye do them." To know things is wonderful, but to do things is the real test. Happy are ye if ye do them. Inactivity is wrong, "for to him who knoweth to do good and doeth it not, to him it is sin." This sin of disuse may cause many to lose their exaltation. Few will lose their blessings because they cannot know. Many will lose their blessings because they will not do.

Even testimony and faith come from works. For Jesus said, "If ye shall do my will, ye shall know of the doctrine." And if we don't give the gospel message to others, we risk losing it ourselves, for great faith, like great fortune, never lingers in the hands with idle fingers. When works dwindle faith dries up, accomplishment withers and blessings are lost. People soon begin to suffer from feelings of frustration and inferiority when they bury their talents in the ground. Such feelings rob us of our strength. They sap our energy and diminish our spiritual values.

How pathetic it is that anyone should needlessly tolerate this destructive, devastating inactivity which leads us even to doubt ourselves. To disbelieve in God is tragic, but to have this destructive disbelief in ourselves may be even worse. The moving cause of all action is faith—not only faith in God but faith in ourselves, neither of which is possible in the absence of works, and both of which must be earned in advance. We get belief by action and disbelief by inaction. When self-doubt and self-distrust get lodged in our minds, they discolor every thought and every activity with a feeling of inadequacy and hopelessness. We sometimes use our minds as dumping grounds for doubts, fears, worries, sins and complexes, causing destructive mental attitudes and failure. Many of the greatest sins begin as sins of inaction.

Everyone in a sense must be his own priest. Everyone must purify his own life. Every man must do his own growing. Everyone must create his own desire to serve. Everyone must be responsible for making the most of every opportunity. The great recipe for success is to make our religion "a religion of action, not diction."

The Second Great Commandment in Action

THE GREATEST NEED in human nature is the need for God. The second greatest need is the need to be appreciated and loved and helped by our kind. Therefore, the first and great commandment naturally concerns our relationship with God, while the second greatest commandment was given to fulfill our need for each other. The Lord said, "And thou shalt love thy neighbour as thyself."

That is tremendously important. It implies an active interest, a mutual understanding, and a devoted service, not merely in giving mental assent, but in actual daily practice. This is a pretty big order and needs a lot of our attention.

Jesus indicated the importance of the second great commandment and gave second place to it in his teachings. The parables of the Good Samaritan, the prodigal son, the laborers in the vineyard, the sower, the lost sheep, and many others have to do with this commandment and cover this vast field of human relationships.

It is not only second in its importance and in our need, but it also stands second in the pleasure it gives us. Many of our greatest satisfactions come from people. We would not like to be isolated from our kind. The sense of being alone or of not being wanted is one of the most devastating of all human emotions. The "second death" is banishment from God. Next in severity would be banishment from our kind. People who love each other find great pleasure in each other's companionship. A mother does not like to be separated from her children. Lovers like to be together. Those happily married over a long period of years sometimes come to look like each other. The Lord has said that "it is not good that man should be alone." Therefore families are bound together for time and eternity. There is also great pleasure to be had from our membership in the larger family of God. Paul says, "The love of Christ passeth knowledge." (Eph. 3:19) And the Lord has said to us, "A new commandment I give unto you, that ye love one another as I have loved you, and by this shall men know ye are my disciples." (John 13:34-35)

It is a comparatively simple thing to understand what these words mean, but it is not so simple to translate them into action and actually practice this fundamental Christian law of love and service. From the very beginning we have had a tendency to separate our works from our faith, our profession from our practice. It is so easy just to give mental consent and then feel that we have discharged our full responsibility.

In the Epistle of James reference is made to what someone called "verbal Christianity." Some well-meaning followers of the Master said, "Depart in peace; be ye warmed and filled," and let it go at that. This was one of the things that the Lord objected to so strenuously about the sectarians of our own day. They practiced drawing near to him with their lips; but their hearts were elsewhere. (See Pearl of Great Price, Joseph Smith 2:19)

But we should check occasionally to see how free we are from this offense. It is so easy to give lip service to our responsibility, to pray for people and then forget them; whereas the effective follower of Christ is the one who initiates action and actually gets the job done. The real Christian is the doer of the word, not the hearer only.

I KNELT TO PRAY

I knelt to pray as day began
And prayed, "O God, bless every man.
Lift from each weary heart some pain
And let the sick be well again."

And then I rose to meet the day
And thoughtlessly went on my way;
I didn't try to dry a tear
Or take the time a grief to hear.

I took no steps to ease the load
Of hard-pressed travelers on the road;
I didn't even go to see
The sick friend who lives next door to me.

But then again when day was done
I prayed, "O God, bless everyone."
But as I prayed a voice rang clear
Instructing me to think and hear.

"Consult your own heart ere you pray:
What good have you performed today?
God's choicest blessings are bestowed
On those who help him bear the load."

And then I hid my face and cried,
"Forgive me, Lord, for I have lied.
Let me but live another day
And I will live it as I pray."

Many of our most serious problems in the Church and in the world could be solved immediately if we could really learn to be "doers" by putting into actual practice this second great commandment.

This may be the area where we commit some of our most serious violations of the will of the Lord. Many people are inactive in the Church, not because they disbelieve in the doctrine of the Church. Many are inactive, consciously or unconsciously, because of some real or imagined offense or because they have felt they were not appreciated or wanted. That is, it concerns some real or imagined transgression of the second great commandment.

A green army recruit heard the general say that there were 13,347,289 soldiers in the service. The rookie held up his hand and asked, "Does that include me?" But that is what everyone wants to know. We all want to know that we are included. Any undertaking acquires a new importance when we know that it includes us. Look at any group photograph and see whose picture you seek first.

How wonderful it would be if we could always take that much interest in our neighbor, especially the one who is in danger of losing his blessings by inactivity in spiritual things. We can improve church attendance by being more friendly ourselves. We usually don't go places where we are not invited or where we feel strange or unwanted, whereas nothing could keep us away if we really felt needed and wanted.

The next time you go to Church and have a wonderful time, try to determine what it was that made the occasion so pleasant. It may be because of something that the speaker said, or because you enjoyed the music or felt unlifted by your own feeling of devotion and worship. But quite likely it will also be because some wonderful friends gave you the pleasant feeling of worthwhileness. But there are people who don't feel warmth and friendliness when they go to Church, and so they stay away. It may be partly their own fault, but that does not change the result.

People will not even patronize a business establishment if they are not treated cordially. A warm, friendly atmosphere and an interested and interesting personality to serve you are the most wonderful business-getters ever discovered.

> The reason people pass one door
> To patronize another store
> Is not because the second place
> Has finer silks or gloves or lace
> Or cheaper prices — But it lies
> In friendly words and smiling eyes.
> The great big difference, we believe,
> Is in the treatment folks receive.
> —EDGAR A. GUEST

Jesus has also placed this friendly interest in our fellow men second in importance only to our relationship to God himself. It is our responsibility to help put this quality of love and friendliness in force in our own lives and in the lives of others. That is, we need more "practice" in this second great commandment, not only in our hearts and in our minds, but in our actual conduct. People need more understandable evidence of our interest and desire to be helpful.

We may think that people should go to Church because they love God, but people can usually be brought to God more quickly through our love and example. We must furnish the initiative.

One of the most detrimental influences in human personality and progress is inertia, that quality which the dictionary describes as the tendency "to remain at rest." We tend just to stay put. We don't even vote at election time unless someone stirs us up a little bit. We also need someone to encourage us to do most of the other worthwhile things in life, including bringing about our own eternal salvation. Certainly we need help and encouragement in the second great commandment, for if someone doesn't intervene in our behalf, we may lose our blessings.

The greatest power in the world to bring about the good of people is the power of love. A sincere interest and a friendly desire to serve our kind can overcome any obstacle. Napoleon said that providence was on the side of the army with the strongest regiments, but in the work of human relations and the work of the Church, success goes to those who have the strongest love in their hearts and are the most industrious to make that love felt. If we really loved our fellow men as we love ourselves, many millions more of our Father's children would get into the celestial kingdom.

We know the tremendous importance of church activity, including a study of doctrine, getting the right spirit, thinking the right thoughts, living the right lives. And one of the best ways of guaranteeing the blessings of the Lord to our fellow men is to put the second great commandment into action. Here are some things we might do:

1. Give the people with whom we work a personal, friendly invitation to church activity, extended in such a way that they cannot help feeling our interest. No general announcement, written or spoken, can satisfy this need for personal recognition. There is absolutely no substitute for the human personality in effective expression. Even the process of extending the invitation can be made a thrilling experience in satisfying this fundamental human need.

2. This invitation to activity should be extended frequently. Very seldom can a great good be accomplished in one exposure. A teacher meets his students many times. Everything, including love and enthusiasm for the gospel, is born small, and growth is a gradual process.

3. When those invited accept our invitation to activity and church attendance, we should be prepared to give them something really worthwhile, including the feeling of belonging. If you invited someone to your home and then slighted or ignored him, you would probably have

great difficulty getting him to return. But some who have been invited to church activity have not felt that they have been cordially treated. We have sometimes promised them bread but given them a stone.

Emerson once said, "There is a great deal more kindness than is ever spoken. The whole human family is bathed in an element of love like a fine ether. How many people we meet whom we scarcely speak to, whom yet we honor and who honor us. How many people we meet in the street or sit with in church whom, though silently, we warmly rejoice to be with." This expression must not be too silent. Inactive members are usually not mind readers.

Missionaries never make many converts by keeping their message a secret, and we will probably never develop great ability in this second great commandment by burying our talents or our friendliness in the ground. We should first recognize the need and then see what we can do about it. A detailed list of ways and means may help us.

One of our principle objectives in the work of the Lord is to make others happy. Sidney Smith said that "to love and be loved is the greatest happiness of existence." People should be happy in the work of the Lord. They should be happy in the worship of the Lord. There are two kinds of love, that which goes up to God and that which goes out to man. "Love," like Shakespeare's "mercy," "blesseth him that gives and him that takes," and is one of the greatest powers for good in our lives.

In Henry Van Dyke's story, *The Other Wise Man*, he said—

> He who seeks heaven alone to save his soul
> May keep the path, but will not reach the goal;
> But he who walks in love may wander far,
> God will bring him where the blessed are.

Seven Success Ideas

THE GREAT SCRIPTURES serve us in many ways. They are very important because of the doctrine and inspiration they contain, but they also serve us as a kind of "how book" for our actual success. That is, they help us to function more effectively in our various assignments and responsibilities. The scriptures tell us many things to do, but they also teach us how to do them more effectively. Success in church affairs, like all other success, is made up of several things, including knowledge, attitudes, skills, habits and personality traits. We can develop these more quickly and profitably when we have proper direction in procedure.

When we really focus our attention upon significant ideas they tend to come to life and exert influence upon our accomplishment which they did not previously possess. This phenomenon of power prompted the question, "By what strange law of the mind is it that an idea long overlooked and trodden upon as a useless stone, suddenly sparkles out in new light and becomes a brilliant diamond?"

The fourth section of the *Doctrine and Covenants* is one of these significant success formulas written by the Lord to bring about our accomplishment. Our problem is like that of a good contractor. If we can carefully follow the blueprint the final objective will be accomplished. Section four is made up of seven sentences, totalling one hundred forty-six words. It takes approximately forty-five seconds to read. But it contains a power all out of proportion to its length.

Suppose we take each of these seven sentences one at a time and see what we can get from them to increase the effectiveness of our church performance.

The first sentence says—

1. Now behold, a marvelous work is about to come forth
among the children of men.

There is a danger that this first sentence may seem a
little too commonplace and therefore escape our notice.
We have become so intimately familiar with the fact of the
gospel's restoration that we may miss its importance. But
in this first great sentence is found the very foundation
of all success.

The first principle of the gospel is faith, but the foundation of *all* success is faith. One must be a convert before
any real accomplishment is possible. Do we really understand the significance of the fact that the gospel is again
upon the earth with the authority to minister in all of the
ordinances having to do with the celestial kingdom? When
this fact is firmly established in our minds and hearts then
all accomplishment becomes easy.

Not only should we feel and understand the tremendous importance of the *work,* but we should also feel and
understand the tremendous importance of the *worker.*
Sometimes people are unable to distinguish between the
two, and they judge the importance of the work by the
quality of the lives of those who carry it forward.

There is another significant implication in the above
sentence, to the effect that we may have as great a part in
this marvelous work as we choose. We may have any
blessing that we are willing to live for. But many of us
fail to reach our maximum possibilities simply because we
do not comprehend the overwhelming importance of this
"marvelous work." This is the greatest and last of all the
gospel dispensations. The other dispensations have been
wiped out by apostasy. But we have been reserved to be
a part of the dispensation of the fullness of times, the dispensation that shall prepare the way before the glorious

second coming of the Lord. What can you think of in the world that is more thrilling than this single idea? How vigorous we should be in performing our part of this "marvelous work" with corresponding skill and devotion.

The second sentence says—

2. Therefore, oh ye that embark in the service of God, see that ye serve him with all your heart, might, mind and strength, that ye may stand blameless before God at the last day.

When we embark in such an important undertaking as the very work of God both our Heavenly Father and we ourselves ought to be assured of our whole-souled effort. We ought to make up our minds once and for all that our service will be enthusiastic, vigorous, continuous and of high quality. Success is not made up of fractional devotion or minimum performance. Success does not come easily to one who is disabled by every little discouragement, nor does it come to one who has a large degree of personal irresponsibility.

Like the first sentence, this one also contains one of the great keys of success in any undertaking. This is the ability to coordinate all of our powers into one cooperative effort. This involves a joint action of the heart, the mind, the might and the physical strength. To serve him with all our hearts means that our love and devotion should be genuine and wholehearted. To serve him with all our might is to employ to the utmost our determination and will power. It does not mean to walk the irregular pathway of vacillation and procrastination. To serve him with all our mind requires a strong, positive mental attitude. It means study, meditation and firm, positive decisions on each of the questions involved. To serve him with all of our strength requires vigorous, persistent, continuous physical activity.

By this process of consolidation and joint action one

may concentrate all of the elements of personal effectiveness into one united, powerful effort. We thereby achieve a centrality in our purpose. Our effort becomes not only highly concentrated but accurately directed. Psychologically speaking, a person whose life is characterized by this united effort is all in one piece, rather than a bundle of many-directioned and conflicting impulses held loosely together by circumstances. Such a consolidated personality is capable of a maximum of efficiency and accomplishment.

3. Therefore, if ye have desires to serve God, ye are called to the work.

A greater success principle than this can hardly be imagined. A consuming desire is the greatest qualification for any success. If our desire is strong enough accomplishment is assured. But if you don't want to do it, you can't do it. A physician judges physical health by the appetite. God judges our devotion by the desire to serve and has made that the outstanding qualification. It is easy to lose our appetite for the things of God if we lack desire. What a great thrill it should give us to hear these qualifying words, "If ye have desires to serve God ye are called to the work." That is not only our opportunity; it is also the big test that each of us must pass. We should learn to hunger and thirst after righteousness. Our greatest need is to learn to want to serve God. We must desire with greater intensity. Desire is the father of initiative, resourcefulness, ambition and all of the other virtues. Desire is the quality that makes us want to "do many things of our own free will." All other powers are inferior to desire.

4. For behold the field is white already to harvest, and he that thrusteth in his sickle with his might, the same layeth up in store that he perisheth not, but bringeth salvation unto his soul.

This is the opportunity sentence. Now is one of the most productive gospel harvest times in the history of the world. This is not a time of gleaning or unproductivity; this is the harvest of greatest abundance. Compare it with the other dispensations. Noah labored for 120 years and converted only his own family. Even the dispensation established by Jesus lasted for only a relatively short time until the apostles had been slain or banished, and the prophecy of Isaiah saw its fulfillment, which said, "For behold darkness shall cover the earth and gross darkness the people." (Isa. 60:2) But in our day we have examples of one missionary bringing into the Church more people in a single month than Noah did in his entire lifetime. What a great time to live and be in the field. May God help us that we may not lack strength.

5. And faith, hope, charity and love, with an eye single to the glory of God qualify him for the work.

One of the most vital qualifications for spiritual success is to have "an eye single to the glory of God." That means concentration, to keep just one thing in our focus. When we start to see double or triple we become confused, and conflict and failure are the natural results. The scripture says that "a double-minded man is unstable in all his ways." "No man can serve two masters." It is easy to serve God if we go all the way all of the time under all circumstances. It is only when we do right things part of the time and wrong things the other part that we get into trouble. Emerson says, "The one virtue in life is concentration." We need to eliminate the conflicts in ourselves. Success comes out of consistency. We must make up our minds about values and directions and then concentrate all of our efforts to one end. A devoted singleness of purpose can always be depended upon to perform a miracle of accomplishment.

6. Remember faith, virtue, knowledge, temperance, patience, brotherly kindness, godliness, charity, humility, diligence.

These are the attributes of God himself. These personality traits determine what we are. Almost all of success is determined by the kind of personality we build in ourselves. This important part of leadership development is discussed more fully in Chapter 33.

The seventh and final of these success sentences is—

7. Ask and ye shall receive; knock and it shall be opened unto you. Amen.

To get all of the blessings of the Lord is as simple as that. All we need to do is to take them. All of the benefits of the gospel are ours for the asking, providing only that we get them in time. Unfortunately we usually don't appreciate our blessings until we lose them. Just suppose that we had unlimited funds and were asked to pay for our blessings at a price which we ourselves would gladly pay to get them back once they were lost. How long would our money last?

That is, what would be a fair price for repentance if you couldn't repent? How much would it be worth to live forever in the celestial kingdom if you had been consigned elsewhere? How much would you be willing to pay to get your family back if they were eternally lost? Try to determine a fair price for the priesthood or a godly character or eternal progression or eternal increase. What would be your appraisal of the value of a celestial body, a celestial mind, a celestial personality, a chance to live forever on a celestial earth with celestial friends and loved ones? We may even share the profession of God, which is to bring to pass the immortality and eternal life of man.

These and a thousand other things have been provided for us. And what do they cost us? Just "ask and ye shall receive; knock and it shall be opened unto you." What a thrilling opportunity! What tremendous ideas are tied up in each of these seven little sentences. What great spiritual wealth and power can be ours if we lived up to them. What a transformation there would be in our personal effectiveness if we strictly followed the blueprint of this forty-five seconds worth of ideas for success given by the Lord in section four.

We should constantly remind ourselves that the one business of life is to succeed. The purpose of life is success. Our mortality is very brief. This opportunity can never be repeated. If we are unfruitful and unproductive in our mortal stewardship we will have all of eternity to remember and regret. To prevent this the Lord has given us these seven key ideas to guarantee our success. We should get them into our minds and hearts and muscles. The Lord had written these for our individual benefit, just as he wrote on the Liahona to guide Lehi in the wilderness. Section four is our great spindle to point out the way. If we follow it, it will lead us to magnificent accomplishment in our part of the work of the Lord.

My Sins Are Mightier Than I

THE THIRD VERSE of the 65th
Psalm says, "Iniquities prevail
against me." Some years ago Harry Emerson Fosdick wrote
an article under the heading of obedience, drawing attention to the destructive power of sin in the lives of people.
He quoted a more picturesque translation of this verse
which says, "My sins are mightier than I," and he pointed
out some of the sources from which sin gets its power.

Sin is the central problem of mankind. It is the obstacle standing in the way of almost every human success
and happiness. Therefore, considered in any light, including that of our own experience, it is entitled to our most
serious consideration. Sin is an old word. For many people
it has been worn out and its teeth have largely been pulled.
There are some people who completely ignore it. Among
some others it has become fashionable even to deny the
existence of sin altogether. But sin does not go into exile
with its name. Nor does it cease to exist because it is
ignored. Those who close their eyes to its existence probably become less competent to deal with it than do those
who recognize the problem and continue to grapple with
its causes. We have every reason to fear our sins, for they
have great powers over us, and in their triumph we may
see the wreck of our every hope.

The biggest problem of our lives and the greatest
responsibility of leadership is the elimination of sin. Our
chief concern and the place where our attack should begin
centers in ourselves. In our own interests, we should find
the source of strength of our sins, for in overcoming sin we

find our only hope for permanent happiness. In the words of the scripture—

1. "My sins are mightier than I" because of their binding power.

If given rein, sin has the power to make itself habitual; it has a binding grip. Habit is more important in determining our destiny than almost any other influence. To give yourself an adequate sense of respect for the power of a habit, just try to break one sometime, even a small one.

As an illustration of the binding power of a habit, or a sin, it is reported that a group of the ancients had an interesting custom for punishing crime. If a man committed a murder, his penalty was to be chained to the corpse of his victim. Wherever he went forevermore he must drag with him the putrifying body of his sin. There was no possible way that he could disentangle himself from the result of his evil act. If later he decided to slay again, another corpse was added to his horrible burden. This he must also drag with him wherever he went forevermore.

Terrible as this punishment seems, life has a plan of retribution that is very closely akin to it. In one way we are always chained to our sins. There seems to be a great power of retribution that constantly watches over the world to see that no sin goes unpunished.

The sentence of one who violates the law of temperance is that a ruinous, driving thirst attaches itself, which drives him further and further down the road of despair. Everyone has seen the pitiful struggles of some poor alcoholic trying to free himself from the monstrous thing that has fastened itself upon him. The sentence of one who fails to study is that he is chained to his ignorance, and wherever he goes forevermore he must drag his ignorance along. While it holds him in its clutches, he can never have relief even for an instant, and there can be no salvation in ignorance. We see pathetic lives burdened down with their heavy load of ignorance as they drag through life this unpleasant and destructive cargo. The sentence of one who practices immorality is that the sin incarnates itself in his soul and leaves him scarred and disfigured by its foul presence. It is the same with dishonesty. It is the same with sloth. It is the same with bad attitudes and negative thinking. It is probable that Paul made reference to this ancient custom of being chained to a corpse when he cried out, "Oh wretched man that I am. Who shall deliver me from the body of this death?" (Rom. 7:24)

One who steps into sin is like one who steps into space from an upper window. If he had only that single act to consider, his problem would be simple, but when he is out of the window and gravity has taken hold of him, he finds himself dealing with a power over which he has no control. He was absolute master of his first act, but he is not the master of the power of gravitation which immediately succeeds it.

Many people blithely play with sin, supposing that the separate deeds which they may do, or refrain from doing, make up their total problem. But thoughts grow into deeds; deeds become habits; habits ripen into character; and character determines our destiny. We commit the separate acts of sin, but our eternal destiny must reckon with the "binding power" of sin.

2. "My sins are mightier than I" because of their blinding power.

No one ever sees his own sin aright. No one ever properly estimates the consequences of his own wrongs. At its beginning, sin always comes in disguise. It may at first call itself by some other name such as liberty, but anyone who ever accepted sin's offer of freedom soon discovers that he has been cheated. One begins by being

free to do evil, free to indulge his baser moods, but he
ends up not being free to stop. Once he has started, he
finds himself a slave, bound to the things he was at first
free to do. Dr. Fosdick says, "He was at liberty to play
with a cuttlefish, but now that he finds himself enveloped
in its long arms and held close by its suckers, he is not at
liberty to get away." The blinding power of sin distorts
the vision. Eyes once perverted in this manner do not easily
regain their focus either to see clearly or to see straight.

It is almost impossible to recognize our own deeds as
being as black as the same deed when committed by a
felon. One of the hardest things anyone ever has to learn
to say is, "I have sinned." We think of our own sins as
"experience." We call them "misdemeanors" or "errors."
By such devices we blind our own eyes and keep ourselves
unaware of the inward malady constantly growing larger
and larger until it destroys us. Sin always gives us a blind
spot which covers up our own offenses from our view. Sin
has so many aliases and disguises that one can seldom recognize himself as the culprit. It is even more impossible
to imagine that ultimately he himself will be lost. Sin in
the slums seems to us gross and terrible; it staggers and
blasphemes and wallows in unmentionable vice. But move
it into a more respectable neighborhood, dress it in refine-
ment and elegance, and it dances before us like Salome
before her uncle, possessing a fascination so nearly irresistible that our happiness almost seems to depend upon it.
But it lures us only in anticipation. Once we are overcome,
sin quickly changes its clothes and alters its bearing. It
passes from anticipation through committal into memory
and will never be beautiful again. We then lock it in the
memory as in the bloody room of Bluebeard's palace where
dead things were hung. At the thought of the sin in our
remembrance we shrink away, and yet back to it our
reminiscence is continually drawn.

3. "My sins are mightier than I" because they are more contagious than disease.

When we care for people as we do our family and friends, we put into their hands an almost irresistible influence over us. We respond with telegraphic swiftness to their words and emotions. What happens to them tends to happen to us. What they think and feel we contagiously receive. When their opinions and practices are involved, we become very sensitive and impressionable. In almost every act of life we are merely following someone else.

When Satan walked out of heaven, one-third of all the hosts of heaven walked out after him. Sin Satanizes men. No one walks down the broad road of sin alone. Each one marches at the head of some kind of caravan. When one becomes a sinner he immediately goes out to seduce his fellows. No drug addict or profaner of the name of deity or violator of the Sabbath Day is ever content until he wins a comrade to his vice. Man's greatest sin is not as a victim but as a victimitizer. He plays Satan to others.

4. "My sins are mightier than I" because of their hardening power

Sin makes the soul callous. It estranges the mind from God. A hardened heart has no fertile topsoil in which the seeds of faith and righteousness may get a foothold. One of the traits that makes salvation most difficult is a hard heart. The Psalmist sang, "Harden not your hearts." (Psalms 95:8) Paul echoes the refrain, "Harden not your hearts." (Heb. 3:8) We might well take up the chorus to banish sin and thereby free ourselves from its hardening power.

5. "My sins are mightier than I" because they bring upon others consequences of evil which cannot be undone.

No man ever built a wall high enough to contain the consequences of his sins. The sins of the fathers are visited upon the children. The sins of the children are also visited upon their parents and upon their associates. Sin once released cannot be stopped. It involves us all. It cannot be overtaken. It cannot be undone. A governor may pardon a murderer, but he cannot restore a life. God can forgive us our sins, but how can he forgive their consequences, or how can even God forgive us of our ignorance or our sloth or the evil influence in the lives of others?

6. "My sins are mightier than I" because of their multiplying power.

Each sin spawns other sins like fish in the sea. One untruth makes another untruth necessary. One man can lead a family or a nation to destruction. Laman and Lemuel destroyed a civilization because the seeds of sin and death were in their characters and soon multiplied sufficiently to kill an entire continent.

7. "My sins are mightier than I" because they can fasten upon me a sense of guilt which cannot be shaken off.

Sin has the power to lodge itself in the memory and incarnate itself in the soul, from whence it cannot easily be dislodged. Sin remains in our hearts to make our lives ugly and unwholesome.

"When on a lonely ocean the floating bell buoys toll, no man's hands cause them to ring. The waste of an unpeopled ocean surrounds them in every direction. The sea, by its own restlessness, is ringing its own bells. So tolls the remorse and guilt in the heart of the damned, and no man's hands can stop it forever and ever." Thus we have "an endless torment whose flames ascendeth up forever and ever." Then sin has had its victory; it has cast its victim down into hell.

Leadership must tear away the aliases of sin and leave it exposed for what it is. Then it may not be able to change its guise so swiftly and gain so great a welcome in any company. We must break the power of sin in our lives both by reformation and by elimination. The better of these is elimination. The most desirable thing is not the home-coming of the prodigal. It is far more desirable for one to keep his character clean by obedience to the highest law that he knows, so that he never has the hard bitter struggle of trying to come back. We must prune away the sprouts of sin and encourage the growth of holiness and communication with God as the ruling principle of our lives. Then we may develop our strength and become stronger than those forces of sin that strive to overcome us.

Something to Wear

A great leader should be well-dressed,
both on the outside and on the inside.

A LOT OF PEOPLE, particularly women, endure a great deal of suffering because of having to skimp on clothes. We especially dislike to appear in public without being what we consider properly dressed. The phrase, "I have nothing to wear" is usually loaded with all kinds of grief and unhappiness. Clothes may not make the man, but they do account for about 95 per cent of what people see of him. We are embarrassed when we are not as well dressed as those with whom we associate. We do not want to stand out from the crowd because of shabby clothing, nor the things that shabby clothing may be a sign of.

In ancient Biblical days if someone was to be humiliated he was dressed in sackcloth and covered with ashes. If he was to be honored he was washed and dressed in beautiful apparel, and some personal adornment such as a necklace of gold was added to improve his appearance. Jesus mentioned "a certain rich man who was clothed in purple and fine linen." Fine clothing has always been a badge of honor and distinction. There are not many things that give us a greater "lift" than to be clean and attractively dressed.

What could be more stimulating than the contemplation of living in the presence of God, with our bodies and our minds and our personalities dressed in celestial glory? Who can understand the loss of those who must be content with something less fine, something less beautiful, something that compares with celestial glory as the twinkle of a tiny star compares with the blaze of the noon-day sun? I wonder if some who fail in their possibilities may not feel like those shabbily-dressed people who are always complaining, "I have nothing to wear." Now is the time to determine how "well-dressed" we want to be in eternity. But there, even more than here, the most pleasing adornment may not be worn on our backs. It is more likely to be in our minds and hearts from whence it will shine out in our faces.

A radiant spirit shines out through the eyes, which have been called the "windows of the soul." Our eyes are also the means whereby people look into our hearts. What we are is often revealed in our facial expression. In eternity even more than now we may be recognized for what we are. Then the most effective measure of worth may be the clothes in which we dress the immortal spirit. Our appearance even in mortality is influenced by our thoughts. But what we are in eternity will be an important factor in our beautification. The immortal spirit is the architect that will clothe itself in a resurrected body to match the beauty and quality of the spirit. The scripture says of Daniel that "there was an excellent spirit" in him. That is also the kind of spirit we should strive to develop, for that will dress the body and character accordingly.

Lincoln was once asked to give a certain man a government position. Lincoln turned him down, saying, "I don't like his face." Someone objected that a man's face should not be held against him. But Lincoln thought otherwise. Lincoln had a great confidence in his ability to read the character of people as indicated in their faces. A similar idea is expressed in the following lines:

> Whenever you cultivate a thought,
> Remember, it will trace
> With telling touch, in pictured form,
> Its story on your face.

Whenever you act upon a thought,
Remember it will roll
Into your being and become
A fiber of your soul.

Whenever you express a thought,
Remember it will be
A force throughout the universe
For all eternity.

Sometime ago an article appeared in the press about the artist Norman Rockwell and how he breathed such vibrant life into his paintings of everyday people. Mr. Rockwell said, "What you are inside shows in your face. Your eyes, sooner or later, become the mirrors of your soul." Mr. Rockwell gave credit for part of his success as an artist to the people who posed for him. That is, he selected people who had lived full lives and who were possessed of those inner qualities that he wanted to stand out in his paintings. He said, "It is not very satisfying to paint individuals who have lost their faith. I could sketch their faces but that inner glow that gives them character would be missing."

He picked up a magazine and as an example turned to the picture of a teen-ager who had become involved in a brutal murder. "Look at that face," Mr. Rockwell said. And then he retold the story of the worthy young man who had posed for the picture of Christ in da Vinci's painting, *The Last Supper.* But this same young man, after becoming corrupt in his mode of living, later posed as the model for Judas. The decay of the betrayer had become evident for everyone to see. Mr. Rockwell looked again at the magazine picture and said, "Who knows but what the same thing may have happened to this teen-ager? Certainly there is little godliness in his face."

No one in mortality has ever seen his own spirit. Have you ever thought about what our own acts may be doing to it? It is a little bit startling to remember what an important part our face plays in our lives. It is even more startling to remember that we will wear our faces forever, and that God and the friends of our immortality may be even more expert than Abraham Lincoln in reading what is pictured there. It is an interesting thing to remember that we are presently dressing ourselves for eternal life. The thoughts that we think and the things that we do and the emotions that stir our hearts are all architects that are fashioning the form and features that we will wear forever.

Have you ever looked into the face of someone who was possessed by the overpowering insanity of some dreadful rage or hate or some unholy purpose? You may have actually been frightened by how the features were distorted and misshapen. A face that may ordinarily be pleasing to behold can change itself into something hideous and grotesque in a second's time. When the unholy period has passed, the features may again assume approximately their previous appearance, though it is doubtful if they will ever be exactly the same. The features, stretched by passion to a new dimension, may never completely return to their proper form. Each disfiguration may make a permanent contribution to deformity. How would it be to wear a face forever that had been frozen at the moment of its greatest distortion? Is it any more comfortable to know that as some passion or thought becomes dominant in our lives that the life tends to take the permanent shape which the thought gives it? Satan became Satan by his own acts and thoughts. Sin not only degrades the spirit; it also disfigures the body. We would certainly not expect to see the same beauty in the demoniac face of the devil as we would expect to see shining from the face of God.

God wants all of his children to be beautiful, and to that end, runs the most effective beauty parlor ever imagined. His program for our exaltation is made up of certain techniques of faith and works and godliness that put the glow of divinity into the human spirit. What the spirit is will eventually shine out through the face in letters of light for everyone to read. Socrates was supposed to have been a very homely man physically, but he prayed, "O God, make me beautiful within." We have all seen plain people who have become outstandingly beautiful by the working of a radiant spirituality. A godly spirit will make the plainest body beautiful. Great spiritual qualities put charm and ease in one's manner. Qualities of great leadership are qualities of godliness. Every great man manifests his greatness in his person. The Lord wants us to develop these traits to their maximum.

Friendliness is godliness. Think what happens in your heart when a beautiful smile with all that it means spreads over the face and shines out through the eyes of one you love. Can you imagine any adornment more beautiful than a radiant, godly personality? We say that someone has a "light in his eye," or "his face beams." Try to imagine that quality when it has become celestialized. Then it goes beyond beauty and we call it glory. The glory of God is so great that no natural man can abide his presence. (D&C 67:11-3) Yet we may have a glory like his. We can only feebly try to understand a celestialized personality with its quickened senses, amplified powers of perception and vastly increased capacity for happiness, love and understanding. It would be interesting if we had a light meter that would register the light in people's faces and then be able to compare the reading with celestial glory, or follow our own progress day by day as we clothe the spirit for the celestial kingdom.

The gospel is not only to be lived; it can also be worn. Solomon in his prayer dedicating his magnificent temple said, "Let thy priests, O Lord, be clothed with salvation, and let thy saints rejoice in goodness." The Lord in our own day has said, "And above all things, clothe yourselves with a bond of charity as with a mantle which is the bond of perfectness and peace." (D&C 88:125)

Between the time of death and the resurrection some wonderful beauty treatments will be given to those spirits who have lived worthily in this life. While separated from the body, the spirit will be cleansed, purified and given its final education to become a celestial spirit. Then the body will also be given its final beauty treatment by being resurrected and quickened to match the celestial spirit. That is, every celestial spirit is permitted to resurrect for itself a celestial body.

In the 88th section and 28th and 29th verses of the *Doctrine and Covenants,* the Lord says, "They who are of a celestial spirit shall receive the same body which was a natural body; even ye shall receive your bodies and your glory shall be the glory by which your bodies are quickened. Ye who are quickened by a portion of the celestial glory shall then receive of the same, even a fullness."

What a challenging thought to try to understand a "fullness" of celestial glory. Those earning the celestial glory are the ones that will be dressed for the presence of God. They will be like God. Think by way of comparison of those who fail to be worthy of celestial glory. They will be excluded from the presence of God, and "where God and Christ are they cannot come worlds without end." That is, those with a spirit and a body and a personality less fine, less delightful, less interesting than the celestial, will not be properly dressed for the presence of God. The phrase, "I have nothing to wear" as we now understand it, may have a great increase in its meaning for those who are thus excluded.

The work of the Lord is the process by which we bring about the blessings mentioned by Paul, who says, "Eye hath not seen nor ear heard, neither hath it entered into the heart of man the things that God hath prepared for those that love him."

Who would like to be shabbily dressed in the presence of God? Alma says, "Can ye imagine yourselves brought before the tribunal of God with your souls filled with guilt and remorse, having a remembrance of all your guilt, yea, a perfect remembrance of all your wickedness . . . that ye have set at defiance the commandments of God." (Alma 5:18)

God will not only be able to read our faces, but our whole souls will be open to his gaze. Not only will God know that we are shabbily dressed, but we ourselves will be acutely aware of our own shame. Mosiah gives us a hint about how we might feel. He said, "And if they be evil they are consigned to an awful view of their own guilt and abominations; which doth cause them to shrink from the presence of the Lord into a state of misery and endless torment, from whence they can no more return." (Mosiah 3:25)

Alma says: "And in this awful state we shall not dare to look up to our God; and we would fain be glad if we could command the rocks and the mountains to fall upon us to hide us from his presence." (Alma 12:14) These folk will apparently feel pretty bad. (We had better be sure that we are not in that situation.) We had better get ourselves prepared so that God may point to us and say, "These are they whose bodies are celestial, whose glory is that of the sun . . . the highest of all, whose glory the sun of the firmament is written of as being typical." (D&C 76:70)

We can develop the most becoming personality qualities so that we will have no concern for "something to wear," either in time or in eternity. The program of the Lord will make us beautiful both on the outside and on the inside, as fast as we will live it. The final destiny of

God's children is the celestial kingdom, but those who cannot live the celestial law cannot attain a celestial glory. So
what we wear depends on what we do. We light up our
homes at Christmas time to commemorate Christ's birth.
How much more appropriate to light up our lives with his
righteousness and clothe ourselves with his attributes and
his abilities, to do his work.

Now is the time to dress ourselves in character and
understanding and determination and skill and industry.
For the Lord has promised those who serve him in righteousness and ability unto the end that "great shall be their
reward and eternal shall be their glory . . . and their wisdom
shall be great and their understanding shall reach the
heavens . . . for by my spirit will I enlighten them." Try
to think of something more wonderful! It might well be
said that these will always have "something to wear."

Stimulants

THE HIGHEST FUNCTION of a leader consists not so much in imparting knowledge as in effectively stimulating the mind and feelings. Success itself is not made up by accumulating information like storing up water in a cistern; it more resembles the opening of a spring. Leadership needs to be concerned with the ability to develop and direct initiative and resourcefulness in people. These are the qualities that tend to overcome basic inertia, that power which holds people bound in inactivity.

One of the first steps toward success is to get movement. Movement can be produced by a process of stimulation. The ability to stimulate is the secret weapon of both mental and spiritual progress. Each one of us has been created in the image of God, and each one of us has been endowed with a set of the attributes of divinity. One of these is the power of inspiration. We talk a great deal about our right to *receive* inspiration from God. We don't understand quite so well either our right or our ability to *give* inspiration. This, however, is one of the greatest of the powers that God has placed in human personality.

One of the most uplifting of our experiences in life is to be in contact with what we call an inspiring person, one that has the power to stir up our spirits and incite us to greater achievement. An inspiring person is one who can "open the springs of the spirit." Such a one initiates impulses and arouses better and stronger desires, appetites and ambitions.

New ideas are not always necessary in this process of stimulation. Stimulation may merely give old ideas more power and greater activity. Old truths can be stamped deeper into the mind so as to be made more impressive and influential. Some ideas convey information; others give power. The function of the first is to teach; the function of the second is to move. The ability of some of our greatest men has been not only to impart truth, but also to get action. By asking questions, engaging in discussion and cross-examination, Socrates was able to draw ideas from people and lead them to make decisions about things which they may have already known but on which no action had been taken. Socrates was able to take a familiar idea already existing in somebody's mind and help to give it a meaning and movement that changed it into an activity. An active idea of lesser quality may be of greater value than a better idea which is only lightly felt in the mind. Non-working ideas usually have only a small amount of usefulness.

Jesus, of course, was the great master in changing the lives of people. By the use of stimulating ideas he helped publicans and sinners to rise to the rank of saints and apostles. This field of stimulation and motivation is probably the greatest opportunity area in the world. It gives active importance and usefulness to ideas which before were inactive and powerless. Stimulation applies to giving ideas, ideals and ambitions more specific assignments and greater work to do.

Everyone has had the experience of having some idea lying dormant and inactive in the mind, and then because it has received some effective stimulation, it has come into activity and usefulness with a maturity and power which its possessor did not previously imagine. This experience can be to us like the awakening of some sleeping giant within us. Many years ago I memorized the fourth section of the *Doctrine and Covenants*. I thought I understood it perfectly and was getting out of it all of the good there was in it. Years later I heard a great church leader talk to a group of young missionaries about this section, and all of a sudden it acquired an importance and influence in my life which it did not previously possess.

Knowledge by itself may be useless, but power comes when that knowledge is activated, harnessed and put to productive work. Ideals and ambitions can be aroused and increased in people, just as the physical appetite can be made stronger. We have some items in our diet that we call appetizers. Appetizers serve a purpose similar to the mechanical process of priming the pump. An appetizer is a small portion of tasty food or drink served before a meal for the purpose of stimulating the appetite. Appetite in one area has a lot in common with appetite in other areas. The dictionary defines appetite as "the desire for food in general or for some special food in particular." But leadership and accomplishment and spirituality are also largely matters of appetite.

A leader is a stimulating person who knows how to use appetizing morsels of thought, motives and ideals to start accomplishment. He is the one who knows how to intensify desire and whet the spiritual longings. Hunger in the human heart produces a power that can overcome such negative influences as timidity, sin or sloth.

Jesus said, "Blessed are they who hunger and thirst after righteousness: for they shall be filled." It is a natural principle that hunger always seeks to satisfy itself. It was the mission of Jesus to increase spiritual hunger in people. It is our mission to use ideas, examples, motives, etc. to stimulate greater accomplishment in ourselves and in others.

Some of the things that we usually think of as stimulants are actually depressants, whereas the dictionary says that to stimulate is—

To Raise Objectives
To Increase Incentives
To Invigorate
To Provoke Thought
To Incite Activity

To Raise Objectives

Most people suffer from unworthy objectives or objectives that are not pointed high enough. A great objective is in itself a powerful stimulant. A popular national magazine once conducted a survey among a large number of people. These people were asked what their main objectives in life were. Ninety-five per cent did not know. They had no definite objectives and therefore lacked the motive power which could have been available to them. Without a firmly-held, challenging objective, the chances for success are greatly reduced.

Almost all of life is a matter of preparation. We prepare for our life's work; we prepare for marriage; we prepare for old age, etc. Our greatest objective should be to prepare for eternal life. This can best be done by a process of self-motivation. Our objectives should be clear-cut and tightly-held. Certainly we should know in detail what we are preparing for. A capable leader can help other people as well as himself to identify and become enthusiastic over worthwhile objectives, pointing finally to the celestial kingdom.

To Increase Incentive

An incentive is something to work for. It is a picture to hold in our minds. It is something to spark ambition. What are the incentives of the gospel, and how can they be used in the best interests of people? Bread alone is not the highest incentive to a worthwhile life. An incentive gives increased power which in turn gives an increased accomplishment. A good leader can help to establish these stronger incentives and more favorable feelings pointing toward the highest objectives. "Gold" or "golf" as incentives to effort are inferior to "God," "glory" and "goodness," held up before our minds by the gospel. One way to increase our incentives is to change ourselves from mere *needers* of religion to *wanters* of religion. If our appetite is sufficiently aroused we soon become *possessors* of religion. For when we love and desire a thing enough, we soon make it ours. To desire enough is to attain; to aspire is to achieve. David indicated a powerful incentive when he said, "As the hart pants after the water brook, so do I hunger after thee, O God."

To Invigorate

What a great ability it is to be able to inspire and strengthen purpose, to fill minds with energy, to arouse vigor and enthusiasm in people. One of the most bitter denunciations ever given by Jesus was heaped upon him who buried his talents in the ground. Jesus called him "slothful." That indicates a lack of vigor. It is a wonderful ability to be able to get excited about the right things. Paul said to Timothy, "Stir up the gift of God which is within thee." Vigorous thinking and acting will stir up your gifts and give them increased ardor and fervor. Enthusiasm supports and drives reason to make it active. Effective stimulation can help to produce zeal which is a vigorous, untiring, vital activity. A well-trained conscience is also an instrument of invigoration.

To Provoke Thought

"Provoke" comes from a word meaning "to call forth." One of our greatest opportunities is to be able to call forth thought. No one is greater than his ability to think. Someone has said that we are like tacks; we can go no further than our heads will let us. Sometimes we fill ourselves so full of prize fights, baseball games, television shows and the stock market that we have no room for thoughts of God and eternal life. When our spiritual intellect becomes poverty-stricken it manifests itself in trite verbal intercourse. Our daily thoughts and conversation should be concerned with more important things, developing deeper longings and more worthwhile hungers. We should learn to love activity involving serious religious thought and spiritual experiences. One of the greatest abilities any leader may develop is to provoke thought in people.

To Incite Activity

Thomas Huxley said, "The great end of life is not knowledge but action." We will be judged not only by what we believe but by what we have done. Activity is the basis for all accomplishment. "You can lead a running stream, but what can you do with a stagnant pool?" An inactive man sometimes suffers a kind of spiritual death on the installment plan. Important mental and spiritual activity leading to more worthwhile accomplishment can be increased in people.

In 1923 there sat in a prison cell in Germany a young man by the name of Adolph Hitler who had been unsuccessful in many things. But now he was writing his book *Mein Kampf*, his plan to make Germany the greatest nation on the earth. The fact that starting out singlehanded he almost upset the world indicated that he had something. How did he do it? The answer is in his book. He said, "The question of Germany regaining her power is not how to manufacture or distribute arms, but how to produce in people that will to win, that spirit of determination, which produces a thousand different methods, each of which ends with arms."

Wars are not won with tanks or guns or airplanes or oil, but with that spirit of determination inside of people. And that's how souls are saved, and that is how we do every other worthwhile thing in the world. William James said, "Whenever life communicates an eagerness to him who lives it, his life becomes genuinely significant."

What does the following idea do to you? "And now after the many testimonies which have been give of him, this is the testimony last of all which we give of him: that he lives! For we saw him even on the right hand of God; and we heard the voice bearing record that he is the only begotten of the Father! That by him, and through him, and of him, the worlds are and were created, and the inhabitants thereof are begotten sons and daughers unto God." (D&C 76:22-23)

God has placed in our hands the great power of stimulation, which is the power to enlighten, the power to produce enthusiasm, the power to plant the seeds of faith. It is the power to get action. By this power we may persuade and convince, arouse and inspire. Stimulation is the power to touch a life and cause it to ripen into something greater than it was. This power is in our hands and we may learn to use it to dispel ignorance, raise objectives and incite activity in the greatest enterprise ever undertaken upon the earth—the work of human exaltation.

Thou Shalt Not

THERE HAS BEEN a great deal of emphasis properly placed on the power of positive thinking, the benefits of which are too numerous to mention here. It is also true that we usually prefer those who build up rather than those who tear down. People would rather be praised than criticized. It is usually more pleasant to add something than to take something away. We like to say "do" rather than "don't." Many educators feel that great care should be taken not to be too frank in calling attention of students to their own shortcomings because of the possible inhibitions or complexes that might result. Systems of grading students have been devised so that even the student himself will not find out exactly where he stands in relation to others. It is believed that to look for the good points and then give praise is far better than to call attention to weaknesses.

With this philosophy in mind, even the Ten Commandments have sometimes been criticized as being on the negative side. Some feel that a religion with too many *don'ts* is out of date and may lose its appeal. It has been thought by some that the Beatitudes and the Articles of Faith are in better form psychologically because they are positive. The Beatitudes are made up of eight blessings; they are the *do's*. The Articles of Faith are also positive. They are thirteen basic statements of faith, beginning "We believe." And then on the other side of the ledger comes the stern and forbidding voice of the Ten Commandments saying, "Thou shalt not."

As important as are the *do's*, it is equally important to have some *don'ts*. That is, there are some things that we just must not do, and nothing gets that idea over quite as well as a plain "thou shalt not." Too much *diplomacy* and beating around the bush may be misunderstood (even by ourselves.) There is no chance of misunderstanding the command "Thou shalt not steal."

There are also a positive and a negative side to the formula of success. The success formula resembles a medical prescription. It is important what the pharmacist puts into the prescription; but it is just as important what he leaves out. This applies particularly to leadership success. Martin Luther once said, "Let a man be endowed with ten virtues and have but one fault and the one fault will eclipse and darken all of the virtues." A banker may balance off one liability with an asset of equal size, but such balancing does not work in the success formula; it does not work in life or in health. That is, you can't balance off a disease in one part of the body with health in another. A strong healthy arm will not balance an exploding appendix. You do no need to have a *majority* in disease in order to die. That is, you do not need to have heart trouble, diabetes, tuberculosis and rheumatism to cause your death if you already have cancer. You may be perfectly healthy in every other organ and yet lose your life if you are fatally diseased in one.

This also applies in our leadership. One well-placed sin gets a person into very serious trouble even though he may be a perfectly wonderful person in a hundred other ways. For example, God said, "Thou shalt not kill." This law could be violated in ten minutes, whereas ten years of piling up assets on the other side of the ledger would not bring the dead man back to life.

In appraising our leadership we don't just balance off a leadership liability with a leadership asset. We reach a balance about as we do when we find a little fly in a big bowl of soup. We don't just dip out enough soup to balance the fly; we throw the whole thing out. We had a recent example of how this works in public life. The chief aid of the President of the United States was "an acknowledged genius in matters of organization, efficiency and discernment in getting to the basic issues of controversial problems." Yet he was eliminated from office because he was suspected of some indiscretions in accepting some articles of clothing and a few other trivial gifts while holding political office. How this principle works within the family was illustrated by the experience of a married man who had been a good provider, a kind father and a faithful husband all of his life. Then one day he kissed the cook on her birthday. That put him in the soup and he was thrown out as a consequence.

It works about the some way in leadership. One weakness can make an otherwise wonderful leader unfit for service. He may be an outstanding leader, but if he is dishonest or undependable or is touched with immorality, his one vice will overbalance ten virtues and make his leadership unusable.

To *add* great virtues is wonderful, but that is not all there is to leadership development. If we fail to *subtract* the vices, the virtues may automatically lose their value. Gamaliel Bradford once wrote a book entitled *Damaged Souls*. This was the biography of eight near-great men who were prevented from becoming what their virtues intended because they also had great faults. Benedict Arnold was one of these. It was said that in many ways Benedict Arnold was a greater general than George Washington, but he also had a great fault. He could not take criticism. His virtues were many and well developed. But because this one fault had not been removed, it fomented in his soul like a deadly poison. We are told that the reason that Benedict Arnold negotiated to sell West Point to the British during the Revolutionary War was that he wanted to get even with superiors who had criticized him.

The fall of Satan came about because he could not have his own way. Satan apparently had great virtues. He was the brilliant Son of the Morning. He had probably been faithful, capable and devoted. But he lost his standing and his future because of his fault. He was rebellious, and when his program was not accepted his fault took control and brought about his downfall.

How often we follow that procedure and let some vice destroy virtues and opportunities that we have spent a lifetime to build. A liability we thought of no real consequence can rob us of every blessing, including the celestial kingdom. Our tendency to take offense if someone doesn't handle us just right causes us no end of trouble. A farmer once became offended at the water master and said, "I will never use another drop of water out of this canal as long as you are the water master." What a needless loss. But how familiar that statement sounds. How many blessings have been lost and how much leadership destroyed by a similar fault. Sometimes we even betray the work of God and our own destiny because we are not able to take a suggestion or a criticism without offense.

But to withhold criticism has often proven to be even more dangerous, for sometimes our success is destroyed because some little sin was not pointed out to us until it grew too big for us to handle. It is the responsibility of leadership to see that sins and errors are eliminated before they involve us in too many serious problems. A little surgery can save our lives if applied in time. That is, if our appendix is about to blow up, our chief concern should not be to hurry to the gymnasium to build up our arm muscles. Subtraction of the liability is then far more urgent than any addition or even multiplication of our assets.

We ought to remember that there is no great leadership without a generous amount of subtraction. If we can get some expert help, so much the better. Abraham Lincoln capitalized upon this idea of criticism by making two of his most bitter enemies members of his cabinet. This was Lincoln's method of keeping himself alert and on his toes. He needed his enemies to test his program as well as himself with the most severe criticism. This was one of the indications of the great wisdom of Lincoln. How different from the disabling, touchy tenderness of Benedict Arnold.

Why should we so bitterly resent criticism? If the suggestion is wrong it need not be followed, but even when it is wrong it sometimes wakes us up and keeps us on guard against our own damaging weaknesses. It also prompts us to "look before we leap."

But mostly we don't think of criticism as help, and therefore we don't get the maximum good out of it. We think of criticism as a "bitter pill" to take. But that is not necessarily true. Criticism may save our lives. It can eliminate our faults and build up our strengths. We should regard criticism as Jacob did the angel with whom he wrestled. He would not let the angel go until the angel had given him a blessing. Most criticisms also have a blessing to give us, and we should not let the criticism go until it blesses us. A good leader should train himself to think of criticism as the most pleasant medicine, as well as the most valuable aid to progress. Criticism is the wonder drug of leadership. About the only question we need to be concerned about is, How well can we take it?

To the wise and alert, criticism makes accomplishment and happiness possible. It steers us around the pitfalls that may otherwise bring us disgrace and disaster. If we have a personality with a diseased appendix or two (and who hasn't?) then while a pat on the back may be a good thing, we may also need a surgeon who knows how to extract

the poison by eliminating the diseased member. Even if
it should hurt a little bit it may still be a good idea. It is
not always possible to eliminate a fault as painlessly as to
remove a ruptured appendix. But pain or no pain, if we
wish to improve our situation we had better take our medicine. More than most other things we need someone on
the sidelines to act as our coach, to observe our mistakes
and warn us against repetition. Most of us have a very
serious potential weakness in our natural "blind spot." One
of our most limiting factors is that we don't see ourselves
as others see us. We need someone on the sidelines with
enough interest and courage to tell us the truth about our
annoying mannerisms, our bad habits, our inexcusable
mistakes. Otherwise, we may fall into the pit of self-
delusion where disaster lurks.

If you really want a means for effective improvement
in your leadership get someone to act as a mirror in which
you may see yourself as others see you. Don't keep thinking
that criticism is wrong or that it is unpleasant to take; that
is only because of the way you think about it. Criticism
is right; it can be used to remove present and potential
unpleasantness from our lives. Without someone to keep
us up to date we may be heading for trouble. As pleasant
as "yes men" sometimes appear to be, they are never really
very helpful or very useful.

When out of the thunders and lightnings of Sinai God
said, "Thou shalt not," he was not just being negative. He
was trying to help us. "God is not an umpire who is trying
to count us out. He is not a competitor who is trying to
outsmart us. He is not an enemy who is trying to punish
us." He is God our Father who is trying to promote our
success and happiness. He is trying to raise us to his own
stature. He sometimes has to get some bad things out of
us before he can get good things into us. And if we first
firmly decide what we must *not* do, then we are more free

to do vigorously what we should do. But whether we are thinking in terms of psychology or good sense or the celestial kingdom, the "thou shalt nots," the negative commandments, in many cases carry a rank as high as, if not higher than, those wonderfully soothing Beatitudes which say, "Blessed are ye . . ." Our leadership attains its most advantageous position when we keep a proper balance between the do's and the dont's. We can multiply our strength if we can learn to take criticism as enthusiastically as we take praise.

I know of a great sales manager who has had wonderful success in building men. His system is a combination of both addition and subtraction. The training program is thoroughly outlined to the trainees in advance. It is understood and agreed that there will be perfect frankness. No one must be held back by fear of criticism or fear of giving offense. The trainer *must* be critical at times; there is no other way. "Spare the rod and spoil the child" is one of the basic concepts of training. But it also offers the trainee his greatest opportunity to get rid of his liabilities. Nothing is harder on the trainee than to be always guessing what is in the mind of the trainer. Why shouldn't the trainee want the trainer to be perfectly honest about weaknesses? Both must understand that faults must be eliminated, bad habits must be discontinued. To add qualities is wonderful, but that is not enough. Pats on the back serve a very useful purpose, but they have never been known to cure a bursting appendix. Exercises are good for growth, but that is also true of frankness and a good elimination system. We couldn't get along very well without the Beatitudes; but neither could we spare the Ten Commandments.

If Lucifer had been up on his "thou shalt nots" he would not have done what he did. If Benedict Arnold had been worked over by a good surgeon in the early years of his life he would never have betrayed his country and stigmatized himself as a traitor. Can we learn to apply these lessons effectively to ourselves and our church work? Each one of us is entrusted with the making of a personality capable of bearing the weight of eternity, and each of us is also entrusted with making our leadership strong enough to guarantee the eternal welfare of others. In both cases we need some "thou shalt nots."

It is not always possible to know exactly the right thing to say or do. No matter how careful or diplomatic one may be, he occasionally touches someone's soft spot. But what advantage is there to being sensitive and touchy? If someone makes an error in his dealings with us, that is his error, not ours. But we should not discourage his help by taking offense. Rather we should learn all we can from his mistakes so that we will not have to make the same errors ourselves. Besides, we can never get the maximum out of our training if the people with whom we work are afraid of us, or if they always have to put on their kid gloves. Some feelings, including our own, are bound to be hurt occasionally, but what difference does it make? It is not reasonable to throw away some great good just to avoid the possibility of a little unpleasantness. A little unpleasantness is sometimes good for what ails us, and there will never be very many unpleasant situations from which we cannot get some benefit if we are really looking for self-improvement.

Jesus said, "Love your enemies." Such a procedure has numerous advantages. At least our enemies sometimes tell us the truth about ourselves, whereas our friends seldom do.

One of the greatest of abilities is to be able to take criticism. It may be an even greater ability to be able to give criticism constructively, effectively and without offense. However, that is not always possible. But we cannot let the work of the Lord fail because we are afraid to make a real effort to help those under our direction. Strengthening people is a very important part of the work of the Church, and the ability to take criticism is a good strength to keep in mind. Criticism in its varied forms is a very important part of most training and supervision. Everyone in the Church is both trainer and trainee at the same time. Each is his brother's keeper. We should give praise generously as it is deserved. But we should never let our desire for approval lead us to indulge in harmful flattery when a more honest and constructive help is indicated. And we should always keep in mind that this helping process consists of both *addition* and *subtraction*.

Twice-Born Men

THERE IS AN old proverb that says, "As you have made your bed so you must lie in it." Like some other things, proverbs are subject to different interpretations by different people under different circumstances. In many cases this proverb is not true. That is, if your bed is uncomfortable you can remake it, and you can remake it so that it will be exactly to your liking. It is also possible to change practically every other undesirable aspect of your life. If your surroundings are incompatible or your habits don't suit you, or if you yourself are not what you would like to be, you may change yourself in every particular to conform to your most discriminating taste.

There are some people who have accepted this proverb at its face value to their great detriment. When so accepted, it often prevents progress, kills potentialities and destroys happiness. One expresses his version of this damaging philosophy by saying, "I am what I am and there is nothing that I can do about it." Someone else says, "I am just not religious," or "I was not cut out to be a teacher," or "I was not cut out to be a leader." We ought to forget this "cut out to be" business, for we ourselves are assigned to do most of the cutting. When we were born we were merely "cut out to be" a baby, and we can outgrow that if we work at it hard enough.

There are some people who feel that their brains have reached their limits, that their personality cannot be improved or modified. Some even feel that their conditions were determined by which star was shining when they were born. Some people have accepted their bad habits and other unfavorable conditions as a part of their destiny from which they have ceased trying to free themselves. Many people would deny with their lips that they believed in any such doctrine, yet their actions prove otherwise. Sometimes we believe a thing in our subconscious minds— where the real issues of our lives are determined—which we deny on the surface.

If we are to make the most of our leadership, it is very necessary that we understand this part of the law of free agency. Except in a very broad sense, our limits are not prescribed either by destiny, heredity or providence. The only real limitations to our accomplishments are those that we set for ourselves.

William James, the great Harvard psychologist, said, "The greatest discovery of my generation is that you can change your circumstances by changing your attitudes of mind." This is one of those truths that sometimes lies so lightly on the surface of our minds that it has no real influence. Our beliefs sometimes don't go deep enough to get into our real mental machinery where they can become action. Everyone wants to change his circumstances but few are willing to change themselves. Subconsciously we sometimes accept our bed, no matter how badly it is made, and we lie in it without remonstrance.

But there are innumerable examples of individuals who have done the opposite. They have completely revolutionized their lives. They have reversed their direction, changed their speed and acquired a new set of attitudes. They have traded in their unprofitable habits for habits of success. They have even remade their philosophy of life and have become new men.

Brains can be revitalized, weaknesses can be turned into strengths. Harold Beebie once wrote a book entitled *Twice Born Men*. It is an inspiring record of people, whose lamentable start in life was more than redeemed by a wonderful conclusion. They became different people. They were born again. One of these twice-born men was Wendell Phillips. Someone asked him when he was born, and he said, "I will tell you. It was one evening in my 25th year after I had finished reading a good book."

It would be interesting by way of contrast to read a book about the unfortunate folk who have only been born once. That would be the story of those who had accepted the bed given them by circumstances and lived their entire lives with only one birthday. Birthdays are not annual affairs; birthdays are the days when we have a new birth and make a fresh beginning.

The Apostle Paul got a new start as he was going on the road to Damascus. Peter, the fisherman, got started over when he came in contact with the life and teaching of the Master. When Jesus told Nicodemus that he also needed to be born again, he was not thinking of any physical rebirth. Bodies are born only once, but ambitions and faith, enthusiasm and devotion can be born several times. It is one of the greatest of abilities to be able to bring this new birth about successfully and each one of us has been given a wonderful potentiality in this direction. We need only to make up our minds to develop and exercise that ability. Everyone possesses an inborn capacity to bring upon himself transforming invasions of power which will make his life over.

Jesus talked with Nicodemus and other people about a new point of view with new objectives. He talked about turning from darkness to light, from failure to success, from the things of the world to the things of God. Such a change is in order right now for many of us. With some of us this change is long past due. More than anything else some of us need to be born again, and we need to be born different. Lyn Yutang said, "An educated man is one who has the right loves and hatreds." When we are born the next time, it would help us if we are born with a little stronger hatred of idleness, a little stronger disapproval of confusion in our work. Maybe it wouldn't hurt us too much to hate selfishness and dishonesty. On the other hand, we could get ourselves born with a greater love of dependability, a greater love of the work of the Lord, a greater love of good habits. Jesus said that Nicodemus should be born of the water and of the spirit. That would both signify and bring about a great change in his life. Change is the only means of progress.

Robert Southwell said, "Not where I breathe, but where I love, I live." A strong love of certain qualities will tend to give them birth in our lives. However, if we love the wrong things, the wrong things will be given birth. When planning our second birth, we ought to get firmly in mind a new set of loves and more worthy objectives. Then we will need a new set of road maps and a bigger gas tank filled with higher octane gasoline.

Walter Pitkin once wrote a book entitled *Life Begins at Forty*. And that may be true in some cases. But life may begin sooner than that. Life may begin every morning. Life begins when we begin. Life begins the minute we are born, whether it is for the first or the second or the third time. Life begins when we start driving the bad out of our lives and antidoting it with good.

But what are we going to do if life has given us a "thorn in the flesh?" We have been told that a weakness points out the place where life expects us to excel. Demosthenes was born with a very bad speech impediment. But it was *because* of this defect that he became the greatest orator in the world. His weakness served to humiliate, embarrass and tantalize him until he made a change. Weaknesses build up pressures in our minds—like water being backed up behind a dam—until they accumulate enough force to sweep everything before them.

Only when we are sufficiently unhappy with the bed we are lying in are we willing to put forth enough extra effort to bring about a change. Once we are sufficiently disturbed, then we will get ourselves born again, and we will make certain that we will be born better. If Demosthenes had been as satisfied with himself as were his classmates who got good marks in their speech classes, Demosthenes would never have been heard of either.

If we don't have something to stir us up or jar us out of our complacency we may go through life with only one birth. Our desire must be strong enough and penetrating enough to bring these changes about. Desire feeds and fertilizes the subsoil of our conscious life. It floods the mind and heart with power. It helps us to uncover the vital stratum of our being and understand the secrets of our own behavior which live in the depths of our subconscious minds. Then we are in a better position to make progress than when we merely let our thoughts lie lightly on the surface of the mind.

But a weakness is sometimes life's way of giving us a good swift kick to put us on our toes. A shock, if great enough, will often start the processes that produce birth. Life very often gives us the shock treatment, not to hurt us, but to help us get born again. That is, some of those who are ground down under the heel of unfavorable circumstances develop in their hearts a determination to rise which cannot be denied. These same defects often compensate by giving birth to a dozen virtues.

The Lord said, "I give unto men weaknesses that they may be humble." Then the humility starts a whole new train of strengths. Sometimes even our complexes and our sins humiliate and punish us until we develop the power to break out of our shell into a new life. Alma, who became a great prophet, was once a very wicked man. But after he had begun a new life he said, "Behold I am born of the spirit. (Mosiah 27:24) My soul hath been redeemed from the gall of bitterness and the bonds of iniquity. I was in the darkest abyss, but now I behold the marvelous light of God. My soul was racked with eternal torment, but . . . my soul is pained no more." (Mosiah 27:29)

This change may be brought about not only in regard to our faith—it can also be brought about in regard to our success or our appreciation or our leadership. Life gave Julius Caesar the weakness of epilepsy. He compensated by becoming the greatest military man of his day. Helen Keller said, "I thank God for my handicaps for through them I have found myself, my work and my God." We often need some such powerful catalyst to make us want to be born over; otherwise the transformation never takes place. But when our weaknesses make us suffer and squirm we sometimes begin to WANT in capital letters. Then our beds have a way of getting made over.

To have a defect is not in itself an advantage; it is what we do about it that counts. When we mend a defect it is often like nature mending a broken twig of an apple tree. The limb was broken in its weakest place, but that section becomes the strongest place after it has been mended. Nature puts on some natural splints. That is also what happens when we mend our faults. Someone said that Abraham Lincoln was not great because he was born in a log cabin; he was great because he got out of it. Alma was great, not because of his sins but because he threw them overboard.

But sometimes weaknesses do not prod us into activity. Some people just accept their lot. They lie in their unpleasant beds and feebly say, "There is nothing I can do about it." That is a sinful misuse of the gift of weakness that has been provided to sting and prod us to greater accomplishment.

A story was recently told of a salesman who let his

record get so bad that the boss told him he was going to be fired. This gave the salesman a severe shock, and for the first time in his life he really began to think seriously about his success. One year later he was the leading salesman in that entire organization. The realization that he was about to lose his job and that he had already lost the confidence of his employer and other people acted as the catalyst to jar him loose from his old habits and helped him become a new man.

A new beginning, a better direction, an increase of speed are all wonderful. But that is not all there is to a new birth. There follows the long steep climb of transformation while the changes are being permanently put in force. Jesus did not try to give the idea to Nicodemus or anyone else that by one single act we could solve all of the problems of our lives. There is no instantaneous success, just as there is no instantaneous salvation. Salvation is not the result of a single thrust at wrong. If a sinful appetite or an unfavorable personality could be changed by one conclusive, permanent, instantaneous victory, life would be simple. But no one should demand such a victory as the price of his effort. It was not even given to Jesus nor is it given to us to meet the foe, to fight the battle and to overcome in a single encounter.

It is usually true with the second birth as with the first, that we are born little and we must do our own growing. We start out by changing some of our mental pictures just as we would put on our clean clothes. The best way to change our circumstances is to dress ourselves up in our best thoughts, our best attitudes and our best habits. We ought to put on our best thinking and exert our best efforts. Only then will we be successful in this art of arts which is self-refreshment, self-renewal, self-rejuvenation. We need to center our minds on uplifting thoughts and revel in worthwhile work.

Higher goals and more worthy ambitions give us greater physical, mental and emotional stamina. They help to make man the master of his circumstances. The Apostle Paul was an expert in this business of being born again. He speaks to us as an authority when he says, "Be ye transformed by the renewing of your mind." That process is difficult. It means changing, ennobling, purifying and refreshing our thoughts. It means stamping new ideas deep enough into our minds to change our desires and ambitions.

These must be adequately supported by industry, and the change must be made under pressure. No accomplishment comes without struggle. The change must go deep. It must be within us. The Bible gives us a helpful clue of what ought to be inside of us when it tells us the reason for Daniel's outstanding success. When Darius, king of the Persians, captured Babylon, he made Daniel the ruler of the whole kingdom because as he said, "an excellent spirit was in him." Today as in the days of Daniel, the thing that counts in a man is the kind of spirit that is in him.

Sometimes our leadership lacks spirit; sometimes our faith and devotion lack spirit. The spirit of accomplishment of every man is what his resolutions make it. It is what his faith and courage demand him to be. If we get an excellent spirit in us as there was in Daniel, then even the Lord will soon be taking note of that fact.

Now here is a good idea. If it suits our purpose we can be born again a little bit at a time. Our determination to be punctual can be born today. A thorough lesson preparation habit may be born tomorrow. An enthusiastic determination to be dependable can be born next month. We can bring into being new character qualities with clocklike punctuality.

When James A. Garfield was asked what he meant to be in life, he answered, "First of all I must make myself a man. If I do not succeed in that I can succeed in nothing."

That is a great place to start our determinations toward a new birth, and we ought to see that this particular quality is well born.

Lincoln said, "Make every occasion a great occasion." That is very important. If the aggregate of our lives is to be what it should we had better put our best workmanship into each part, including the original determination. We ought to stick to our good resolutions and let nothing cause our decisions to waver or vacillate. Nothing dispels enthusiasm for a thing like a lot of exceptions. Exceptions cause the subconscious mind to become divided and confused. If we open the door to just one little evil several greater evils will invariably slip in. It does not take very many exceptions until we are worse off than we were to begin with.

The prospect of a new birth is a thrilling thing to contemplate. Just think about it. How would you like to become a brand new man? How would you like to be an inspiring leader? How would you like to be a "savior upon Mt. Zion?" How would you like to do the kind of church work that would please God?

Here is how to do it. Just make a list of all of the things that you would like to know and all of the abilities that you would like to have, and all of the objectives that you would like to reach. Then as Paul says, "Put off the old man which is corrupt and be renewed in the spirit of your mind." (Eph. 4:23) That means to repent and stay repentant. Then get the spirit of accomplishment. Get the spirit of the gospel. Get the spirit of your Heavenly Father. Get a firm determination to go forward. Then get yourself born again and include every one of your desired qualities and accomplishments in your new program.

Expertness in the techniques of bringing about a rebirth is one of the most profitable of all skills. It is the process by which we can remake our beds exactly to our tastes.

Who Is My Enemy?

THE INSPIRING story of the Good Samaritan was given by Jesus in answer to the lawyer's question, "Who is my neighbor?" As people have pondered the answer for 1900 years, some very constructive ideas have been impressed into our minds. An appropriate story illustrates and clarifies ideas in a way that sometimes makes them even more valuable than the actual experience itself would have been. Helpful thoughts must first be clear and then they can be stamped deeper and deeper into our minds to acquire greater influence in our behavior.

The other day someone asked another question. After some discussion and confusion about some personal problems, he said, in substance, "Who is my enemy?" That is a pretty good question to think about, and we don't always get the right answers. Just as we are sometimes unable to pick out the villain in a mystery movie, so we are sometimes unable to tell our friends from our enemies. Jesus was the best friend that the people of this earth have ever had, and yet in his own day, as in ours, he is not always so recognized. "Mistaken identity" is one of the common misfortunes of human experience. Wolves in sheep's clothing are an everyday occurrence. With great frequency people unknowingly turn their backs on their best friends.

Friends and enemies, like blessings, sometimes come in disguise. But even without any disguise, our batting average has not been very good in identifying either. We don't always recognize our parents or our teachers or our religious leaders in their true light. And at the same time, we allow enemies in the most flimsy disguises to infiltrate our ranks and rob us of our blessings without even realizing that they are being taken. "Who is my enemy?" is a timely question. To think about it may sharpen our skills in the processes of identification. Another story may help us to see some of the answers more clearly.

One of the most instructive stories of any age is the story of Mark Antony, the friend of Julius Caesar. The story begins just after a group of thirty-eight conspirators had assassinated Caesar with the intention of taking over the government of the Roman Empire. Then Mark Antony came onto the scene and by an effective argument at the funeral of Caesar, started the ball rolling away from the conspirators. Then Antony and Octavius Caesar organized forces and began a long, fierce struggle with the conspirators for power.

Plutarch, the great Greek moralist and historian who lived about the same time as Antony, tells how Antony, armed with his convincing speech, his logic, his courage and his ability to lead men, took the world away from the conspirators. Antony went from one success to another to become the world's most illustrious and powerful man. He overcame every difficulty. He endured the most arduous marches; he lived for long periods on rations of insects and the bark of trees. He shared these most extreme hardships with his men with wondrous good cheer. He gained the unquestioned loyalty and devotion of his soldiers who were willing to follow him in every enterprise.

But when the power of Antony seemed secure and further need for struggle unnecessary, Antony became idle. He fell in love with the bewitching Queen Cleopatra of Egypt and became a victim of the soft luxury and perfumed elegance of the Egyptian court. His great mind became clouded with the fumes of wine. He lost interest in the processes that had brought about his success. He became what Plutarch calls "a fishing rod general," and Shakespeare says he was transformed into a "strumpet's fool."

As so many others have done since, Antony abandoned his better self. It was not long therefore before he began losing his power. His prestige began to slip, his winning personality went into an eclipse, and his ability to perform began a swift decline. He lost his sense of morality and responsibility. He lost the loyalty of his men, the admiration of the people and the support of Octavius. Soon the magnificent accomplishment of Antony was reduced to rubble. Finally Octavius sent soldiers to Egypt to take Antony into custody. Antony avoided arrest by seeking death on his own sword.

And while he lay dying he recounted to Cleopatra the stimulating idea that there had been no power in the world sufficient to overthrow him except his own. Antony had been undone by himself. He said, "Only Antony could conquer Antony." William Haynes Lytle has put into verse Antony's supposed last speech, addressed to Cleopatra. As Caesar's soldiers were almost knocking at Cleopatra's door, Antony was saying to her:

> Let not Caesar's servile minions
> Mock the lion thus layed low;
> 'Twas no foeman's arm that felled him—
> 'Twas his own hand struck the blow.
> He who pillow'd on thy bosom,
> Turned aside from glory's way
> When made drunk with thy caresses,
> Madly threw a world away.

Everything in the world that Antony desired, he had held firmly in his own hands. There existed no earthly power sufficient to take it from him, except his own power. The opposition of the conspirators only made him more determined; the stimulating challenge of difficulties called forth his greatest effort; the deserts and mountains which he conquered made him stronger. His problems actually increased his abilities. But when he "turned aside from glory's way" and set himself against his own best interests, there was no power that could save him. He deliberately laid himself in the dust. Of his own accord, he "madly threw a world away."

Many people at this instant are in that same situation. They have every blessing within their easy reach, but they are deliberately throwing them all away, including the celestial kingdom, and all that goes with it. God has given us great power over our own welfare. If we fail it will be because, like Antony, we have destroyed ourselves.

Aristotle recited to Alexander the Great an important truth that we should be familiar with. He said, "The greatest enemy that ever confronts an army is never in the ranks of the foe, but always in your own camp." This is not only one of the most important truths in the world, but is also one of the hardest to learn. It is very difficult to protect ourselves against ourselves. This applies to individuals, churches, armies and nations.

For example, who is the greatest enemy of America? It is not Russia nor China. The greatest enemy of America is weakness and sin inside of America. Who was it that sold the atomic secrets? Who is it that causes our strikes, our bitterness, our distrust, our extravagances and our ignorance? If America is overthrown, who will be responsible? There is only one answer. America. Every other nation that has been destroyed upon this land, including the great civilizations of the Jaredites and the Nephites, destroyed themselves, just as certainly as did Antony.

Or who is the greatest enemy of the Church? Is it other churches or governments? That is ridiculous. No possible power outside the Church itself can stop its progress. The only people that can hold back our part of the work of the Lord are those in our own camp. As early as 1834, the Lord said that "were it not for the transgressions of *my people* . . . they might have been redeemed even now." (D&C 105:2)

Sometimes we destroy ourselves over the most trivial things. Thomas B. Marsh, one of the early leaders of the Church, apostatized as a result of a dispute over a few pints of milk. Others throw their blessings away with no better excuse. Probably no one was ever "reasoned" out of his faith. Faith is lost because of offenses, sins, sloth and idleness.

The Prophet Joseph Smith was less fearful of the acts of the mob than he was of those who might prove to be traitors among his own people. Before the city council of Nauvoo he made this significant statement in December 1843:

> I am exposed to far greater dangers from traitors from among ourselves than from enemies from without. All the enemies upon the face of the earth may roar and exert all of their powers to bring about my death, but they can accomplish nothing unless some who are among us, who have enjoyed our society, have been with us in our council, participated in our confidence, taken us by the hand and called us brother, saluted us with a kiss—join with our enemies, turn our virtues into faults and by falsehood and deceit stir up their wrath and indignation against us and bring their united vengeance upon our heads.

The history of the following few months clearly shows that Joseph was right in his fear that traitors within his own ranks would do him harm. One of his own counselors, William Law, assisted in betraying him into the hands of his enemies, and on June 12, 1844, Constable David Pettisworth of Carthage arrived in Nauvoo with warrants for the arrest of Joseph and Hyrum, an arrest which finally resulted in their deaths. These warrants were issued upon

complaints sworn by Francis M. Higbee, a former member
of the Church.

Enemies in our own camp have always been our biggest problem. Who was it that betrayed Jesus? Who
denied him? Who doubted him? Who was it that slept
during his most critical hour? The source of the problem
has not changed. President McKay said, "The Church
is seldom, if ever, injured by the persecution of ignorant
or misinformed or malicious enemies. A far greater hin-
drance to its progress comes from fault-finders, com-
mandment-breakers, and shirkers inside the Church."

We need to be able to identify the present enemies
of the Church if we are going to do anything about it. Who
is stopping the progress of the various wards and stakes?
Who is responsible for blessings being lost by a large number of inactive members? Who is responsible for the unpaid
tithing and the neglected ward teaching and the ineffective
leadership? There can only be one possible answer. The
difficulty lies with the members of the Church, both those
who fail to lead and those who fail to follow.

The Lord will not hold us guiltless. He has said, "It
must needs be that all men must be left without excuse."
(D&C 88:82) And that applies to those who fail to hear
and even more particularly to those who fail to teach.
Leaders must bear the prospective condemnation of Paul,
who said, "Woe is me if I preach not the gospel."

It is easy to fall a victim of that serious weakness of
human nature wherein we tend to justify ourselves in the
things that we do that are wrong. We pass very lightly over
our own shortcomings. We have a most serious blind spot
which prevents us from seeing our own weaknesses. Almost
more than anything else, we need to be able to analyze
and criticize and look objectively at ourselves.

The Lord has indicated the great joy that will be ours
if we bring one soul unto him. Isn't it logical to believe

that the pain will be in proportion if we lose one soul through our negligence or mislead one soul through our' bad example? The Lord says, "Woe unto him by whom the offense cometh."

Our own weakness or lack of integrity or inferior leadership may prove a more effective stumbling block to others than any deliberate opposition that could be given, and if we are not conscious of our problems, our offenses may grow larger and more numerous. We should make sure that the work of the Lord will not be cut down from within, by us.

We might apply this queston of "Who is my enemy?" to ourselves personally. Who is it that keeps me ignorant and poor and unsuccessful? There is only one answer. How can we fail to be impressed with this tremendous idea that the Lord has placed before us every blessing and every opportunity in time and for eternity? The celestial kingdom for ourselves and our neighbors is within our easy reach. There is no power in the world sufficient to keep us from those blessings, except ourselves. "Only Antony can conquer Antony." Even Satan himself cannot force us to do wrong against our will.

> All the water in the world
> However hard it tried
> Can never sink the smallest ship
> Unless it gets inside.

> All the evil in the world
> The blackest kind of sin
> Can never hurt you the least bit
> Unless you let it in.

No one can hurt us but ourselves. The thief steals from himself. The sinner brings about his own condemnation. The sloth loses the blessings of the work which he fails to perform. If we lose the celestial kingdom, it will be only because we ourselves have "turned aside from glory's way," and deliberately thrown our blessings out of the window, for there is no power in the world that can stop our eternal exaltation and happiness, except our own.

Cannon Farr stimulates us with the following lines. He says—

> I am only one, but I am one.
> I can't do everything, but I can do some things.
> What I can do, that I ought to do,
> And what I ought to do, by the grace of God, I will do.

If we put this determination in force in our lives we will not only become friends of God, but we will be friends to ourselves as well.

Worshipping the Net

HABAKKUK was a prophet of ancient Judah who lived some 600 years B. C. His writing is included as one of the smallest of the books of the Old Testament. Habakkuk seemed to have a lot of problems trying to get people to do as they should. This may indicate that the world hasn't changed very much. One of the weaknesses of that day which Habakkuk tried to point out to his people was the tendency of some of them to worship their nets. Habakkuk worded his complaint as follows:

"They catch fish in their net and gather them in their drag; therefore they do rejoice and are glad. Therefore they sacrifice unto their net, and burn incense unto their drag, because by them their portion is made fat, and their meat plenteous." (Hab. 1:15-16)

Habakkuk gives a graphic visual picture of the successful fisherman of his day, and reminds us of his counterpart in our own time. We see through the eyes of the prophet a very prosperous fisherman, skillful in his occupation. We see a net bulging with fish. The fisherman is elated by his success and the good fortune that comes from his business of fishing. He is naturally very happy. "His portion is fat" and "his meat is plenteous." The means of his production is his net. It is because of the fruit of his net that he is so prosperous. He is so absorbed by his successes and so delighted at his good fortune that he proceeds forthwith to "sacrifice to his net," and "burn incense unto his drag."

Ludicrous as this situation may appear at first glance, it is a problem that is still with us. The dictionary says that "worship" is an intense love of or a show of reverence or devotion for some particular thing. We really are not bothered by any shortage of devotion in general. Our problem comes from the fact that our devotion is so often misplaced or misdirected. We frequently have too much devotion for the wrong thing. For example, too much of our devotion is often directed toward material things. It is one of our common failings to lose sight sometimes of the real objectives of life, and worship the means by which our "portion is made fat" and "our meat plenteous."

Suppose we put on the spectacles of Habakkuk and see how many of us are presently "worshipping our nets," which translated would mean our modern means of production. However grotesque the idea may appear, it is still an important part of our society to "sacrifice to our net" and "burn incense unto our drag." For some the "net" or means of production is science. It is not unusual for science to be deified in the minds of its devotees. But this is not our only "net." The contest in our minds between God and Mammon has been long and difficult. Sometimes we spend 200 hours per month serving our business and two hours per month serving our God and our own souls. It is small wonder that these interests hold a place in our lives more or less comparable to the relative time and devotion which we lavish upon them.

Jesus made a comparison of the difficulty involved in a camel getting through the eye of a needle and a rich man getting into the kingdom of heaven. I suppose that not all rich men are necessarily worse than poor men, but rich men sometimes have a stronger grip on their nets, and consequently their nets get a stronger grip on them. We become absorbed by what we do. In one way it is like developing faith, inasmuch as faith usually doesn't take hold of us until we take hold of it. William James said, "That which holds our attention determines our action."

The greater the attention, the stronger the hold. The first step even toward worship is to center the attention firmly Men have a natural inclination to worship something, and when the attraction of the "net" reaches a certain intensity, it overpowers the tendency to worship God.

Jesus also pointed out the difficulty of trying to serve two masters. Two dominant ideas usually seem to have more trouble with "peaceful co-existence" than two dominant nations. Jesus said that the reason that only a "few were chosen" out of the many who had been called was that "their hearts were set so much upon the things of the world." That is, the things of the world had crowded out their spiritual interests. That almost always happens when too large a proportion of one's available time is spent burning incense to the drag. There are some men who bow down before the state for that reason. Others kneel before peculiar ideologies. Others just get so busy with other things that they crowd God out of their lives, without ever meaning to do so.

The story is told of a young man who wanted to go to college. He had the good fortune of finding a family that was willing to furnish him with a room and let him chop their wood in payment. This the young man was delighted to do. The neighbors across the fence agreed to furnish him with his meals if he would chop their wood. A family down the street offered to pay his tuition if he would chop their wood, etc. It wasn't long before this young man was so busy chopping wood that he had no time to go to college. The means had overcome the end. He had made too great a sacrifice to his net.

It is a very frequent mistake that we make in getting things out of their proper place. We confuse the means of livelihood with the purpose of life. Solomon reminds us that there is a time to be born and a time to die. And there are certain very important things that should be done in between. Solomon seems to give the inference that to budget our time might be a pretty good idea. If a man had an income of $400 per month he should probably not spend the whole $400 on housing; neither would he spend limitlessly on automobiles and leave the other necessities unprovided for. Yet we often get this kind of an imbalance in our personal program by giving limitlessly to our nets and only letting God and our souls have what time, if any, may be left over.

In our household affairs a wise manager works out a proper balance of his expenditures and then holds the line and does not allow one need to encroach upon the rights of the other. It would be very wise if we would do that same thing with the twenty-four hours that are allotted to us each day. Part of that ime properly belongs to the net. Part belongs to society. Part belongs to our own souls. And part belongs to him who created us and supports our every breath. *We* must work out the proper balance.

Count Tolstoy had an interesting discussion devoted to the important of wealth and the proportion of our "time budget" that should be allotted to the net. He tells of a Russian peasant trying to decide how much land a man needs. At first he lived very happily with his wife and family on his five-acre farm. And then someone suggested that five acres was not enough, and so he got ten acres. Then he got a hundred, and then a thousand acres. And then someone gave him a chance to acquire all of the land that he could run around in the course of a twelve-hour day between sunrise and sunset.

The next morning when the contest was to begin, he was on his mark, and as the sun came up he began to run north as fast as he could, and he ran north for the first quarter of the day. Then he ran east for three hours. During the third three hours he ran south. Then during the last quarter of the day he ran west to the point of beginning.

And just as the sun was about to drop into the west he dragged himself back across the finish line and fell over dead. Then his friends buried him in a plot of ground four feet wide and six feet long and six feet deep. And then for the first time he found out how much land a man really needed.

That may not be the amount best suited to every man's need, but it indicates that there is a point of diminishing returns when we limitlessly sacrifice to the net. Our relationship to the net can easily become a serious violation of that great commandment that still thunders down across the centuries saying to us, "Thou shalt have no other gods before me." Probably the most common form of idolatry, particularly in our day, is our tendency to "worship the net." The old sun worshippers looked upon the sun as their source of supply. The sun sent them energy and heat and food, therefore they worshipped the sun; others have worshipped earth out of which their food was taken; others have worshipped various things in whatever form they may have been, as long as they made "their portion fat," and their "meat plenteous."

Isaiah refers to a man who cut a beautiful piece of cedar from the forest. He burned a part of it to warm himself. A part of it he used to cook his food. And with "the residue thereof he maketh a god, even a graven image; he falleth down unto it, and worshippeth it and prayeth unto it, and saith, Deliver me; for thou art my god." (Isa. 44:17)

We also frequently say to that which gets material things for us, "Deliver me for thou art my god." In this man's ignorance it probably seemed a proper thing to worship that which warmed him and cooked his food. In many cases we still fail to look behind the "means." We imagine it is the cedar that provided the fire and the net that produced the fishes. In a measure, we are like the blind men from Indostan who went to see the elephant; and because of their own limitations one blind man thought that the elephant was like a tree; another thought the elephant was like a serpent, etc. We make even a greater mistake when we think that the sun or the rain or the soil or science or the cedar or the net is God. Sometimes we worship the attributes of God rather than God himself. We say "God is love," etc.

Some people worship pleasure. A man once said that inasmuch as Sunday was his only free day he intended to enjoy it with his family. And so each Sunday he took them into the canyons and resorts in search of pleasure. But in so doing, he took his family away from their church meetings and the spirit of the Sabbath Day. Their understanding of the gospel was thereby retarded and undermined. This man was using the Sabbath to teach his family to violate the commands of God and center their minds on their fishing rods and their guns and their golf clubs. Over the years his family have naturally gotten farther and farther away from the Church until now they are almost completely inactive. What a great sacrifice this man has made to his net! Because he sought the companionship of his children in the wrong way, he may actually lose their companionship throughout eternity.

Recently a friend remarked, "Someday when I get a little time I am going to surprise everyone and start coming to church." But who knows how much time he has left? Of such a one it was said, "Thou fool, this night shall thy soul be required of thee." (Luke 12:20) Time is precious and none of us has too much, even from the beginning of our lives. In 1776 the average length of life in the United States was 35 years. In 1900 it was 48 years. Now it is nearly 70 years. Since 1900 there has been an additional 22 years of life added to our "second estate." This is extra time for us to prepare for eternity. But what are we doing with this time, and are we any nearer to being ready to meet God now than the people were in 1900?

If we had a stop watch to time our efforts, how much of this additional time has been spent in "our Father's business"? If we would give to God the amount of time that we spend on trivial things, or on pleasure, hobbies, bad habits or waste—or just suppose that we devoted the "excess" of that time we spend at our nets—in that time we could save our souls and the souls of many others of our Father's children.

As leaders in the Church, we have been called to labor in the greatest enterprise ever undertaken upon the earth. It is the work in which God himself spends his entire time. We ought to set aside an appropriate amount of our time for this purpose, including time for an adequate preparation. There is a time for our nets and a time to worship God.

It takes a lot of time to build up attitudes and abilities. It takes time to develop an interest in spiritual things. Someone was telling of the time involved in courting his wife. His friend said, "Why didn't you just call on her once?" Interest and ability and love are accumulative, even in the things of God. It might be a good idea for us if for a while we would carry *two* stop watches. Let the one run while we were working at our nets and run the other when we were doing the work of the Church. We may be impressed, as Habakkuk was, that we are sacrificing too much to our nets and burning too much incense unto our drag.

Your Gift

RALPH WALDO EMERSON once said, "I have never met a man who was not my superior in some particular." It is a very interesting fact that each person has been given some talent or some potentiality wherein he may excel everyone else in the world. That is, if you knew everything there was to know about any particular person you would probably find that that person had some trait or some ability superior to your own where he might be expected to uplift and inspire you. It is also a part of our nature that everyone *needs* to excel in something. The Creator has given us "gifts" to supply this need, and he in turn requires that we develop them to their maximum, and then use them for the benefit of all.

In the days of Socrates it was customary for some of the leading men to get together for discussion and dinner. They would sit around in a circle on the floor, each one leaning against the one next to him. Socrates once said to his neighbor that he was glad to sit close to him, for said he, as water can be made to flow by means of a syphon from a higher to a lower body, so wisdom can be made to pass from the greater to the less among men.

When we raise the level of our own attainment a natural outpouring takes place which supplies those around us with benefits. Jesus was the greatest leader because he bestowed the greatest benefits. He spoke of "living water" which he freely offered to others, and as these life-giving streams refreshed and revitalized those around him his own supply was not diminished.

In leadership the benefits also flow naturally from the greater to the less. It is very difficult to get water or wisdom to run uphill. It is difficult to get leadership to run from the emptier to the fuller. If we are to make a worthwhile contribution to others our own leadership level must be high. When our cask is full it raises the level in the emptier vessels by which it is surrounded. Jesus said, "Ye shall instruct and edify each other." (D&C 48:8) That is most readily done by first raising the level of our own gifts.

We might follow the interesting custom of some merchants who develop what they call "trade leaders." They select some particular item and make it their specialty. They build an attractive bargain around it, or give it a reputation by developing its outstanding quality.

We might proceed in that same way. The Lord has said, "To every man is given a gift by the spirit of God. To some is given one and to some is given another, that all may be profited thereby." (D&C 46:11) He wants us to have these "personality leaders" and give them power by development. He has said, "Seek ye earnestly the best gifts, always remembering for what they are given, for verily I say unto you they are given for the benefit of those who love me and keep my commandments." (D&C 46:8)

It is a wonderful thing to fill our lives with excellence. Excellence should be introduced into our program as early as possible by a maximum development of our gifts. The Lord has said we should select the best gifts. This process is like selecting majors in college. One may major in English or mathematics to a point where he becomes an authority. In our leadership we may major in particular abilities or traits of character. We may major in virtues. We may build up the importance of little things. We can major in minor as well as major virtues.

Seneca said, "Shun no effort to make yourself remarkable in some talent." When we develop one trait fully there is a tendency for that trait to pull all the other traits up to its stature so that the whole personality may be finished symmetrically.

But we need our majors to lead the attack. Lincoln majored in honesty. His major gave his personality its power. The Lord himself was the author and designer of these majors or gifts, but he insists that they are not wasted or ignored. He said to the Prophet Joseph Smith, "You shall have a gift to translate the plates, and I will grant unto you no other gift until it is finished." (D&C 5:4)

Everyone has been put under bond for the successful development of his gifts. The parable of the talents indicates that the Lord sometimes forecloses unused talents. He also exacts a heavy forfeit under some circumstances. On the other hand, he gives us abundant gifts on the basis of appreciation and use. He has said, "Behold thou shalt have the gift if you wilt desire of me in faith." (D&C 11:10)

There are special gifts for leaders, and we may have as many as we will adequately use. The Lord said, "Unto some it may be given to have all those gifts, that there may be a head in order that every member may be profited thereby." (D&C 46:29) Leaders can develop this important muscle of mastery through service until finally we may qualify for the greatest of all gifts, eternal life, "which gift is the greatest of all the gifts of God." (D&C 14:7) But for this greatest gift, as for all of the other gifts, we ourselves must first qualify.

Now here are some good questions that everyone should think about and answer for himself. What is my gift? How did the Lord intend me to excel? How does the Lord want me to serve? Do I desire the right gifts? Do I desire them intently enough? Am I displeasing the Lord because I fail to recognize the gifts that I already have? Is the disuse of my gifts disqualifying me for an increase? Am I burying my talents in the ground and running the

risk of losing what I already have? Specifically, what shall
I do about these questions?

First, we must identify the gifts we already have.
Second, we must know what we want. Third, we must
desire to have these gifts. Fourth, we must have faith that
we can get them. Jesus said, "All things are possible to
them that believe." We must believe that we were meant
to excel and that we can excel. Reed Smoot once said that
"an ambition to excell is indispensable to success." An
ambition to excel is also indispensable to leadership, and
must back up our faith with our works.

This idea of excelling in some trait was once mentioned
to a group of missionaries and after the meeting one rather
skeptical missionary said, "How could I excel in anything?"
Then he proceeded to express the idea that in his opinion
he had no talents worth mentioning. He more or less
accused the Lord of passing him up when the gifts were
distributed. That is the usual pattern of failure. One of
our biggest sins is our own negation of our gifts. This trait
we mistakenly think of as modesty or humility. This missionary was a fine young man of substantial potentiality,
most of which was going to waste. It seemed never to have
occurred to him that God was his father and had endowed
him with all of his own attributes. All of his life this young
man had greatly underestimated his own possibilities. He
had accused God by his severe lack of faith in himself.
Naturally his lack of effort at self-development and service
had been in proportion to his lack of faith. He was sinfully
taking the great gifts that the Creator had given him and
destructively depreciating their value. The fault of not
being aware of our own possibilities is very common, very
destructive and very sinful.

I had noticed that this missionary was about fifteen
minutes late in coming into the meeting, and so it was suggested to him that probably the Lord intended him to excel
in punctuality. That was one area where he would not

have too much competition. But think how that one trait would have put the glow of success on his personality. It was suggested to this young man that he might try to excel in having a more positive mental attitude about himself.

We should not be so easily fooled by what may seem to us a lack of gifts. Sometimes gifts, like blessings, come in disguise. People often excel at the very point of what they thought was their greatest weakness. Think about Abraham Lincoln, Mahatma Gandhi, Winston Churchill, Joseph Smith, and many others. All were thought to have less than average possibilities at one time. Lincoln was homely, uneducated, awkward. He was "born without a chance." Gandhi lived as an "untouchable" in a mud hut. At one time he had an ungovernable temper and an overpowering inferiority complex. Churchill failed three times in his examinations to enter the British military school at Sandhurst. One of Churchill's friends said that he couldn't see how Churchill could possibly have gone through Sandhurst; he must have gone under it. Who would have thought that young Joseph Smith had ahead of him such an all-important mission and destiny? Therefore isn't it possible that you also may not understand your own potential importance?

After looking at the report that this missionary kept of his work I suggested that inasmuch as the Lord expected him to excel at the point of his greatest weakness, the Lord must have intended for this missionary to excel in getting up in the morning and becoming outstanding in industry and enthusiasm. The small number of calls shown on his report indicated that he was not only burying his talents in the ground, but he was covering them over with concrete. No wonder he was losing faith in the reality of his own possibilities. I tried to point out to this young man that it is pretty difficult to develop any quality in which he himself did not believe. Disbelief is highly antagonistic to any success or progress. If we firmly believe that gifts are impossible to us we will by that process make them impossible. Disbelief sometimes becomes the chief characteristic of some people. It was said of one person that his ability to disbelieve was unbelievable.

I once heard a great salesman speaking to a large sales convention. He was trying to point out one of the reasons why salesmen fail. The hotel had placed some large pitchers of ice water and trays of glasses on the long speaker's table. All of the glasses were turned upside down on the trays. The speaker took the first pitcher and began pouring the water on the upturned glass bottoms. The water splashed all over, but not one drop got inside of any of the glasses. He continued to pour until everything was wet except the inside of the glasses where the water was supposed to be. Then he took the second tray of glasses and turned them right side up and repeated the process of pouring the water over the tray of glasses. But this time, because of the different position of the glasses, they were all soon filled with water.

Sometimes some of us get our mental attitude turned wrong side up. Then when the Lord pours out his gifts we don't catch very many. That isn't becase the Lord is trying to slight us; we are just not in a position to receive anything. The Lord can only pour the blessings out; he can't accept them for us. He has said, "For what doth it profit a man if a gift is bestowed upon him and he receive not the gift?" Such a man "rejoices not in that which is given unto him, neither rejoices in him who is the giver of the gift." (D&C 88:33)

To become a good "receiver" one must rejoice in the gift and in the giver. We can't receive the gift and reject the giver. If we know how to "receive" then we may take our choice of "many gifts." We may have the gift of knowledge if we are willing to study and develop a love of learning. We may have the gift of wisdom if we will practice always thinking straight. We may have one of the greatest of all the gifts, which is the gift of faith if we have the works and follow the Lord's direction.

Think of the multitude of other wonderful gifts. How would you like to have the gift of courage, or the gift of industry, or the gift of great accomplishment? If you so desired the Lord could give you the miraculous power to turn water into wine, but as a practical, everyday matter, wouldn't it be much better to develop your gift of becoming an expert Sunday School teacher? How would you like to have the gift of great administrative ability and execute skill? That means the ability to be dependable, to learn to plan and think and follow through. All of these wonderful gifts may be yours if you are willing to receive them.

If someone gave you the deed to a gold mine you would still have to dig out and refine the ore. It is the same with your gifts. And it takes a strong desire and a lot of digging to get the job done properly. God put the gifts of silver and gold in the earth. But he put far greater gifts in his own children. They are the gifts of his own attributes. However, it does no good for our minds to accept a gift if our ambitions refuse to qualify.

We should not only have our glasses right side up, but we should also be in the right place when the Lord is pouring out blessings. Certain of these gifts and blessings are given out only in certain places. The Lord has designated the temple as the only place where certain blessings may be received. Others are passed out at Sacrament meeting. If we don't go to priesthood meeting we will miss certain others. Some places are out of bounds for blessings. That is, the pool hall is not a distribution center for divine gifts. A loafing place is not where the gift of industry is bestowed. It is pretty difficult to receive

any blessing if our glasses are wrong side up or if we are
absent when the pouring takes place. If we want to enjoy
a spiritual feast, or any other kind of a feast, we had better
go where the feast is, and then make sure that our plates
are right side up.

Psychologists have told us that a majority of people use
only a very small percentage of their potential abilities.
That is not because the gifts have not been bestowed—it
is because they have not been received. Why should the
Lord give us any more gifts if we don't develop and use
those that we already have?

The Lord said to Joseph Smith that no other gift was
forthcoming until he finished the work for which the present gift was given. Just think of the number of gifts we
may be missing on that basis. Or think of the great volume
of our "unfinished business" if we are to get our present
gifts in good standing. When we develop our ward teaching gift to its ultimate or do our planning as effectively as
it can be done, then the Lord might be persuaded to give
us some other gifts.

The ancient Athenians had a rule that before anyone
could qualify for an important post he must have first
filled some lesser posts well. If we can develop our gift
of study and work and learn to be faithful in little things,
then we will be preparing ourselves for excellence in the
greater things. To major in some minor virtue is far better
than to minor in some major virtue. But if we will major
in a minor virtue we may soon find ourselves majoring in
a major virtue.

The best way to be a great leader in large affairs next
year is to be a great leader in small affairs this year. The
best way to be a great soul in heaven is to be a great soul
here. The best way to get greater gifts is to use to the
utmost those that we already have. And a good place to
start is to make ourselves remarkable in some talent.

Summary

IN THE FOREGOING pages we have considered fifty-two of the subdivisions of leadership. There are hundreds more that should be given equal consideration. While leadership can never be completely mastered, it must never be forgotten or laid aside even momentarily. We must keep asking ourselves, "What is it? What are its values? How can it be developed, and what are we doing about it?" Leadership is at the very heart of our success and welfare. Our ability to produce it in our own and other's lives determine every worth-while accomplishment.

As the times in which we live are different, so our leadership is more important than ever before. We live in the age of the greatest wonders, the greatest power and the most enlightenment ever known in the world. We also have the biggest problems to solve, but we have the most resources with which to solve them. So far as material advantages are concerned, we live better and faster though more dangerously than any king lived just a hundred years ago. We live in a day when the available knowledge of health can give us stronger bodies and clearer minds. Since the days of George Washington this increase of knowledge has doubled our life's expectancy, and has therefore given us more time multiplied by greater opportunity.

We live in a time when the gospel has been revealed to us in a fullness (and with a responsibility) never given to any other people. We live in a day when we may have all of the education that we desire. One of the most important decisions that our first parents were asked to make when they were placed in the Garden of Eden was whether or not they would eat the fruit from the tree of knowledge of good and evil. After they had eaten, the Lord said of them, "Behold, the man is become as one of us, to know good and evil." (Gen. 3:22) We might remind ourselves that the right kind of knowledge still tends to have that effect upon people. Though in a different way, we are being asked to decide the extent to which we will eat the fruit from the tree of knowledge. Our answer and what we do about it will largely determine the quality of our leadership. In the Garden of Eden the Lord placed a flaming sword to guard the tree of life. But there is no flaming sword preventing us from acquiring knowledge, and the right kind of knowledge will help us win eternal life. Isn't it wonderful that in this day when knowledge is so important that each of us may eat from the storehouse of knowledge to his heart's content.

Our forefathers lived on what some of them conceived to be a flat, stationary earth and plowed their ground with a wooden stick. We live in a world of power steering, jet propulsion, atomic power and guided missiles. We now even contemplate communication and transportation beyond the boundaries of the earth on which we live, and we need character and leadership qualities to match the momentous times and the tremendous opportunities of our day.

Long ago the prophets foretold that in the latter days the Lord would release an increase of knowledge in the earth. That carries with it a corresponding responsibility. Standards are constantly being raised; the tempo of life is being speeded up. The values at stake are getting greater. Our leadership must keep pace by taking advantage of every possible means for increasing our effectiveness as leaders. Spiritual leadership is the most important responsibility in the world. The Apostle Paul said, "And now abideth faith, hope, charity—these three, but the greatest of these is charity." (I Cor. 13:13) Without any disposition to reduce the comparative importance of these wonderful qualities, it is pointed out that they all depend primarily upon good leadership and cannot flourish without it. The kind of leadership we provide influences every attitude and activity among us. It is the ruling factor from the beginning to the end of our lives.

Years ago an unknown priest gave voice to a popular philosophy by saying, "Give me a child until he is seven and I care not who has him in charge after that." Walter Pitkin finds serious fault with the judgment of this statement. Mr. Pitkin makes this saying more to his liking by adding two letters to one word so that the amended proverb now reads, "Give me a child until he is seventy and I care not who has him in charge after that." But it would still be very easy to find the shortcomings of this leadership adage, even in its enlarged scope. Leadership was an all-important factor in the council in heaven before this earth was created. Many noble and great spirits were there developed and appointed to leadership responsibility. Certainly we may be sure of the fact that leadership in its highest form will continue with increased importance throughout eternity, with God, the greatest of all, carrying the chief executive responsibility.

Leadership was our most important obligation in the pre-existence. It will be our most important obligation in the hereafter. But this life is the period specifically set apart for us to prepare ourselves and others for eternity, and right now is our finest opportunity to develop and practice this most important of all of the abilities—the ability to lead in the work of the Lord.

Index